THE
YOUNG & RUBICAM
TRAVELING CREATIVE WORKSHOP

THE
YOUNG & RUBICAM

Traveling Creative Workshop

HANLEY NORINS

PRENTICE HALL
Englewood Cliffs, New Jersey 07632

Prentice-Hall International (UK) Limited, *London*
Prentice-Hall of Australia Pty. Limited, *Sydney*
Prentice-Hall Canada, Inc., *Toronto*
Prentice-Hall Hispanoamericana, S.A., *Mexico*
Prentice-Hall of India Private Limited, *New Delhi*
Prentice-Hall of Japan, Inc., *Tokyo*
Simon & Schuster Asia Pte. Ltd., *Singapore*
Editora Prentice-Hall do Brasil, Ltda., *Rio de Janeiro*

©1990 by

PRENTICE-HALL, Inc.

Englewood Cliffs, NJ

Material from *The Compleat Copywriter* is used by permission
of the International Group, McGraw-Hill Publishing Company.

10 9 8 7 6 5 4 3 2 1

Library of Congress Cataloging-in-Publication Data

Norins, Hanley.
   The Young & Rubicam traveling creative workshop / by Hanley
Norins.
      p.   cm.
  ISBN 0-13-973116-4
  1. Advertising. 2. Advertising copy. 3. Creative ability in
business. 4. Y&R Media Research. I. Title. II. Title: Young
and Rubicam traveling creative workshop.
HF5827.N67 1990
659.1—dc20   89-22880
                                              CIP

ISBN 0-13-973116-4

PRENTICE HALL
BUSINESS & PROFESSIONAL DIVISION
A division of Simon & Schuster
Englewood Cliffs, New Jersey 07632

PRINTED IN THE UNITED STATES OF AMERICA

Once again, to Marcy and Wendy, with love

About the Author

Hanley Norins was associated with Young & Rubicam for 32 years. He served as Associate Creative Director, New York; Sr. V.P. and Creative Director, Y&R West; Creative Consultant to Y&R at large. Norins was one of the three-member faculty of the Young & Rubicam Traveling Creative Workshop, which served 40 Y&R offices in 21 countries.

With Y&R, Norins developed campaigns on such accounts as Time Inc., Goodyear Tires, Procter & Gamble, Bristol-Myers, Security Pacific Bank, Kaiser Industries, Remington Shavers, Gallo and Italian Swiss Colony wines. His advertising credits include lyrics for the Brylcreem song ("A Little Dab'll Do Ya"); Peach-and-Brush TV demonstration for Remington Shavers; Cheer "Eye-Witness" commercials (first of the Candid Camera campaigns); "Go-Go-Goodyear" non-verbal TV series, Gold Medal winner for best International campaign of 1963; Security Pacific "Looking Forward" campaign; "The Gourmet Jug Wine" Colony campaign.

Norins currently specializes in group problem-solving seminars for clients who have been as diverse as: Ringling Bros. Barnum & Bailey; *Sunset* magazine; *The San Francisco Examiner*; Heublein wines and liquors; General Consumer Electronics; and the University of Florida School of Journalism & Advertising.

His publishing credits include "The Compleat Copywriter" (McGraw-Hill, 1966), the book from which Y&R derived the "Whole Egg" title for its worldwide integrated communications concept; three feature articles in the *S.F. Examiner* Sunday supplement, *California Living*; six poems in the *Wall Street Journal* op-ed "Pepper . . . and Salt" section; a popular song ("Peace of Mind"), recorded by RCA Victor; reporting and features as New England Editor of *The Exhibitor*, motion picture trade magazine.

Acknowledgments

The acknowledgments for this book break down into five categories.

The first category is what I might call "the prime movers." Foremost among these is Bette Schwartzberg, Senior Editor at Prentice Hall, who, besides having been my friend, guide, and mentor throughout the preparation of the manuscript, actually *originated* the *idea* for the book itself!

My second acknowledgment in this category goes to Lin Gander. Lin had retired from Young & Rubicam ten years ago, when he was the head of the Account Coordinating Department (which I always prefer to call by its old name: The Traffic Department). Through the account coordinator flow all the facets of an account. He or she has to be sensitive to client relations, to see that all the schedules are met, and material delivered to publications, while at the same time striving to give creativity a chance to breathe. Moreover, the account coordinator has to understand the details of production.

On February 1st, I had finished my final draft and elatedly sent it off to Bette Schwartzberg. But the author's job, with such a book, still has a long way to go. He is responsible for locating the final artwork for the exhibits, for getting releases, and for many other details. Later that same day, I learned that I had to undergo a massive operation (three, as it turned out), and that I would be hospitalized for many weeks, completely "out of it" (even for consultation).

I appealed to Lin to take over as my surrogate, and his immediate response was, "It would be a labor of love." During the ensuing weeks, he and Bette collaborated on the enormous task, and somehow carried it through, constantly reassuring me, with solicitous messages to my intensive care room, that there wasn't a thing to worry about!

The third acknowledgment, in this category, goes to Nick Rudd, who had started the Resource Center ten years ago. Although he had since been promoted, to direct *all* Management Services, it was Nick who had first to pass upon the concept, to help chivvy it through its many stages, and, indeed, to perform a miracle of intellectual gymnastics when he read my first draft in one sitting and delivered a crystal-clear, detailed critique, page by page, down to suggestions for punctuation.

The fourth member of these "prime movers" was that monument to patience and forbearance, Bill Foley, present Director of the Resource Center, who somehow managed to conduct his seminars and get his own complex job done while, one by one, responding to my queries for information and sources. I count, in my correspondence file, more than a hundred screeds I would fire off to Bill Foley, and lo and behold, the answers always came back.

The fifth hero, in my first list, is Bob Stone, literally the nation's leading teacher, writer, and expert on direct marketing and direct response advertising, who consented, at short notice, to write the chapter on that subject when I was completely flummoxed by a specialty too alien for me to handle competently.

Finally, my sixth prime mover was John Rindlaub, Y&R's newly appointed Director of Corporate Relations. John was following in the footsteps of Mark Stroock, who had held that crucial job for some thirty years. Here was John, with a thousand new tasks and critical decisions to be made, whose *last* need was the subtle shepherding of my manuscript through the yeas and nays, the legalities, the company policies, and what have you. John, I humbly doff my beret to you, and add my deep affection as well.

The second category of acknowledgments goes to all the people whose names and quotes and opinions you will specifically find in the book. Although many of these worthies appear more than once in the manuscript, I am listing them, one at a time, in the order in which they first appear:

John Eighmey, Nick Rudd, Alex Kroll, Ray Rubicam, Bob Work, Ed Ney, George Gribbin, Mark Stroock, Art Klein, Jim Morey, Jim Kobak, Ed Barnes, Pete Peabody, Frazier Purdy, Sam Cherr, Bill Foley, Peter Georgescu, Hanno Fuchs, Joe Plummer, Shirley Simkin, Howard Krieger, Alex Osborn, Mary O'Meara, Daniel Starch, John Ferrell, John Rindlaub, Art Harris, Bob Czernysz, Bill Taubin, Roger Mader, Clark Frankel, Gary Goldstein, George D'Hussey, Clay Felker, Milton Glaser, Arthur Hettick, John Mack Carter, Hal Silverman, Andre Demarais, Klaus Schmidt, Manny Perez, Don Egensteiner, Laurie Kahn, Hunter Murtaugh, Sid Hecker, Stephanie Kugelman, John Kelley, Bob Mayer, Jenny Bowen, Muts Yasumura, Gene Ptachinski, Bill Power, Jim Castling, Alan Zweibel, Douglas Haley, Harold Burson, Jim Burke, Jim Dowling, Al Schreiber, Jerry Welsh, Bill Rylance, Dave Berman, Barbara Delfyett-Hester, Frank Zingale, Arthur Cohen, Joe De Deo, Ed Thomas, Norman Kappler, John Hatheway, Niels Menko, Ted Levitt, Philip Kotler, Kenschi Ohmae, Jerry Wind, Mary Alice Kennedy, John P. McGarry, Jr.

The third category of acknowledgments go to many people whose names do not appear in the manuscript, stalwarts too numerous to list here, but those who actually "dug up" the material and/or paved my way to the information I needed. I think specifically, for the digging up, of Margaret Hasselberg, of the media department. For the paving of the way I especially credit David May for his editing of the IC section, and Bill Hammons, Senior Vice President and Director of Training and Development Worldwide at Burson-Marsteller. Bill led me through the maze of an organization I had never experienced, and provided most of the material contained in that chapter. (A thousand thanks, Bill, and to you others of Burson-Marsteller, I feel I know ye!)

The fourth category is the entire Y&R family, in every department, in every associated company, in every office around the world. For training to be effective—to be more than just an imposed body of guides and rules—you have to have employees who really want it, people who have the *will* to excel. Everywhere at Y&R I have found this common spirit, an eagerness to learn and improve.

Finally, for my fifth category, I must borrow from Alex Kroll's felicitous phrase, "the usable past." On every one of these pages, in all these precepts and basics, live and glow the generous teachings of those Y&R-ites who are no longer literally with us. Just as Ed Ney fondly remembered his first mentor at Y&R, Lu Weil, just so every one of us has in mind a teacher or teachers who inspired us. I see and hear, in my mind's eye, the genial art director, Jack Anthony, who seemed to "throw it away" but could never have a layout or idea that was not fresh. I see the brilliant writings of a Dick Olmsted, freshly inspiring me, saying, "go thou and do likewise." I see that tough topkick (who was really a pussycat at the core), Tony Geoghegan, running a Media Department that couldn't make a move without a touch of class and often breathtaking boldness. I see a feisty Sam Cherr, when Y&R's Merchandising Department was a force to be reckoned with. Of course, I constantly think of my friend, George Gribbin, Scholarly gentleman farmer who, I do believe loved nature even more than his thoroughly stimulating occupation. I remember Sig' Larmon, the Chairman of the Board who used to take prospective clients "up to the top of the mountain and show them the view"—the one leader, I think, who especially set the tone for Y&R's permanent dedication to high ethics and public service. And in the more recent "usable past," I am in mind of Ed Ney, now U.S. Ambassador to Canada, who led the agency during its period of greatest growth.

These visions of Y&R past remain constantly fresh. They are the living embodiment of the continuity of Y&R, whose traveling creative workshop has *always* been with us.

Long may the breed improve!

As the author of this book I have considered myself to be the conduit for relating the historical development and application of Y&R training programs. Chapter 9 is the exception. And with good reason.

Through serendipity, I might say, I found the one person capable of writing the chapter on direct marketing. And he's an alumnus of Y&R. So it's all in the family.

Bob Stone has been teacher to decades of direct marketers around the world. He's taught and lectured throughout this country and in England, France, Germany, Holland, Sweden, Japan, and South Africa. He serves as adjunct professor of direct marketing at both Northwestern University and University of Missouri/Kansas City.

His landmark book—*Successful Direct Marketing Methods*—is now in its fourth edition. This book is in the best-seller class among business books and is the required text in marketing classes in close to 100 universities around the world.

Bob Stone has written over 200 articles on direct marketing for *Advertising Age*. His awards are many. He is a member of the Direct Marketing Hall of Fame. He's a recipient of the Edward N. Mayer, Jr., award for contributions to direct marketing education as well as the John Caples award for copy excellence. Bob Stone has also received the prestigious Irving Wunderman Award for a decade or more of unique creative work.

Sandwiched between Bob's training and writing has been an illustrious business career. He co-founded Stone & Adler—the first full-service direct marketing agency in the middle west—in 1966. The agency grew to be one of the world's largest. Chapter 9 starts at the point S&A was acquired by Y&R. You will learn in detail how Bob Stone created and orchestrated the first Y&R direct marketing workshop.

Three Commentaries About the Author and His Book

By Alex Kroll, Chairman and CEO, Young & Rubicam, Inc.:

Last week, I got a call from the creative director of a major competitor.

"I'm giving a speech to the American Association of Advertising Agencies," he said, "and I want to illustrate a point I'm making with a Goodyear commercial called 'When there's no man around, Goodyear should be.' Could you send me a copy?"

This is not a particularly unusual request except for the fact that the commercial was created in 1964. We're in a business whose product is novelty, and there aren't many 25-year old advertisements that one remembers, let alone finds interesting. But this commercial is one of them. It was the first commercial that made an emotional appeal for a practical, down-to-earth product like a tire. The inspiration behind this breakthrough was Hanley Norins.

Hanley has been breaking rules and creating "firsts" since he joined Young & Rubicam as a copywriter in the new television department in 1951. In the early days of television, when most advertising writers were so contemptuous of the new medium that they delegated it to the most junior writer, he explored its possibilities with the enthusiasm of a kid who has just been given a new toy.

He created the first television commercial that didn't use a spoken word ("Go. Go. Goodyear."), the first hidden-camera commercial ("Cheer Eyewitness."), and the first commercials that took advantage of the new medium's amazing ability to demonstrate (such as shaving a peach and brush to demonstrate the gentleness and power of a Remington Electric Shaver.)

Besides raw talent, the most precious trait a creative person can have is "openness"—being open to ideas, to people, to experience, to change. Hanley is one of the most open, least-judgmental people I know. He's the kind of man who discovered the Beatles before his kids. In fact, I remember one of our colleagues saying, "Can you imagine having Hanley for a father? You'd have nothing to rebel against."

Hanley is not only interested in everything, he collects everything. Long before there was such a thing as a Walkman, he carried a tape recorder everywhere he went—to meetings, to the movies, and for all I know to bed—sopping up every sound and word he heard. David Ogilvy has written that he likes to hire people with "well-furnished minds." Hanley's mind is furnished like the Collier brothers' apartment.

And Hanley has the creative person's ability to relate and connect and combine his vast collection of ideas and experiences in new and arresting ways. To use the phrase that he often uses himself when he's urging copywriters and art directors to new heights, he knows how to "make the strange familiar and the familiar strange."

His physical appearance attests to his creativity. He looks exactly like Groucho Marx (familiar). But he wears a jump-suit (very strange). For years, Hanley wore nothing but jump suits—a testament to his originality and his continence.

In 1960 our West Coast client Kaiser wanted to launch a corporate image campaign that, instead of simply talking about their company, would capture its essence by discussing seminal ideas from many different fields. Who could do it better than our human idea attic, Hanley Norins. So Hanley was sent to San Francisco to be creative director of our office there and head up work for the Kaiser account.

But after a year or two without Hanley, his biggest New York client, Goodyear, became restive and insisted that he be brought back to work for them. By this time, however, Hanley had fallen in love with San Francisco and a tiny town called Mendocino on up the Coast. California's youthfulness and openness—its sense of limitless possibility—seemed a metaphor for the man. Nothing—not even money—could persuade him to return to New York.

Goodyear had to have Hanley. So for half a dozen years, Hanley was the creative director of the Goodyear account in our New York office, commuting every week from San Francisco to New York by way of Akron. He habitually called his New York writers and artists around 10 P.M. California time. Courteous to a fault, his opening words were always, "Is this a good time to talk?" Once, when he interrupted one of his writers in the midst of making love to his wife, he was finally told that the answer was "no."

In addition to talent and openness, the third requirement for success on the creative side of advertising is resilience—and that's something else Hanley has more of than anyone else I know. Proof of the point is the fact that he holds the agency record for length of time on the Gallo account.

But the most impressive thing about Hanley isn't what he has done but what he has helped others to do. In New York, in San Francisco, in Los Angeles—in every office where he's worked—he has coaxed and badgered and bullied and loved a whole generation of creative people into being the very best and brightest in our company and in our business. If I were to list everyone whose creative talents have been helped and honed by Hanley, there wouldn't be room between these covers for his book.

Because he is such a great teacher—by precept, by example, by the sheer contagiousness of his enthusiasm—I coaxed Hanley out of retirement in 1978 and asked him to help start a Y&R Traveling Creative

Workshop; to be one of a trio of Y&R sages who would travel to each of our offices all over the world reminding our people of the basics of advertising creativity.

The workshop turned out to be a breakthrough idea. And since Hanley doesn't throw anything away, it's all here. The book also includes much additional material he has managed to inveigle from others that broadens the scope of the original workshops.

The printed word can't replicate a Groucho Marx look-alike in a jump suit conducting a brainstorming session at which he writes down every dumb idea that comes into your head as if it were as brilliant as $E=mc^2$. But here is as fine a course in advertising creativity as you can find in a book.

By Ed Ney, former Chairman and CEO, Young & Rubicam, Inc., now United States Ambassador to Canada:

Norins' book is an enormous contribution on what makes great advertising—examples galore from New York to Hong Kong. Norins knows what he's talking about—he was one of a worldwide creative traveling team which taught in every office of Young & Rubicam. A creative superstar himself ("Go, Go, Goodyear," Remington Electric Shaver and the Peach," etc.), he's one of the great teachers in advertising history. This is the best book of its kind that I've ever seen.

By John Kelley, former Advertising Director, Goodyear Tire and Rubber Company:

Hanley Norins and I worked together for a number of years, Hanley as Y&R Creative Director on Goodyear, of which I was VP Advertising.

As I look back on it now, all of us connected with Goodyear advertising at that time—both at the company and at Y&R—were in creative training by Hanley.

The reason was that, up to that time, much of creativity in advertising had to do with tinkering with words and pictures. Hanley's approach to advertising was a whole new world. His creative thrust dealt not so much with words and pictures as it did with the Big Idea—a creative happening—around which words and pictures fell swimmingly into place.

These would be Big Ideas which would allow us to build-in our own advertising excitement, an especially significant thing when you're dealing with a product which isn't itself very exciting. Thus, the advertising wasn't tedious and self-conscious, which is what bores most advertising viewers to death.

Examples of Hanley's Big Idea: To demonstrate a new kind of steel belted tire, Hanley had us build a road of axe blades, knives and saws, over which we ran and photographed our tires. For a new kind of studded snow tire, he had us field two cars in the famous Monte Carlo Over-the-Alps auto race, and follow them through the race in cinema verité style, from which we made commercials. For a run-flat tire, Hanley had us address male tire buyers over the shoulders of women, for the first time in tire advertising ("When There's No Man Around, Goodyear Should Be").

These campaigns were all big hits and won all kinds of advertising awards. Better yet, they helped Goodyear reach a totally dominant position in the domestic tire business at that time.

How did Hanley train us—agency and client—to take these creative risks? He did it with his rare ability to immerse everyone connected with his creative projects in his tireless and unending quest for the Big Idea. We weren't frittering our time tinkering with the advertising, we were centered on searching for an all-encompassing idea.

The result was an outpouring of focused creative energy. Everyone contributed, and Hanley was the conductor. It transcended the usual petty client-agency squabbles about words and pictures. The Big Ideas went beyond all that and got our full attention.

In those days, Hanley was 20 years ahead of his time, and he still is. Hanley's new book reflects the fact that the best training is in generating exciting advertising by energizing the people you work with, training them, in effect, to zero-in on and devote their energies to a core idea with power.

The quest for the Big Idea is elusive—much of the advertising we see today still hasn't found it. The people who are preparing this advertising will, hopefully, read Hanley's new book and learn how.

Note: John Kelley's 40 year background in advertising includes work as a writer and account executive for Batten, Barton, Durstine & Osborn, as President of his own agency in his home town of Columbus, Ohio, as an Advertising Manager of Monsanto Chemical Co., and for 25 years, as VP Advertising for Goodyear.

During that time, he was also Chairman of the Board of Directors of the Association of National Advertisers in New York, as well as Chairman of the Board of The Advertising Council of New York, the nation's premiere Public Service advertising arm.

About the Origin of This Book

In 1987, Bette Schwartzberg, acquisitions editor of the Prentice Hall Business & Professional Publishing division, having known about the original Y&R Traveling Creative Workshop, suggested that I write a book about it.

It sounded like a good idea, but I told her that the first traveling workshop was just the tip of the iceberg. An enormous effort and investment in Y&R training for creativity had gone on ever since 1978, and the book should be about the whole story.

It had been my privilege to have served, along with Shirley Simkin, on the faculty of that first traveling workshop. Our leader was the late great George Gribbin, former chairman of the board of Y&R, who selflessly came back from retirement to attempt the energy-sapping task of two years of world traveling and teaching. During much of the second year, when I served as creative director pro tem at Y&R West, John Rindlaub, now Y&R director of corporate relations, generously took my place on the faculty.

That initial worldwide training program, and all the training since, came about because of organic necessity. In 1923, John Orr Young and Ray Rubicam had left N. W. Ayer, to found their own agency on a literal shoelace (their first account was a shoelace company). Their second account was a little-known health drink called Postum, the first assignment from General Foods, one of today's oldest and most cherished Y&R accounts.

The original single Y&R office started in Philadelphia, but soon moved to New York. Shortly thereafter, John Orr Young departed for other commitments, and Ray Rubicam led the agency through its initial growth. During the ensuing 65 years, Y&R would have six more chief executive officers, and they were all dedicated to Ray's initial injunction, to "Resist the Usual." But the tiny "boutique" would always have the age-old problem: how to maintain the spirit, daring, and creativity that enabled the agency to grow in the first place, while, at the same time, offering clients the advantages of a large agency's comprehensive services.

In 1976, in a period of unprecedented growth, Ed Ney, then chairman of the board, and Alex Kroll and Alex Brody, presidents, respectively of Y&R U.S.A. and Y&R International, boldly launched a drive to achieve "Worldwide creative leadership by 1980."

How to do it? Training. Institute an expensive and ambitious program to train each and every member of the growing family in the qualities that had always accounted for Y&R's success.

Ney and his lieutenants were more readily able to effect such an investment because Y&R was then, and I daresay always will be, a private company, owned by its employees.

Our Traveling Creative Workshop was one of the first parts of that ambitious training program. And as might have been expected, by the time 1980 had arrived, Y&R's management remained dissatisfied. Confident as we all appeared to be, it was obvious that in four short years, the agency could not achieve its goal. Moreover, even if we had, we would have to continue the effort just to maintain our leadership.

The most important result is that we had helped to foster a momentum. The training activities summarized in this book are the result of a never-ending quest for excellence.

Hanley Norins

Hanley Norins,
Little River, California

Introduction

This book is a distillation of 65 years of Y&R experience. Here, for the first time in one place, you will find a summary of the principles and practices that have made Young & Rubicam the most consistently successful large agency in advertising and allied forms of communication.

Y&R has been named "Agency of the Year" so often by the trade that it might well be called "Agency of the Century."

It stands to reason, therefore, that you would be hard-pressed to find anywhere a more authoritative guide.

The book is entitled *The Young & Rubicam Traveling Creative Workshop*, but it is actually about *two* traveling creative workshops. The first was the vanguard:" a peripatetic school, that traveled for two years (1978 and 1979) to 40 offices of Young & Rubicam, in 22 countries, conducting two-day seminars each year on the Y&R basics of advertising creativity.

The second "traveling creative workshop" is both metaphorical and actual: metaphorical in the sense of the day-by-day training by Y&R supervisors and actual in the far-reaching educational activities developed since that first traveling school, by Y&R specialists in creative subjects and the company's Resource Center in New York.

Y&R invests over $6 million each year in all forms of training. The principles and practices revealed in the following pages are a kind of dividend for you. In this book you will find:

- Five guides for creating the ideal environment for creativity.

- How to develop a brilliant strategy and how to turn it into an exciting campaign.

- What creativity is and the process for achieving it.

- The shocking truth about print advertising readership and how you can magnify *your* ads' memorability and effectiveness.

- The one inviolate rule and five guides for creating successful television commercials.

- What the best print and TV producers do and how they do it.

- The secrets of Y&R's success in using research (ever since Ray Rubicam started the first agency research department, with George Gallup at its head).

☐ How Y&R's direct marketing agencies cultivate consumer relationships.

☐ Insights into the esoteric world of design and sales promotion.

☐ The training disciplines of Y&R's specialized company, Burson-Marsteller, world leader in public relations.

☐ Creativity in the exploding new medium of event marketing.

☐ State-of-the-art information about the changing world of media.

☐ Some essential lessons for integrated communications and creative global marketing.

It is a tribute to Young & Rubicam's open spirit that its management has permitted the revelation of so much priceless information. It is in the tradition of this unique, still privately owned agency to share its knowledge. In fact, Y&R's leaders, owing to the agency's success, have a profound sense of obligation to help improve the breed. And that is why so many other leaders, in agency and advertiser organizations, are Y&R alumni.

As Alex Kroll, chairman and CEO, has expressed it, "Growing people should be every agency's tithe to the agency business."

Contents

CHAPTER

1

How to Create the Environment for Creativity

John Eighmey,
former Manager, New York
Y&R Creative Department

I was a former academic, a college professor, someone trained in the behavioral sciences. I had mastered the logic of proof, which is setting up concepts, theories, and methodologies for proving and investigating, and I always felt that the fit between the real world and the conceptual world of theory was not a good one. To come into an atmosphere where I was deeply involved with creative people, and my job would help create an environment that supported them, that's where my thinking changed about what communication is, and how we communicate, and to deeply appreciate how fragile ideas are, and how important the environments are which give rise to ideas and let them grow.

Creativity, like a delicate flower, needs the ideal atmosphere in which to flourish. The first Y&R Traveling Creative Workshop, of 1978–1979, attempted to provide that atmosphere for all the agency's employees around the world. We tried to carry, in a sense, the environment of the entire agency with us—what Alex Kroll has called its "usable past"—as well as its mission and the principles and practices we all hoped would help to ensure a prosperous future.

Throughout the years that followed, the agency continued to have a "traveling creative workshop," which has become a veritable Y&R university. It consists, first and foremost, of the day-by-day education every creative director and management supervisor transmits to his or her staff. In addition, there is Y&R's extensive Resource Center, which develops and administers countless individual workshops and the month-long Advertising Skills Workshop; dispatches a constant stream of videocassettes, literature, and speeches by key executives to offices around the world; and provides specialized instructors to offices where their expertise is desired.

In the following chapters you will read about the specific lessons our traveling workshops have provided. But, first, let's consider the setting in which those lessons are learned.

FIVE WAYS TO FOSTER CREATIVITY IN YOUR ORGANIZATION

I have distilled, from all my notes and interviews, a summary of five ways to achieve an ideal environment for creativity. These five guides are as follows:

1. Have a high goal and commit yourselves to it.

2. Cultivate a company culture, an attitude, a way of approaching problems.

3. Constantly provide incentives for improving creativity.

4. Keep renewing yourselves, reinventing yourselves, by making stimulating changes.

5. Constantly provide the best possible tools and the best possible training.

I hope that what has succeeded for Young & Rubicam will give inspiration to you. Whether you work with an organization that has only one or a few offices or, like today's Y&R, has more than two hundred, whether you have 10 employees or the more than 12,000 of a Y&R, the principles we have learned, about this fragile living thing called creativity, can be the same for you. Everyone is potentially creative, and the degree to which that creativity flourishes depends to a major extent on the environment.

Guide 1: Have a High Goal

Nick Rudd, head of Y&R's Management Services, speaking to the Conference Board on "The Adaptive Organization," once said that "organizations are places in which people seek meaning." There is no better way, for you and your fellow workers to give meaning to your workaday life than to share a common goal. That simple formula is the way to convert an amorphous group into a cohesive team.

Here is what Alex Kroll, Y&R's current CEO, has to say about goal setting:

If there's one thing that I can attest to, that I have come to believe more fervently than anything else, it is to *have a sense of purpose.* The greatest creators have it. Most of them are stimulated in and of themselves. They work in lonely places. *But in a company it can be the collective purpose, and the higher it is and bolder it is, the more creative energy you release.*

What do I mean by a purpose? I think it's when people really believe in their business life that they're adding some new value or advancing a good cause in their commercial lives. I'm not referring to *Pro Bono* advertising, although that is another area in which we have devoutly become leaders. I mean in this business, as a business, we're advancing a cause, we're on the high road to making the business better and making ourselves a better value, a greater bargain. I think what came together when we acquired the major direct marketing agency and the major public relations agency and the major sales promotion agency, and the major medical agency—all with a view to the integration of people of special expertise—we brought something new to the game. We could together offer combined communications that didn't exist before.

We have an outer-directed mission, which is *to be the best at creating ideas which can build a client's business,* change his history for the better, his cause, whatever you want to call it. That's important, to come to work and say we're here for a cause—we're not a bucket shop, we aren't here to squeeze as much out of the plant as we can for as little, or to do it the easy way. It's often a painful process, to hew to our goal, but we must keep trying to do it—*to expand the possibilities of creative communication in the commercial field,* of inventing things, of new kinds of research, of sharper kinds of communication, of better kinds of integration—all that is in our annual plan (and it *is* in our annual plan!)

When you get these agglomerates of companies, with no purpose but bigness and profit, not only is there loss of jobs, there's a real loss of identity. What does the management expect? Well, a great return on investment, increase in stock value. But what do you expect from me as a worker, not me as an income-producer. They don't know. *Where there's an absence of purpose, or it becomes blurred or quiescent or ambiguous, then the quality of the output inevitably deteriorates.*

Y&R's Success Formula—A Guide for You   Y&R, in its 66-year history, always did have a mission statement of a sort. Ray Rubicam expressed it first with three words: "Resist the Usual." A couple of decades later, Copy Supervisor Bob Work devised the *Golden Ruler*— "to reach the best possible prospects, with the best possible message, at the lowest possible cost." When you break down that statement, it legislates that you work very hard to identify who your best prospect is, that you have a clear enough understanding to determine the best possible message for that particular prospect, and that you create the freshest, most provocative idea so that your ad will get the highest noting and reading—hence you are delivering the message at the lowest possible cost. That's a pretty good and inclusive formula for fulfilling the mission of creative advertising.

During the early 1970s Ed Ney, who succeeded Ed Bond and George Gribbin as heads of the agency, extended the goal of "creative advertising" to that of "total commercial persuasion," which would include public relations, direct marketing, sales promotion, and so on.

At the time of our first traveling workshop, in 1978, everyone involved felt a need for a refresher, a summarizing statement about the goal our workshop would inaugurate. So George Gribbin, who had written so many great ads in the past, sat down and wrote what would turn out to be his valedictory. His "ad to the agency" was set in beautifully spacious type and dispatched, in large poster form, to every office of Y&R. Some offices had it blown up to billboard size (Figure 1–1).

This credo called for the agency to be "better than the competition in every category, in every medium, and in every market in which we do business." That meant that "we must produce work that accomplishes its selling objective with consistently more flair and imagination than the advertising created for competitive products."

Y&R

YOUNG&RUBICAM I

FIGURE 1–1

"Grib" went on to say that such advertising can only be created "in an environment where leadership is strong, sensitive, and inspiring, and where the creative staff has great joy in doing its work." He concluded by defining the major characteristics by which one could recognize creative advertising.

During the years that followed the first traveling creative workshop, many changes occurred in the life of the agency, including the continuing acquisition of those specialized agencies and a massive effort to integrate them into what came to be known as "The Whole Egg." At the same time, Y&R had to digest more than $4 billion in billing, which was quadruple what it had been when our workshop began. In 1985, to get back on the main track, the management launched a second concentrated "Creative Leadership" program, with the following:

MISSION STATEMENT

Our aspirations are high.

We intend to be the best in the business of creating marketing and communications ideas which can help a business grow.

To be that

We need ideas which are fresh, hot and consistently more original and productive than our clients can get elsewhere.

We need people who can create those ideas and inspire others to create them.

We need understanding which will give us a truer sense of our audiences and how to reach them than our competitors have.

We need profit which will fuel new growth and reward those special people who can make our aspirations come true.

And finally, we need to have fun at this business, because the best ideas are often the spontaneous sparks of minds released from tension.

And after all, it's just nicer to work that way.

Commitment: The Critical Need It then remained for everyone to get behind those words. And this is where the crucial need for commitment comes in. Often you will find companies declaring mission statements that, like motherhood and the flag, are then honored in the breach. They are empty clichés and bombast. Instead, your mission statement should be an actual blueprint on which to build a solid future. Consider what explicit directions you get from the foregoing mission statement. If you are truly resolved to live up to such a goal, countless expensive and time-consuming actions must take place. *To be the best*, the agency must constantly monitor its competition and measure its work against its competitor. *To get ideas that are fresh* requires an infinite degree of creative activity. *To have the best people* requires a special recruitment program and superior training. *To understand the agency's audiences* requires an immense investment in consumer research. *To make a profit* requires savvy management methods that, while controlling costs, do not inhibit creativity. To do all this, and *to enjoy doing it*, requires planning and execution which will constantly challenge your ingenuity.

And it all starts with the company leader. Says Mark Stroock, Y&R's public relations director for 30 years:

If the CEO doesn't do it, it doesn't get done. He's got to have a mission, and he's got to commit himself to it, and then he's got to put teeth into it and commit the whole agency.

A short time after our first traveling creative workshop began, Nick Rudd was appointed Y&R's training officer. His mission was to set up the finest educational program in the profession, and he succeeded so well that when other agencies wanted training programs, they naturally looked to Y&R's example. N. W. Ayer's Bill Marx was named director of training in 1984, and he called Nick for advice. Reported *Television/Radio Age*, "Marx recalls that the first thing Rudd said was, 'Before I waste your time, who at Ayer made you the training director?' When Marx replied, 'Lou Hagopian,' Rudd then settled back with, 'Okay. Let's talk.' . . . Explains Marx: 'What Nick meant was that if anybody except the top man in the organization is the one who believes in training and wants to do it, training is very likely to be one of the first projects overboard, the first crunch that comes along. But if the man who's running the show is the one who's pushing training, then it's likely to be around awhile.'"

Guide 2: Cultivate a Company Culture

A dictionary definition of the word "culture" is "the totality of socially transmitted behavior patterns, arts, beliefs, institutions, and all other products of human work and thought characteristic of a community or population."

Defining a company's culture is a little harder to express than its mission, because a company consists of so many disparate individuals, and the larger the company the more difficult the task. Yet it's important to have and to perpetuate a culture because it helps to bind people together and to give them a sense of belonging.

Often the culture becomes the long shadow of one person, the strong personality, say, of the founder, as was the case for so many years with the Bernbach and Ogilvy agencies. From a long-range standpoint, this can be a risky kind of culture, because it tends to inhibit flexibility in its output and because it may disappear when that one strong progenitor is gone.

Can you describe the culture of *your* company? If it is a large and long-established company, it may or may not still have a common culture, but if it has been consistently successful, the chances are that it does. On the other hand, if yours is still a small company, you have the opportunity to start now to plant the seeds for a consistent culture to evolve. What should that culture be? Perhaps you will want to emulate the example of Young & Rubicam.

Y&R's Company Culture   I have always found it fascinating to speculate on how, through the tenure of seven different leaders, a predominant culture has continued to exist at Y&R. My analysis is that "like goes to like." Young & Rubicam people have always had a hard core of sincerity, honesty, and caring, *the kind of attitude that makes for doing a job well, not just for power, money, or praise, but simply for the sake of doing it.* Nor are Y&R people the kind who "put up a front" and tend to the sham or the phoney. If you are not a Y&R type of person, you probably would not be hired in the first place, or if you have been, you would not feel comfortable being there and would leave, or be asked to leave.

If I had to liken this huge organization to a well-known individual, in a personality statement, I think it might be to Fred Astaire, who always had a touch of class and was the consummate craftsman.

The Three Requisites for Greatness   Ray Rubicam once said that an agency cannot be great unless it excels in three qualities: "One is ingenuity, another is thoroughness, and the third is restlessness." That last quality, restlessness, has always been a pervasive part of this company's culture. It is because each generation eventually realizes that the essential purpose of the company is innovation. Says Art Klein, President of Y&R New York:

There have been a few times when we have strayed, but we keep coming back to it. There is the highest management emphasis on the creative product. You can never forget the business we're in, and I think some of our competitors are forgetting it. We're in the business of ideas, pure and simple. *You've got to have ideas, and you've got to execute those ideas better than anyone else. If you do that, all the rest falls into place.*

The Small-Team Spirit   Another part of Y&R's culture has been the stubborn maintenance of "The Product Group." This group consists of the fewest possible specialists from each discipline who make up the tightly knit, spirited team which every day does the creative work for each account.

The Wall Street Journal, in a lead story of the early 1980s, concerned with the trend toward bigness, headlined this solution as news:

Manageable Size

**Some Firms Fight Ills
Of Bigness by Keeping
Employee Units Small . . .
Benefits of Type Z Behavior**

Long before such a development was considered news or Type Z behavior had been invented, the culture of Y&R's Product Group inherently helped to solve the problem of the agency's constant expansion.

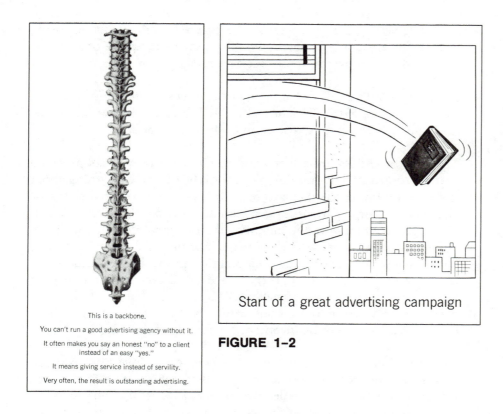

This is a backbone.

You can't run a good advertising agency without it.

It often makes you say an honest "no" to a client instead of an easy "yes."

It means giving service instead of servility.

Very often, the result is outstanding advertising.

Start of a great advertising campaign

FIGURE 1-2

Self-fulfilling Prophecies Another way Y&R has carried on its culture is through its advertising for itself—the famous Y&R house ads (Figure 1-2). They put the agency's best foot forward and are directed at the external audience we wish to influence. But they inevitably speak at the same time to our employees, who take pride in their messages and are impelled to live up to them.

Culture and the First Traveling Workshop Our first Traveling Creative Workshop helped to perpetuate the culture of the company with two presentations, both by George Gribbin. One, at the beginning of the workshop, was "Y&R Past and Present." The other, at the end, was "The Best of Y&R." These presentations made their point primarily by showing telescoped versions of the agency's best work. The company's culture was implicit in those presentations. And Grib, who had lived that culture for so long, and felt it so deeply, would conclude the workshop with these words: "The show is over. And I would just like to say, it's a good business that lets you do work like this, and that is your agency, and it is a very wonderful group of people."

Guide 3: Constantly Provide Incentives

John Eighmey spoke earlier about the fragility of ideas, and how important the environments are that give rise to them. If you are drawing your blueprint for encouraging creativity, you could begin with this checklist of the incentives Y&R developed through the years: the concrete monetary and future security rewards, the rewards of knowing you are appreciated by those you work with, the incentive of healthy competition within the agency, the incentive of winning awards from your peers and of having your good work publicly recognized, the incentive of being educated every day by the work you do, and the incentive of an atmosphere where people stay loose and have fun.

Let's begin with the environmental incentives we developed during those two years of the Traveling Creative Workshop in the late 1970s. As I said, this was to be a reflection of the agency at large.

Most of the offices announced the coming of the workshop with a fanfare, and many had fun doing it. From the outset, everything about the workshop was calculated to be a positive experience rather than a chore. We knew, from our long experience as supervisors, that *there is nothing more stimulating to creativity than a can-do spirit*. Individual writers, who often get writer's block, and artists who find themselves fallow, know all too well how demoralizing is a feeling of inadequacy. But sports teams in a slump, if they have spirit, can sometimes call on inner resources they hardly knew they had and suddenly make a comeback. So too with the writers and artists, and other creative people in our agency, who need the incentive of a feeling of confidence.

The very fact that the agency's management was investing so much time and money to reach out to branch offices which often felt isolated was in itself a boost to morale. We encouraged further confidence by setting aside periods during the workshop when the offices presented their work and enjoyed positive feedback. We didn't hesitate to criticize poor practices, but there was plenty of praise to go around, and we realized how vital it was for morale to remove, as quickly as possible, any vestige of the offices' feeling threatened by these experts from the home office.

To encourage that family feeling of intimacy, we began each seminar with a warmup game, which had nothing to do with the work at hand. Grib would light a candle and say, "Imagine that you have died and have been reborn. You can come back to earth as anything you want to be *except* a human being. Now write down what you would like to be and why."

After an interval, with everyone scribbling, we would raise the lights and go around the group as people read what they'd written. There was always much laughter and expressions of surprise and admiration. People revealed their sensitivity and imagination: "A ray of sunlight, that is always slanted between a birch tree and a cabin, even when it's not visible." "An oatmeal box, because then children could play with me, use me as a telephone." "An eagle, because he represents the concept of freedom and the ability to look down on the world without being constricted." "A Siamese cat, because cats are loving and curious creatures." . . .

Such a warmup game served to put people at their ease and to set the tone of intimacy for the hours to follow, when we would constantly encourage participation. Grib explained the purpose of the game:

You can see how different each one of you is from another. And one of the very fine things about a good organization is that it brings together people of many different backgrounds, of many different ways of thinking, much range of feeling. And I have found that there is a temptation in the advertising business for people to classify themselves in groups. But the best creativity comes out of diversity and the opportunity to draw on the ideas of many different kinds of people.

We would also, in the workshops, use the stimulus of competition, by dividing the groups at large into small teams, which replicated "The Product Group" system. These teams competed against one another in problem-solving sessions, with an award given to the team voted the most successful.

Another spirit-inspiring device was the practice of each office throwing a party at the end of the first day's session. The offices vied with one another to give the most creative parties—in Austria a party in a *Weinstübe*, with entertainers wearing folk costumes, in Hong Kong the party on a Chinese junk, in Paris the party at a fine restaurant featuring what was then the new vogue of *nouvelle cuisine* (some 32 courses were served).

Of course, *one of the greatest incentives of the traveling workshop was the feeling of pride it left in its wake.* The participants had seen many examples of exciting work, the kind of creativity they could then aspire to. They had critiqued advertising in the light of the creative principles we reviewed. Jim Morey, president of Hutchins/Y&R in Rochester, expressed the inspiration of the workshop in his remarks at its conclusion:

A meeting like this is like being reborn. . . . We have some tools we didn't have before. But none of it will be meaningful unless we follow it up.

We were finding fault with multimillion-dollar accounts. That's kind of exciting. But we're saying, look at what they're lacking. They're missing basics, they're not grabbing attention up front.

We're looking at the Burke scores, and we're seeing the tiny little things you can do to increase recall.

The account people are asking the same questions that the writer and the art director are asking themselves—is it a stopper, very basic; if nobody stops, if they're thumbing, when they're getting that two or three second exposure to a magazine, we're nowhere.

I'd like to see us, starting from today, really make a total commitment to the quality of our creative product, of fighting, if not to the death, at least to the point where you can't debate any more with a client, on the campaigns we really believe in.

I said that our workshop reflected the agency at large, and Y&R had always had an arsenal of incentives for creativity. These had helped to make it the most popular of the large agencies, as trade journalists and writers of books about advertising had often highlighted; for example, according to Martin Mayer, in *Madison Avenue, U.S.A*, "[Y&R is] . . . by far the best *liked* agency in the business, by agency people. 'If I were a client,' says the head of a considerable rival agency, 'I wouldn't give my business to us; I'd give it to Y&R.'"

To begin with, Y&R pioneered benefit packages that included an employee trust fund and generous year-end bonuses decades before the custom became widespread. In later years, after the phenomenal growth in accounts and numbers of employees, Ed Ney had the temerity to eliminate that universal trust fund and to substitute an equitable pension plan, *plus* programs called "P.I.P." and "M.I.P."—"Profit Incentive Program" and "Management Incentive Program"—so that *those who did the most meritorious work could enjoy a greater percentage of the profits.*

In addition, there were innumerable "perks": posh birthday presents for every employee; special occasion gifts placed on the desks early in the morning; Easter and Thanksgiving baskets; umbrellas with the Y&R logo to mark the advent of spring showers; hundreds of Mickey Mouse dolls for having won the $40 million Disney account. It's always great fun, during the commuter hour, to see the astonished look on passers-by faces when hundreds of employees disgorge into 42nd Street displaying such gifts.

The Importance of Awards   One should not underestimate the importance of the winning of awards, for unlike authors and artists, our creative people do not have the satisfaction of signing their works. And so, expensive and time consuming as the multiplying award events have become, it's worthwhile to enable your creative people to aspire to as many gold medals and "best of shows" as they can.

Y&R has also constantly encouraged interagency awards, displays, and distribution of "the best ad of the month," "the best TV commercial," and so on. After George Gribbin's death, the agency established the "Grib" award for creative excellence, which was a fine sculpture of Grib's noble head. Most recently, to give the greatest possible impetus to the second "Creative Leadership" program, "The Gang of Ten" (creative directors from the company's ten largest offices) culled through hundreds of agencywide submissions in various categories. The first Y&R "Academy Award" took place in 1986, at Disneyworld, in Orlando, Florida, where the agency flew in the winners from all over the world. The prizes were incentives indeed—$25,000 for the best campaign, $10,000 each for the best print ad and TV commercial, as well as generous awards for posters and radio commercials.

More Incentives for Creativity   But all these tangible incentives are only frosting on the cake of *the incentives that we who are in charge should provide for our creative people every day they come to work.* There are all kinds of encouragement to be given, to stir up what I like to call "our playful minds." For example, Alex Kroll found that the statement of a problem, for a team effort, could be an irresistible incentive:

I think the best thing we can do for creators is to structure the problem. What I did, as a creative supervisor, that felt good unconsciously, came out of my experiences as a football player. I made games out of these things, with fields and boundaries, because I could always visualize problems, almost as tangible, visible things: "This is where we're going on Cheer, Dash, or Spic & Span. That's the goal, here are the boundaries—you can't go left of that or right of that, but down the field, and we have to overcome these obstacles, and let's go!"

It was a kind of enthusiasm, because it was a game. And what I didn't realize until years later (you're sitting around on the rocking chair, y'know) is that that took a lot of tension out of the situation. Nobody doubts for a moment that we're in this for commercial purposes, with a lot of real money riding on it. But for that moment, as we all sat there, it was a game, and the team said, yeah, let's win the game. And winning the game is a lot more fun and a lot looser an enterprise than working on the next Spic & Span backup campaign.

There are many different ways to play "the ad game," and the sheer pleasure of it can be the greatest incentive of all, if only we don't take ourselves so seriously as to squeeze the joy out of it. There is no more exciting game I know and no more exciting people to play it with—stimulating people, with wide-ranging interests and a sense of humor.

My own special method of helping the game along is "planned chaos." (I shall elaborate on this in Chapter Three.) When I first became a creative director, I asked one of the art directors to make a sign, in large, frivolous, multicolored letters. I would hang the sign on the wall of whatever office I occupied, throughout the country and the world. The sign said, "ENJOY YOURSELF!" It remained a fixture of our brainstorming sessions until one day a sly character on the staff wrote in small letters under my command: "(. . . or I'll kill you!)."

Guide 4: Keep Renewing Yourselves

I take my caption from John Gardner's book *Self-renewal*. He emphasizes that if you are sensitive to the changing world around you, you are acutely aware of the need to change *yourself* in order to cope with it. *Making changes is not only a good policy for the contemporary world, but also because a company can become smug and even bored after using the same methods and same system for too long.* A company needs novelty and variety, just as every individual does.

I mentioned that restlessness has been part of Y&R's culture, and there have been several watersheds in the company's history which have called for deliberate major changes.

The "Usable Past"   The trick is to make such changes without disrupting and demoralizing the whole organization. Says Kroll:

You've got to keep evolving, by deliberately making changes. Some of them are to keep up with changes outside that are already happening, some of them to anticipate change, to stay ahead of the crowd. For example, we all recognize now the biggest change of all, for our business. Twenty-five years ago we were still in that delightful age of homogenization—mass markets, mass industry, mass production, mass media. Today we're just the opposite, fragmented in everything, so our clients have a much more complicated task in persuading the people they want to—in reaching them in certain media and doing it in a cost-effective way. It's a much more complicated way.

You've got to keep making changes, but at the same time, I've become more respectful of Edmund Burke's views on change—of doing honor to your traditions while making changes, rather than tearing the temple down every time. One of the real accomplishments I hope I'll be remembered for is my constantly trying to interpret what I call "the usable past."

This blending of past and future, the conflict between maintaining traditions and creating new ones, can be alleviated by working from within, enlisting the people of your organization to be as creative about organizational changes as they are about creating advertising.

One example of how this was done was when Y&R was at an unusually low ebb. Profits had been off and a brand-new CEO had taken over in the person of Ed Ney. He felt that some drastic changes had to be made, but he wanted to be circumspect about them. He began by asking for the help of Jim Kobak, a friend and neighbor who was the leading consultant to the magazine industry:

I asked Jim to come in and take a look at Y&R in New York, to talk to a lot of our executives and see what he saw in this company, what were the problems and what was not going right.

Jim spent a lot of time with us, and he gave us two or three pieces of advice which to me were unbelievably good. One was his report, the pros about Y&R versus the cons. He said, you've got a tremendous reputation as a company. You have a number of strong, good clients. You have a lot of people who believe in the idea of Y&R. You've got a few bucks in the bank. And he stopped there.

Then he gave us the cons, which took the next hour! Disorganized, bad morale, conflict between creative and account management, uncertainty about the new leadership, concern about people's jobs, shaky accounts, lack of an international company in any strength. And he went on, and it was terrible, just terrible. We were all so depressed.

But it was marvelous, it had to be done. The second good thing he did was this: He said, here's my recommendation to you people—rather than right away getting a McKinsey for a more in-depth plan, telling *you* how to do it, I recommend that you *set up a bunch of task forces.* Take some of your youngest and brightest and make them head of the account group, the media group, the creative group, and give them some of these problems, and let them have access to anything they want—the books and the this and that of the company. Give them time, a couple of months, and have them come back and report to you. And when they report, answer within a specific time, whether you agree with them or you don't. . . . Well, that became over time an electrifying thing for a lot of people.

Setting Up Task Forces: The Advantages   Those electrifying sessions and reports, which took place during more than a year that followed, resulted in many far-reaching changes which the management made, gradually but decisively. The first half-a-dozen task forces were broadened to include more people, who contributed to the final outcome by attending evening "rap sessions." Thus, the important changes, when they came, had already involved hundreds of the most creative people in the agency. They felt that they were *their* changes, and in addition to the efficacy of the changes, the process that was used to arrive at them was a boost to morale.

Another advantage to developing such a process is that, having proved its effectiveness, it can become standard operating procedure when the next seminal changes have to be made. The first "Creative Leadership" program was a change instituted five or six years later, and more and more of the rank and file were deeply involved in its creation. Our traveling workshop was just the tip of the iceberg, and *none of the facets of a broad master plan could have become so smoothly operational if it had not been for the use of task forces* and the intense work of many people, usually after hours. When you make changes, you have to communicate about them, and what better form of communication than for those they affect to have been actively involved in their inception.

Guide 5: The Best Possible Tools and Training

There are *four categories* of activity which can provide the tools and the training.

The first is an open, one-on-one daily interchange between highly motivated and creative individuals.

The second is having an ongoing creative workshop—in Y&R's case, the first peripatetic school and the innumerable workshops that followed. These workshops discuss such tools as the Creative Work Plan, the Strategy Selection Outline, the Competitive Advertising Summary, scoring methods for assessing TV commercials and print ads, and so on. And they train the participants in how best to use those tools.

The third category consists of publications, videotapes, and other interagency communications which constantly provide information and impetus to the agency's mission.

The fourth category is marketing the important changes you make through carefully planned major meetings.

Let's discuss these four categories more fully.

Training Category 1   The first category is what you might call, in educational terms, "the tutorial system." Young & Rubicam has traditionally promoted from within, and therefore the creative and management supervisors have usually gone through the tools and training of the agency's usable past. They are steeped in its mission, for they have helped to shape it.

At the heart of the Y&R structure is "The Product Group" I mentioned earlier: the smallest number of people necessary to handle an account efficiently, each of those people coming from one of the departments—management, creative, media, research—and each, according to whatever level of competence he or she has reached, having a mentor such as the creative supervisor or creative director.

Each mentor, of course, has his or her own distinctive personality and way of approaching and solving problems. This is good for the vigor and variety of the agency's creative output, because the young writers and art directors, or account coordinators and account executives, are being exposed to the stimulation of a variety of minds.

Taking into account the diversity of influences your personnel may encounter at your shop, it's a good idea, at least at the beginning, to move people around a little—expose them to various mentors and discover where the compatibilities lie. Just so, it is wise, if possible, to assign them to the kinds of accounts or responsibilities where their chemistry is best and they can use their best abilities.

It is the obligation of conscientious supervisors to enhance the abilities of those who will come after them. Ed Ney, speaking of his early years, said:

When I came to Y&R in 1951, I guess we took training for granted. There was a form of it in the Junior Executive kind of thing. It was a time of growth within the industry and Y&R, like other agencies, was stockpiling young people, and my experience, like that of others, was that I came under the tutelage of a first class trainer—a person who gave me a marvelous example—a fellow named Lu Weil. Y&R was to me more professionally managed than other agencies, and all the young people had their mentor.

I remember most vividly one of my mentors, Ed Barnes, a top management supervisor. He was a tough-spoken curmudgeon with a jowly face. Ed scared me at first—but how he championed creativity! I remember, when a client's sales manager insisted on cramming four or five sales points into a powerful singleminded commercial, and I moaned about it to Ed, he clapped his hat on his head, rushed to a plane, and went straight to the president of the company, growling, "This [EXPLETIVE] has got to stop!" He won that case, and many others, because clients respected his judgment, and he always protected the integrity of our work.

There are teachers and teachers. Walter Lippmann, the famous columnist, was called "The Great Simplifier," and some of the best teachers have been able to cut out the nonsense and get to the heart of things. Pete Peabody, one of Y&R's creative stars in the 1950s and 1960s, used to say, "There are only two things to consider, 'Who are you talking to and what's the best thing to say?'" International Creative Director Frazier Purdy, years later, working with a group whose assignment was to revise the creative strategy system, recalled Pete's ultimate simplification, and that triggered a watershed program which is now a complete workshop in itself.

My favorite way of boiling down an assignment for the people I supervise is: "What would you tell a friend?"

Some teachers don't even go that far, in their simplified instruction. Nick Rudd, when asked a question during the Advertising Skills Workshop, will more often than not reply: "What do you think?" He is encouraging independent thinking.

In that regard, the following story appeared in *The Link* (Y&R's alumni magazine) about Sam Cherr, who founded Y&R's Merchandising Department in 1925 and remained its director until he retired 32 years later:

Once a young marketing man prepared a report and left it with Sam for approval. A few days later he walked into Sam's office and asked him what he thought of it.

Sam held the report up. "Is this the best you can do?" he asked.

When the young man hemmed and hawed Sam handed it back to him. "Better take another swing at it," he said.

In a few days the report was dropped off again. And again the young man asked Sam's opinion.

"Are you sure," Sam said, "that you can't do a little better than this?"

He handed the report back.

"Give it another try," he said.

The third time the young man didn't wait for any comment from Sam at all. He plunked the report down on the desk and said, "This is the very best I can do. If you don't like it you'd better fire me because I can't do any better."

Sam was satisfied.

He picked up the report and said, "Good. Now I'll read it."

One of the greatest influences on Y&R creative people was George Gribbin, who came back from retirement to lead our first traveling creative workshop. *The Link* editorial, when he died, described him as "a gentle teacher who guided writers but always told them, 'Don't write to please me. Write to please yourself.'"

Cherish the best tutors in your organization. Search them out, reward them, give them the tools and responsibility to carry on. The best workshop, after all, is one-on-one, when a dedicated teacher shares his knowledge and experience with an eager student and encourages that student to think for himself. That was the Socratic method, and so it was appropriate that we called our first traveling creative workshop, in the Greek tradition, a peripatetic school.

Training Category 2   Workshops, as I said, are the second category of educational activity. What they teach, and how they teach it, have a common thread.

We discovered that thread after much soul searching when we were planning the curriculum for the first traveling workshop. We had a quandary. How could we possibly condense our experience of a combined hundred years into an activating two-day workshop? We knew that there were commonalities of subjects which all the offices would need—guidance for print and broadcast advertising, for creative research, for the development of strategy, and so forth. We made a list of modules and started to prepare an agenda. But what was the *big idea* of the workshop—the one unifying concept which would be easy for each student to remember, and to act upon, the day, week, month, and year following our departure?

Then came a revelation which, when I think of it now, should have been obvious. *Our central idea should be this: to teach, preach, and practice the basics of creative advertising.*

There *were* certain basics, we agreed, which would be common to all the work of all the participants. They would bridge the different problems and products and nationalities. Such basics as (1) every ad should have a stopper headline and/or visual, so the viewer or reader must perforce pause and participate, and (2) every commercial should have an opening of sufficient interest to hold the viewer who might otherwise be distracted from the interruption.

These were not rules, per se. They were truisms, overriding principles for creative advertising. They were as true for contemporary times as they were long ago when Y&R was young.

Would they be too simple? Would we be stating the obvious? They would be if they were not so often honored in the breach. How often, during the rush of deadlines, had all of us allowed ourselves to settle for tired old headlines, tedious, boring TV sales pitches—or allowed clients, fearful of the unexpected, to persuade us to settle for the clichés of the trade.

We realized that our creative workshop could not be too simple. Consider the basics of human experience—for example, the Golden Rule. If it were universally remembered and practiced, at all times, by everyone, all the problems that divide human beings would be permanently solved.

We all need to be reminded, constantly reminded, of the fundamentals. Bill Foley, director of the Resource Center, describes what happens in a training situation anywhere:

Creative people already know the fundamentals of good advertising. In a workshop, we *reawaken what they know*, with questions, games, great commercials. They rediscover the principles. They look at those principles with a fresh eye, understanding once more how advertising really works. And it is basically the same in any culture, anywhere in the world as far as the principles are concerned.

People make their own rules, which is why Y&R has none. This also means that when they break rules, it's possible to reach breakthrough advertising.

Our job in training is to challenge their thinking, get them to share experiences, get them to rediscover what makes good advertising, so then they can decide what to do about it back on the job.

The basics, which our first traveling creative workshop stressed, became the cornerstone of all the training programs Y&R has instituted since—and they should be yours, too. They are the heart of the Advertising Skills Workshop, the most ambitious program of the Resource Department—a four-and-a-half-week immersion that is attended once or twice a year by 30 carefully selected up-and-comers from offices everywhere. The attendees are a United Nations from all disciplines in the agency, and they are exposed to intensive training in some 50 subjects, by a faculty of the company's top experts. The instructors deal with the basics of each of those subjects, and the students are plunged into round-the-clock practice of those basics. They develop strategies, they plan campaigns, they go through the step-by-step process of each discipline, and they do it in a concentrated atmosphere, with the best leaders the agency has to offer. *The total experience is a comprehensive demonstration of how to do the best creative advertising.* And even though *these* students have already had an average of five years' experience with the agency, and have been chosen because they are the cream of the crop, the workshop is always a revelation. "I came here tired and bored with my work," said one graduate of a class. "I'm leaving rejuvenated."

I mentioned that there have been innumerable workshops since our 1978–1979 effort. You may want to emulate the training practice which has gone on at Y&R now for many years. As each activity occurs, the methods and examples are encapsulated into a self-contained "workshop." One example was a two-year agencywide push for improving creativity in print advertising, which our management decided was essential because print had taken a back seat to the more glamorous TV. That thoroughly worked-out curriculum became the syllabus for future generations.

Another example is the latest guide to strategy making, which Frazier Purdy describes as "a complete package, with all the material a supervisor may need, including an instructor's guide. I can take it off the shelf and give it to you, and you could run the workshop—it's that complete, and it's flexible enough for you to adapt local advertising to the workshop."

Y&R now has, at its Resource Center, complete off-the-shelf workshops on some 75 subjects, ranging from "Low-Cost TV Production" and "Brand Personality" to "Selling by Design" and "How to Judge Ideas." Those workshops are never allowed to become dated. They are revised, or replaced by workshops attuned to the times.

Training Category 3   The third training activity, interagency communication, includes well-edited house organs and the cassettes and proofs which are available to all product groups and all offices.

In addition, you should consider having a series of internal-external publications on special issues and thoughtfully produced seminars for the clients and staff of your organization. Some of those seminars at Y&R have featured guest speakers as prestigious and diverse as George Will, Barbara Walters, Brendan Gill, Nora Ephron, Vernon Jordan, and Ben Wattenberg and a number of U.S. senators and congressmembers. Other seminars, to stir the creative juices and trigger techniques, are often organized by individual creative directors, with guests from outside the agency business, such as fine artists, film directors, composers, writers, and entertainers.

Training Category 4   The fourth category is the activity of holding annual or biannual meetings, usually of three days' duration, which are like the retreats of religious groups and the human potential movements. They are meetings which often require months of preplanning, with a theme and a program, and they are deliberately designed to spearhead major advancements in the agency's goals and practices. As Nick Rudd puts it: "These meetings are to market what amounts to, in business school terms, 'a large-scale systems change' and in day-to-day advertising agency terms 'getting great work out of everybody everywhere in the world.'"

The retreats coincide with the objectives of the agency's annual plan, and for them Y&R goes first class. The meetings have been held in such stimulating venues as Venice, Marbella, Jamaica, Bermuda, San Francisco, and Santo Domingo. Some of them have been gatherings of creative directors, some of management supervisors, some of the boards of directors, and some of all these executives combined. To cite the latest example, there was a series of *four* such major meetings, over a period of *three years*, all to plan and implement the elements of the second creative leadership program, which is today a comprehensive, all-pervasive agency drive for excellence.

Such time-consuming thoroughness illustrates how dedicated you should be to the longevity of your training if you want to have a truly superior organization.

. . . .

A CHECKLIST FOR THIS CHAPTER
The Five Guides for Creating the Ideal Environment:

. . . .

1. Have a high company goal.

2. Cultivate a company culture.

3. Provide constant incentives.

4. Keep renewing yourselves.

5. Provide the best possible tools and training.

EXECUTIONAL ELEMENTS FOR THE FIVE GUIDES
. . . .

1. Develop a "mission statement" which is a *blueprint* for specific actions to fulfill the mission . . . such actions as measuring yourselves against competition, investment in recruitment and training, investment in research, cost control, constant planning for fulfilling your mission.

2. To cultivate your company culture, if you are an established company, analyze your current culture and determine whether it needs substantiation or change; if you are a relatively new company, and do not yet have a culture, decide now what it should be. In either case, proceed to cultivate the qualities you wish to instill—for example, ingenuity, thoroughness, restlessness—and summarize its

primary purpose—for example, innovation.

3. Incentives: financial rewards, provision for future security, constant benefits and "perks," constant recognition and praise for good work, public recognition when possible, the advantage of a perpetual education, an enjoyable atmosphere—making work fun.

4. For self-renewal, observe the changing world, make changes to cope with it, use the company's "usable past," enlist everyone's collaboration in making changes—for example, with task forces to implement changes.

5. For providing the best tools and training: provide a system for an open, one-on-one interchange—for example, tutorials, finding the best tutors, blending individuals with suitable chemistry—provide ample internal communications—for example, publications, stimulating guest speakers—market the company's changes with carefully preplanned meetings and seminars in attractive venues; and make annual plans with explicit objectives and specific assigned people to provide the tools to fulfill those objectives.

. . . .

CHAPTER

2 How to Determine Your Creative Strategy

You can really fly
once you know where you're going.

We believe that the sharpest advertising strategies provide the greatest creative freedom. Only when you know exactly where you're going can the imagination soar free, without fear or formulas.
YOUNG & RUBICAM INC.

FIGURE 2–1

As Figure 2–1, a Y&R house ad, dramatizes, creativity begins with a sound creative strategy. Says Alex Kroll, in that regard: "The best thing we can do for creative people is to structure the problem; we can't solve it for them." . . . Says Peter Georgescu, President of Y&R Advertising: "We are always seeking a brilliant strategy and a surprising execution." . . . Says Hanno Fuchs, a former creative director, now a Y&R consultant: "You can't have great executions without great strategies."

I shall comment, in this chapter, as to why this is so. Suffice to say here that strategy has always been the foundation of every Y&R effort, and never more so than in today's environment.

Strategy is, of course, another way of saying "positioning," and it has been the essence of the successful campaigns we all know. It is often based on facts, but it is determined by insight. Here is how it was expressed by Joe Plummer, former research director of Y&R:

An insight into the consumer is the engine that best drives advertising strategy. Usually, that insight is an emotional one. . . . Avis tapping the inherent sympathy for the underdog; Clairol's insight that second only to her age, a secret to be preserved, is the real color of her hair and the need to relieve that anxiety by promising only your hairdresser knows for sure; Miller Lite's assurance that the boys won't think you are a sissy for drinking a light beer; or the reverse snobbism which comes from Perrier giving you permission not to have a cocktail if you don't really want to.

Among Y&R's many cases of successful positioning are (1) the drive that vaulted Dr Pepper from a tiny regional soft drink to No. 3 nationally through its description as "America's most misunderstood drink," (2) the strategy for Kentucky Fried Chicken built on the insight that 85 percent of all American housewives felt some latent guilt about the fast foods they served their families, and the reassurance that KFC was guilt-free, and (3) the positioning of the Merrill Lynch brokerage as "a breed apart."

When we speak of advertising strategy, we are not discussing marketing strategy. But the former is the child of the latter. The marketing strategy, in turn, is born directly from the advertiser's marketing plan, which is "a detailed statement of the methods by which a predetermined marketing objective is to be realized." Joe Plummer explains these family relationships as follows:

The entire process has to work in order for advertising strategy to have some leverage. It starts with a corporate objective of the firm, the division or the brand.

This is then translated into a marketing objective. The most typical broad objectives are (1) accelerate or maintain growth; (2) hold share or profitability; (3) reenergize growth; and (4) introduce new products, brands, or lines.

Marketing strategy expands or interprets the objective in marketing terms—the consumer's behavior, the competition's behavior and the firm's behavior. These usually are stated in familiar strategic terms—increase consumer trial or consumption, develop a new positioning to new segments, diversify usage occasions, develop a profitable line extension, gain share from brand X.

The main point is that until you have one or more clearly stated marketing strategies, productive and leveragable advertising strategies can't be and shouldn't be brought to life. . . .

This means that we need a "bridge" between marketing strategy and advertising strategy—advertising objectives. This requires a "translation" from marketing strategy in rather fundamental terms before the right advertising strategy can be generated and agreed upon.

The "bare bones" of the advertising objective are rather simple and are concerned with three aspects of a question:

> **What ideas, facts, perceptions about our brand?**
>
> **Do we want to put into whose mind?**
>
> **For them to do what we hope they will do?**

To get at these "bare bones" issues about the objective systematically we need to (1) examine options, and (2) focus on the key issues.

The tools for examining options and focusing on key issues, which our first traveling creative workshop provided, were the Strategy Selection Outline (SSO) and the Creative Work Plan (CWP).

All the facets of these family relationships—the marketing strategy, the advertising strategy, and the creative work plan—are ideally worked out in close collaboration between the advertiser and Young & Rubicam's product group. It is for this reason that Y&R, throughout the years of training, has often invited clients to attend its workshops and has, in daily contact, communicated about its tools with its clients. However, the division of responsibility is, for the most part, for clients to initiate marketing plans and strategy and for the agency to initiate the thought processes that go into preparation of the SSO and the CWP.

Our traveling workshop devoted one module to both the SSO and the CWP. In this Chapter, I am reviewing the scaled-down version. Since our workshop concentrated on the *creative* aspects of advertising, more time was spent on the Creative Work Plan than on the SSO, which was the "enabling" tool for the CWP. Let me first, then, outline the presentation for the Creative Work Plan.

In Grib's introduction to the Y&R workshop, he showed a recent commercial from each of the agency offices. On that reel was a commercial from the Brazilian office, which featured the demonstration of an army tank atop an automobile to illustrate the car's amazing durability. Shirley Simkin would begin her talk about strategy (entitled, "The Groundwork for Creativity") with this comment: "Remember that automotive commercial Grib showed you from our Brazil office, with the tank being carried along by the car? There's a title at the end of the commercial and the literal translation says 'What is on the bottom must be as strong as what's on top.' That's a good way to think about strategy. If it isn't strong, no amount of creativity will save the situation."

THE CREATIVE WORK PLAN

The five-point Y&R Creative Work Plan was a one-page document, (Figure 2–2), with its five simple and explicit directions. There are many excellent methods for determining strategy, and the one described here is not the end-all and be-all. In fact, at this writing, Y&R is experimenting with a new, streamlined method which is proprietary and confidential. What I am reviewing, however, is *the kind of thinking* that goes into sound strategy making. Our Creative Work Plan had already been in use for a half-dozen years when our workshop began. But Shirley Simkin, when she presented it, made the point that she had never seen an office that could not use it a little better than they were doing, and that we could never practice the method too much. Just as a gymnast, a high diver, a concert pianist, all practice daily so that their skills will become second nature.

FIGURE 2–2

Creative Work Plan

1. KEY FACT

2. CONSUMER PROBLEM THE ADVERTISING MUST SOLVE

3. ADVERTISING OBJECTIVE

4. CREATIVE STRATEGY
   A. Prospect Definition:

   B. Principal Competition:

   C. Consumer Benefit:

   D. Reason Why:

5. (IF NECESSARY) MANDATORIES AND POLICY LIMITATIONS

_____   _____   _____
    Product   Date   Creative Supervisor

During her review, Shirley encouraged participation; the following is the gist of her explanation, with illustrations of some of the examples.

1. The Key Fact

The key fact should be the one fact that is most relevant to the advertising of the given brand at a given time. It must be a fact upon which advertising can take action. There may be other facts that are truly important about the brand. It may be spoiling on the shelf in a matter of two weeks. That's not a key fact for an *advertising* Creative Work Plan. It can be a fact about product performance or improvement—maybe you do something nobody else does, maybe it's got some exciting new thing that's been added. It can be a fact about consumer attitudes or usage patterns. Maybe a third of the people are concerned about their health, a little worried about tension and nerves. Yet they never tried Sanka coffee, never tried *any* decaffeinated coffee. That's a key fact that advertising can do something about.

Maybe it's a fact about competitive activity—they've made a product change, they've gotten into the market first with something—and that could be a key fact on which advertising must take some action. It can be a fact about a marketing situation: if a certain segment of the market is shrinking rapidly and that's the segment you've been going after, maybe you'd better do something about that. It can be a fact about economic trends: the high price of gasoline.

It's one kind of fact if you're selling a big car, another kind of fact if you're selling a compact car, but a very key fact that advertising can do something about.

Important point: **A key fact can come from many places, and if the key fact isn't right, the rest of the work plan usually doesn't hang together.**

It's very wise to start wide and focus narrow on *one* key fact. It is not just a summary about all the marketing information somebody has about the brand. It's the one fact where you think advertising can have the greatest leverage. One of the most helpful ways to think about a key fact is in terms of the biggest *opportunity* that advertising can help a brand to seize at that time, if the brand is to really move ahead, or the biggest *obstacle* that advertising can help a brand overcome, if the brand is going to survive and be successful. You can list opportunities and obstacles and then ask: Can advertising do much about this? Well no, it could do a lot more about these—you can check them off and finally arrive at what is the best key fact.

Here are two examples, one an opportunity, the other an obstacle. The first one is for Sugar-Free Dr Pepper, and it was an opportunity. Here is what the work plan said was the key fact:

Sugar-Free Dr Pepper has a unique and delicious taste that effectively masks the saccharine after-taste which most people find unpleasant in other sugar-free soft drinks.

SUGAR FREE DR. PEPPER   7/21/76   30 SECONDS

WOMAN: Here's your diet
soft drink, Honey.

WOMAN: She made a mistake.
MAN: She said it was a

diet soft drink. W: This
tastes fattening.

W: Everybody says it
tastes too good to be

true. W: It's Sugar Free
Dr. Pepper. WOMAN SINGING:
Sugar Free

Dr. Pepper. MAN SINGING: It
tastes

too good to be true.
CHORUS: It doesn't taste

like a diet soft drink.
It tastes too good to be
true.

FIGURE 2-3

Figure 2–3 shows one example from a large pool, all stemming from that one key fact. This was one of the most expensive commercials on the reel, but that facet, a production value, had nothing to do with the strategic consideration. Furthermore, there was a big difference between the theme used in the execution—"It tastes too good to be true"—and the way the work plan expressed the copy strategy, that Dr Pepper's unique taste "effectively masks the taste of saccharine." There are no words about execution in the work plan. *It simply says what we intend to do, not how we intend to do it.*

The second example of a key fact is based on an *obstacle* rather than an opportunity. It was a corporate strategy for Gulf Oil, and the key fact was stated in rather formal language, which had little to do with the informal, human tone of voice which was used in the executions:

Continual negative publicity for Gulf Oil and its industry has made even Gulf's most intimate public—that is, Gulf's customers, stockholders, and especially employees—dispirited to the point of cynicism and/or passivity.

It was important not only to influence the public positively, but to give back some feeling of pride to employees and stockholders if the company was to continue to prosper. The series was designed to show how hard and conscientiously Gulf people worked, and it helped employees to be proud of themselves and their company, while influencing associates, as well as stockholders. Before-and-after attitude studies showed that the campaign worked exceedingly well.

2. Consumer Problem the Advertising Must Solve

This statement of the problem should be related to the key fact, and most important, it should be stated in terms of the prospect. This is the part of the work plan where most people have the most trouble. There is a temptation to talk in terms of what the *brand* needs. But what the brand needs belongs in a marketing plan; what the consumer needs belongs in a Creative Work Plan.

Important point: **It must be the consumer point of view.**

There are statements that say that our brand is losing Nielsen share of market in a level to declining market, while we have a smaller budget than our competition. That is a problem, but it's a brand problem, not a consumer problem. And a Creative Work Plan has to talk to the consumer—consumer problems, consumer needs, what's inside the consumer's head, why the consumer is not buying or doing as we would wish him or her to do.

Here is an example and some background about it. This was the problem for Jell-O brand gelatin, and it took three tries before the right problem was identified. There had been a dessert research study by General Foods, which makes Jell-O, among the younger housewives it was anxious to influence. It showed that most of the housewives knew Jell-O well and thought it was a good dessert to serve to their families, but when it came to the question, "How often do you serve Jell-O?" the answer was "Very seldom." Something was wrong. Sales were declining. What was the consumer problem? They asked the housewives, and the first thing they said was that Jell-O takes two or three hours to set in the refrigerator before it's jelled, so they did not think to make it in time to have it ready for dinner. The product group produced a commercial to overcome this problem, but sales did not improve, and when they considered it further, they realized it could not be the essential problem—if women wanted to make Jell-O, they'd think to make it ahead of time.

So they probed some more, and the women said, well, we used to serve Jell-O a lot, the children liked it. But there have been so many new desserts, new packaged desserts, frozen desserts, ice cream, pies, cakes. Maybe the problem was that Jell-O seemed too simple to mothers; maybe they felt guilty about serving something as simple as Jell-O, and didn't realize how much fun kids could have with it, because it wiggles and wobbles, and you cut it and it jiggles on the plate. So they made another commercial—children having great fun with Jell-O. Still not enough to affect sales.

They finally arrived, on the third try, at what the real problem was, and it did not come directly out of the research, because when questioned, the women didn't really know they had the problem. The problem statement finally was this:

Younger housewives are not familiar with the variety of exciting, colorful desserts, snacks, and salads they can make with Jell-O gelatin. And they don't realize how simple it is to layer, whip, combine with other ingredients, mold, unmold, and so forth.

In other words, the consumers did not know what to do with Jell-O except to serve plain red, plain yellow, and plain green.

That problem made especially good sense because Jell-O had not had any recipe advertising for many years, and there was a whole generation of housewives who had grown up without knowing what to do with Jell-O except to serve it plain—so they didn't serve it often. It was something they would not express in the research study, because *they didn't know that they didn't know what to do.* But as soon as the client started giving them recipes, using both TV and women's magazines, the sales turned right around and started upward. Said Shirley, "The campaign is still running. They're doing fine. That was the answer. Women needed to know what to do, and they loved the recipes." Jell-O put out a recipe book. There were special recipes for summer, for holidays, for salads, for desserts. (See Figure 2–4.)

That was a real woman, not an actress, identified at the beginning. And it was one of the very successful series that turned sales around.

Important point: This experience showed that one sometimes has to try more than one problem to arrive at the really important, long-range problem.

The key fact and the problem are closely related. In the case of decaffeinated coffee, mentioned earlier, the key fact was that a large percentage of the population were worried about their health, but they had never even tried decaffeinated coffee. The problem, closely related to the key fact, was that they thought when you took the caffeine out, you took the flavor out. They thought it would taste poor so they didn't try it. The objective that followed was to convince them that Sanka was really a fine-tasting cup of coffee, which it is. The three items of the work plan can be quite close, but it is a progression of steps. "People are not aware" is not important enough as a problem. The problem should be action-oriented—a real problem the consumer has which, by taking an action as a result of the advertising, can be solved.

---

3. The Advertising Objective

This third point in the Creative Work Plan should simply say how advertising proposes to solve the consumer problem. The key to a good statement of objective is: *Be specific.* It is not very helpful if you say, "We want to convince people that we are the best, the premier brand in our category." Who doesn't? Far too general. And it's not enough to

CLIENT: GENERAL FOODS
PRODUCT: JELL-O GELATIN

TITLE: "JAN DeWITT"
LENGTH: 30 SECONDS

ANNCR: (VO) To make desserts that your family will love, start with Jell-O Brand Gelatin.

JAN DeWITT: Let's make strawberry slopes.

ANNCR: Like Jan DeWitt of Albuquerque.
JAN: Here's all it takes.

Just half-fill dessert glasses with thickened strawberry flavored gelatin and chopped apples.

Now my trick.

Tilt the glasses in the fridge.

Chill 15 minutes.

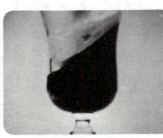

Add whipped topping,

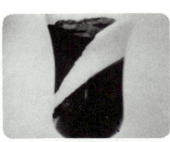

more gelatin. Chill upright.

Then guard the door till dinner.

ANNCR: (VO) Watch for exciting Jell-O Gelatin recipes in women's magazines.

Start with Jell-O.

And start with Jell-O Gelatin.

FIGURE 2–4

say they're not aware. You need to be quite specific. Among the things you can try to get people to do: You can get them to change their ideas about a product or a brand, to switch from some other brand to your brand, to use a product more often, to use a product in a new way, to buy a new product, to move up to a more expensive model or style, if it's a more expensive product, to simply consider the brand before choosing. One commercial isn't going to convince them to write a check for a refrigerator or a car or a TV set—they're going to go look. And all that advertising can do is to get them to go look at your brand before they make up their minds. If you have a large share of market, 80 or 90 percent, that share needs to be solidified—you may never get the additional 10 percent. Keep people satisfied. Don't let somebody else get them away. Be specific about your objective.

How the Key Fact, Problem, and Objective Intertwine   The following example of White Owl cigars illustrates how closely allied are these three headings.

White Owl was a large, inexpensive cigar, and it had no distinguishing characteristic.

> *Key Fact.* Sales of big cigars were declining, little cigars increasing. Little cigars had recently been introduced and were getting very popular. And White Owl sales were declining even faster than those of other big cigars.

> *Consumer Problem.* Smokers did not hold White Owl in high regard. Those who had positive feelings about big cigars didn't like the White Owl. It did not have a good image.

> *The Objective.* "To restate the White Owl quality story in such a way as to make it synonymous with smoking enjoyment and to awaken consumer interest in trying or retrying the brand."

That was an ambitious objective, since the cigar had no special characteristic. It called for all the executional ingenuity the creative people could muster, and Figure 2–5 shows how they did it:[1]

That was a *very* successful commercial. They had a pool of commercials, but this one featured George Irving, and his tone, manner, and message were so engaging that they were able to give that one commercial considerable exposure, and sales responded accordingly.

The Dr Pepper commercial was a very expensive production. This production for White Owl was decidedly inexpensive—a limbo background, a package, and a cigar. Irving was generously paid, but not excessively, since he had not been a celebrity to begin with, at that time.

Important points: (1) Such a commercial shows that it is not necessary to have a big, fancy production to achieve your objective. (2) The objective was "to make White Owl synonymous with smoking enjoyment and to awaken interest in trying the brand."

---

[1] Copyright White Owl Cigars. Reprinted with permission.

WHITE OWL CIGARS   "GOTCHA"   30 SECONDS

MAN: Sooner or later

you're gonna try a small White Owl, a small White

Owl. And when you do, we

gotcha. Maybe we'll get you with a White Owl

miniature. Is that a real cigar, heh, heh? Oh, you

like a tip. The White Owl

Demi-tip, either way you know we're gonna get ya.

(MUSIC)

FIGURE 2–5

The theme that resulted was "We're gonna get'cha." *The work plan does not include executional statements, so it does not inhibit creative people.* It simply says, this is what we're setting out to do—*you figure out how to do it.*

---

4. Creative Strategy

a. The Prospect Definition   The prospect definition should be a characterization in terms of one of three things:

- Demographics (age or geography or occupation).

- Product usage (is the product used in the morning or night, or is it used by a specific group of people, or how is it used).

- Psychographic (life-styles, attitudes—young people are cynical, this is an old product and we're going to position it to young people, thus the prospect definition could be stated in terms of psychographics).

But don't state it in terms of all of these things. Have the courage, in a Creative Work Plan, to be specific in every part of the plan, and if the prospect definition is just a catchall, it doesn't help anybody who's trying to create a campaign—especially a commercial that is 30 or 15 seconds long!

An excellent example was the spot we did for Band-aid Brand Adhesive Bandages. The key fact was that most mothers consider themselves experts in the treatment of wounds, knowing which ones require covering and how long they should stay covered. But the problem was that they usually stop covering a wound when a scab begins to form, which is considered before they should. What Band-aid was out to do was *to get people to use bandages for a longer period*, because if you take it off too soon the scab might come off and the wound would be back. So the prospect definition was this: mothers with children 2 to 12 years of age. The prime age of children falling down and getting cut is 2 to 8, and they gave it a little latitude—2 to 12—but *it was that specific*. They probably said 2 to 8 to the producers, because when they cast the commercial they would want to show children in the prime age group. The Prospect Definition specified: "Mothers of children from 2 to 12, who probably cover most wounds when they first occur, but remove the bandage as soon as the scab begins to form." The executional result was a commercial that dramatized a child about to fall on a wound that had happened before, and the admonition, "Let it heal longer."

b. Principal Competition   This item, in your Creative Work Plan, should not be filled out by just a list of brands. Again, one should be more explicit, to give greater guidance to the creative people. The market segment could be the source of sales, it could be the competitive environment, it could be the area of positioning. The principal competition could even be something completely outside your field. For example, for detergents, the principal competition could be the fact that women are sick of advertising claims, and they don't believe anybody cleans whiter or cleaner, and therefore the principal competition could be apathy, indifference.

The example was Eastern Airlines, but the principal competition was not other airlines. Eastern wanted to get people to take summer vacations, and Eastern traveled a long distance down South. The key fact was that approximately 42 million American families took one or more summer vacations every year, yet only 4 percent of those vacations in the summer involved an airline flight. And nearly two-thirds of all family vacations were taken within 200 miles of the house. The problem: most heads of households don't think of flying on their family vacation; moreover, the economy at the time was in a recession, which tended to discourage the consideration of an expensive vacation to an exotic place. The advertising objective: to convince family vacation prospects of Eastern's ability to provide unique and rewarding family vacation experiences and further to establish the psychic and/or educational benefits of an Eastern vacation. In other words, they had a very rough job to do—to get people to go from 200 miles to 1,000 miles.

The prospect definition was *families in the middle-income group, who have or have not flown as a family group before*. The principal competition—a unique departure—was *the traditional vacation areas*—that is, those that people kept going back to, again and again, because they felt secure and comfortable there. Second only, all other special package vacation deals.

That was a very courageous, bold work plan, because any airline could have gone into the same advertising area. But all the airlines were stressing better food and more courteous stewardesses and more experienced flying. The Y&R people recommended *preempting an area nobody had gone into before.* They also tied it in with vacation packages, so there were certain bargain advantages.

By making its principal competition a whole area of vacations, Eastern had a tremendous sales success.

Important point: **You will often discover that when you are original enough to preempt an area, one that really satisfies the consumer want or need, if you're the first one to do it, people are going to be loyal to you.**

They heard it from Eastern Airlines, so they went to Eastern Airlines. An example of the copy: "A summer to remember, at a price your family can afford." A father taking his son on a great experience, and the other advertisers were not offering such an emotionally fulfilling benefit. The campaign dramatized many ways that families could experience something new and exciting. They ran headlines like this: "Take your family to a place where it's nowhere like home." It was a first for Y&R because it was really a new *kind* of advertising—*experiential* advertising, rather than just trying to persuade somebody.

c. Consumer Benefit

1. *The consumer benefit should be expressed in terms of the specific consumer you are targeting, not just anyone's benefit.* You might have come up with a promise for Jell-O gelatin, that it could be used in many ways, but the work plan would have been incomplete if the prospect definition had not been "younger housewives with families" who would have pride that their families would appreciate those recipes.

2. *The benefit definition should be as competitive as possible,* not merely generic. There is a difference between competitive and comparative. You may not have a comparative claim that you will wash 20 percent whiter, but you can preempt whiteness, as Cheer detergent did. Another example was Bufferin, which was a headache remedy with the claim "works twice as fast as aspirin." When the firm temporarily lost that claim legally, it called itself "Bufferin, the Fast One." It continued the competitive attitude.

3. The benefit *should be a consumer benefit, not a product attribute.* It shouldn't be just "this product has XL70, the Blue Magic Whitener"; it should be what the product will do for your clothes ("Cheer washes whiter").

Here's an example we used: Clairol Herbalessence Shampoo, which at the time of its introduction was a completely new kind of shampoo, made with lots of herbs, a natural kind of product. Most of the shampoos at that time were showing beautiful girls with wavy hair and were promising cleaner hair or more beautiful hair—hackneyed promises. Clairol Herbalessence Shampoo was so different that it deserved to be positioned in a totally new way. The promise was that "Clairol Herbalessence Shampoo provides a uniquely sensual shampooing experience," which in fact it did. Once people were reminded of it, it could deliver the promise. The commercial execution turned out to be in animation, with beautiful artwork, and the technique was different from that used by any other product in the category. The music was different, sensual music. The announcer they used was different, carefully cast, with a sexy, foreign-sounding voice.

Important point: **Everything added up to fulfill the promise of the work plan.**

---

d. Reason Why   Finally, the reason why. This is quite simple.

1. *It should simply state why you can make that offer*—give the reason why you will do what you just promised you would do, why you can offer the benefit you have just offered.

2. *It should come out of the product performance,* what the product itself will do if it does something.

3. *It should be as competitive as possible,* at least in intent—it doesn't have to be comparative.

4. *It should be a single fact,* never a catalog of facts. There's a temptation here to put down all the good things you know about the brand—clients often like to see a long list of reasons. It's not what you need here.

Important point: **You need the one reason it will do what you promise it will do.**

It's hard enough to get people to remember one thing at a time, much less a great number of things.

Here are two quite different types of examples. The first is for Excedrin, an extra-strength analgesic and one of the first brands to introduce a safety cap, a feature it was felt was worth advertising, at least briefly. As an extra-strength product, Excedrin thought parents might worry even more about Excedrin being exposed to children and children getting into those bottles and taking the tablets. Here are the Promise and then the Reason Why:

Promise: **"Extra-strength Excedrin helps protect small children from getting at and consequently swallowing the tablets in this bottle."**

Reason why: **"It has a safety cap that is almost impossible for small children to open, although it's easy for adults."**

ARROW "ULTRESSA"   60 SECONDS

AN: Arrow has a shirt that's so   soft and sensuous, people can't   keep their hands off it.   (MUSIC)

(MUSIC)   Arrow calls this shirt Ul-   tressa. It looks like silk,   feels like silk but since

it isn't silk, it doesn't cost   (MUSIC)   (MUSIC)   Ultressa's for work and
like silk.

play so you can be irresistible   no matter what you're doing.   Arrow, no wonder American men   look so good.

FIGURE 2-6

The second example concerns Arrow Ultressa shirts. Ultressa was a new fabric just brought out in the spring.

Promise: "Arrow Ultressa shirts will help men look and feel like a million without costing a lot." *Reason why:* "Ultressa looks and feels like silk, but does not cost as much as silk." (See Figure 2-6.)

5. (If Necessary) Mandatories and Policy Limitations

This is by way of a postscript in the work plan, and it says "if necessary." Some people seem to think that they should invent something or they haven't finished the work plan. If you don't have any, write "None" or leave it blank. Remember: Don't put down a mandatory unless it really *must* be done or *must not* be done.

It should be a real mandatory—medical restrictions or legal or sometimes media mandatories (the commercial has to work in both a short length and a long length—let creative people know, so they don't do a beautiful demonstration that will only work in 60 seconds but not in a 30 or 20 or 15). Sometimes there are corporate considerations, such as every ad or commercial must end in a certain way (maybe it's an anniversary year, and every commercial must end with "50 years of progress and service to the nation"). If you've got something like that, let the creative people know. Sometimes there are certain models or styles to be featured. If it's mandatory, put it there.

COLLABORATING ON A CREATIVE WORK PLAN

Following discussion of the CWP, it's a good idea, in such a workshop, to have everyone participate in the hands-on activity of filling out one or more work plans. Figure 2-7 gives examples of such work plans in progress.

These same work plans will be the basis of our problem-solving team efforts in the discussion on creativity in Chapter Three. Thus, our workshop was designed to have a continuity, of what should happen in reality during the offices' real activities. The groundwork for creativity would be followed by the creative process of getting ideas for possible campaigns, which would eventually be followed by executions. This continuity, during the first day of our workshop, naturally led to the subjects of creating better print, TV, radio, and so on.

If you are planning such a workshop, think of it as your organization's real life telescoped into two days, and it provides a concept for blueprinting your plans for the seminars.

To illustrate how real these activities became, many workshops led immediately toward improving the branch offices' work on accounts, and therefore toward solidifying client relationships. In two offices (Hong Kong and Denmark), our workshop actually contributed to the acquisition of new business. Hong Kong won the Longine watch account and Denmark the account of a new chain of Danish resort hotels, *both as a result of the Creative Work Plan strategy and the ideas we had generated* during the workshop sessions.

Creative Work Plan
for SANKA®

1. **KEY FACT**
   Twenty-nine percent of the coffee-drinking households say they are concerned about caffeine, but resist trying SANKA® brand.

2. **CONSUMER PROBLEM THE ADVERTISING MUST SOLVE**
   Prospects don't think SANKA® brand would taste as good as caffeinated coffee, and they also resist its somewhat medicinal image.

3. **ADVERTISING OBJECTIVE**
   Convince prospects that <u>SANKA® does indeed taste as good as caffeinated coffee</u> and has the added benefit of being caffeine free.

4. **CREATIVE STRATEGY**

   A. Prospect Definition:
   Our prime prospects are mildly concerned about caffeine but haven't switched to decaffeinated coffee. They are probably somewhat more hyper than the average coffee drinker, more health aware, and perhaps even self-conscious about giving in to a decaffeinated coffee.

   B. Principal Competition:
   The regular coffee prospects are currently drinking. Secondarily, any other decaffeinated coffee they may consider switching to.

   C. Consumer Benefit:
   You will be surprised how good SANKA® tastes, and it has the advantage of being caffeine free.

   D. Reason Why:
   1. In blind taste tests, SANKA® brand decaffeinated coffee is at parity and sometimes superior to competitive caffeinated coffees.
   2. Good taste has helped it become the third largest coffee brand in America.

5. **(IF NECESSARY) MANDATORIES AND POLICY LIMITATIONS**

_____   _____   _____
Product   Date   Creative Supervisor

FIGURE 2–7

Creative Work Plan
for Security Pacific Bank–Hispanic

1. KEY FACT
The Hispanic population within the state of California is enormous, having increased 92 percent to 4.5 million within the past decade. The majority are urban dwellers with an average annual income of $16,300. Additionally, over 30 percent have achieved incomes over $20,000.

2. CONSUMER PROBLEM THE ADVERTISING MUST SOLVE
Affluent Hispanics, like their Anglo counterparts, feel concerned and insecure about their economic futures.

3. ADVERTISING OBJECTIVE
To convince affluent Hispanics that SPB is capable in every way of helping them solve their financial problems and is fully committed to providing them with all of the benefits and attention that the bank has to offer.

4. CREATIVE STRATEGY

A. Prospect Definition:
Top 30 percent of the Hispanic population (annual income in excess of $20,000).

B. Principal Competition:
All commercial banks and S&L's in California, especially Bank of America (45 percent share).

C. Consumer Benefit:
SPB is committed to giving you all the personal service you deserve and can help you in every way to make the most effective use of your money.

D. Reason Why:
Case examples that prove not only SPB's capabilities, but its personal commitment to its Hispanic customers.

5. (IF NECESSARY) MANDATORIES AND POLICY LIMITATIONS

Security Pacific Bank– Hispanic	6/23/83	Norins/Cervera
Product	**Date**	**Creative Supervisor**

FIGURE 2–7 (continued)

Creative Work Plan
for LUSTUCRU Noodles

1. KEY FACT
The only purchasing motivation for the range of
LUSTUCRU Noodles in Sauce without any negative
counterpart is the possibility to make an original
meal of noodles.

2. CONSUMER PROBLEM THE ADVERTISING MUST SOLVE
Women who try and vary methods of serving noodles
only think of a limited number of ways in which to do
so (butter, cheese, tomato sauce).

3. ADVERTISING OBJECTIVE
To inform women that LUSTUCRU Noodles in Sauce
enable them to offer different original noodle
meals to their families.

4. CREATIVE STRATEGY

A. Prospect Definition:
- ABC households: Two children
- Modern housewives, receptive to this type of
  product and willing to vary their noodle dishes
  without going into elaborate culinary
  preparations.

B. Principal Competition:
- Basic ingredients (butter, cheese, tomato
  sauce)
- Bottled, tinned, or packet sauces

C. Consumer Benefit:
LUSTUCRU Noodles in Sauce enable you to vary your
LUSTUCRU fresh egg noodle dishes in a most
original way.

D. Reason Why:
A range of original sauces prepared by LUSTUCRU,
using its own unique methods.

5. (IF NECESSARY) MANDATORIES AND POLICY LIMITATIONS

Product	Date	Creative Supervisor

FIGURE 2.7 *(continued)*

Strategy Selection Outline

	STRATEGY I Current English	STRATEGY II (Preferred)	STRATEGY III (Alternate)	STRATEGY IV	STRATEGY V
PRODUCT CLASS DEFINITION					
TARGET GROUP SELECTION					
MESSAGE ELEMENT SELECTION					
RATIONALE BASED ON INFORMATION AND/OR JUDGMENT					

FIGURE 2–8

At the close of most of the "groundwork" sessions, a brief time was devoted to explaining the Strategy Selection Outline. This is the Y&R one-page discipline that helps to simplify and clarify advertising strategy from a marketing standpoint. (See Figure 2–8.)

THE STRATEGY SELECTION OUTLINE

The purpose of the SSO is to help you think through some of the elements that go into a Creative Work Plan. If you have two or more options, this will help you set them forth in a logical manner and to evaluate which direction might be the best. If you have already done a CWP, the SSO might help you to evaluate your plan against other possible directions you could go.

This form has space already printed for five strategic options. You could fill in more or fewer options, with the rationale for their selection.

Figure 2–9 is a partially filled-in SSO that illustrates only two options, strategy I and strategy II. It's for Sanka brand decaffeinated coffee. The "Product Class Definition" represents your area of competition, your source of sales, where you're going to position the brand. The "Target

Strategy Selection Outline
for Sanka

	STRATEGY I (PREFERRED)	STRATEGY II	BASIS OF PREFERENCE
PRODUCT CLASS DEFINITION	All coffees—caffeinated and decaffeinated.	All beverages (especially those that have replaced coffee).	Strategy I is preferred.
TARGET GROUP SELECTION	Adult, upscale, caffein-concerned. Nontriers, light users. Health-oriented, tense. Want flavor. Aware of Sanka's health benefits.	Youthful, health-concerned nondrinkers of coffee. Not compatible with their values and life-styles.	More prospects (30 percent of adults). Easier to persuade. Youth change more difficult.
MESSAGE ELEMENT SELECTION	Sanka is surprisingly good, real coffee-tasting coffee.	Coffee (Sanka) "belongs" in most refreshment situations. Is no health hazard.	
RATIONALE BASED ON INFORMATION AND/OR JUDGMENT	Caffein-concerned are good prospects. Flavor doubts can be met by Sanka's parity performance.	Big coffee decline among youth, who see coffee as stodgy. Sanka fits current health/natural orientation.	INFORMATION NEEDS: More data about caffein-concerned nontriers, in relation to age groups.

FIGURE 2–9

Group Selection" is your consumer prospect for your sale; and the "Message Element Selection" is what you're going to promise that prospect. The "Rationale Based on Information and/or Judgment" says what's good about strategy I or what's good about strategy II.

In the column on the far right is your "Basis of Preference," and here you fill in: "We prefer strategy I because . . . or we prefer strategy II because . . . ." Also in this column you can add "Information Needs," which you do not yet have, and which may therefore call for more research.

Let's put one of these together—for Sanka brand decaffeinated coffee. For the sake of time, we'll consider just two strategy options. We could position ourselves, in strategy I, against "All coffees—caffeinated and decaffeinated," or in strategy II, against "All beverages (especially those that have replaced coffee—e.g., soft drinks, fruit drinks)."

Those are two broad categories of competitive positions. Who would the two target groups be for those two options? In the first case, they would be adults, upscale in income, concerned about caffeine: people who have not tried decaffeinated coffee or are very light users; people who are health-oriented and tense, who want flavor but think decaffeinated coffees don't have flavor; they know that Sanka has health benefits but they haven't tried it.

In the second strategy, against all beverages, our target group might be younger people who are health-concerned and are nondrinkers of coffee. They feel that coffee is not compatible with their values and life-styles.

If we were to use strategy I, what would we offer to those people? We could promise them the benefit that Sanka gives them a surprisingly good, real coffee-tasting cup of coffee. If we were to use strategy II, for our young people who are drinking other beverages, we could promise them that coffee—Sanka coffee—belongs in most refreshment situations and is no hazard to health.

Now let's consider what is good about the first strategy and what is good about the second. In the first case, our caffeine-concerned people are good prospects, and their doubts about flavor can be met by Sanka's quality performance. In blind taste tests Sanka has proven to taste just as good to panels as regular coffee.

In the case of the second strategy, the strength is that Sanka decaffeinated coffee fits perfectly with their current interest in health and natural-type foods.

Which strategy is stronger and why? That preference goes into the last column, and strategy I is preferred because there are more prime prospects in this group than in the second group. Thirty percent of adults fit into the first group. And this group is easier to persuade than the second group because the younger people are more difficult to change when they already feel that coffee should not be part of their lives. The first group are already part way there. They aren't sure that Sanka is going to taste good, but it's easier to reassure them because you have a parity performance in blind taste tests. So you've got more prospects, and those prospects are open to information about caffeine, since they are concerned nontriers in relation to age group.

This is a simple example of how you can chart options and evaluate them. If you have factual data to put against your options, as is the case in the following example, so much the better. This is a strategy for Gaines Puppy Choice dog food. It was a soft moist product, one of the first in that category. You open the cellophane package and put it in the bowl. Dried products you would have to mix with water, and canned products require opening and disposing of the can.

In this case, Gaines was introducing its first food for puppies, and there was already a popular dry dog food especially for puppies. (See Figure 2–10.) Notice that the target group is the same across the board. It would be—it's for housewives in homes with puppies, under 12 months of age, slightly upscale households to be able to buy a commercial dog food. They probably have children and are high in concern for their puppies.

Strategy Selection Outline
for Gaines Puppy Choice

	STRATEGY I	STRATEGY II	STRATEGY III	STRATEGY IV
PRODUCT CLASS DEFINITION	All commercial dog foods used by puppy owners.	The leading dry puppy brand.	All dry brands used by puppy owners.	All dry and canned brands used by puppy owners.
TARGET GROUP SELECTION	Housewives in homes with puppies (under 12 months). Slightly upscale; with children. High in indulgence and concern for their puppies.			
MESSAGE ELEMENT SELECTION	All the special nutrition your puppy needs in a form he likes.	Three ways better than Purina Puppy Chow.	The real meat your dog has been missing.	Not only the best but also the most convenient.

FIGURE 2-10

Where should Gaines position its product to have the best chance of getting sales? Against all dry and canned brands used by puppy owners? Or against the leading dry puppy brand (the only other on the market yet)?

If you compete against the first, you can promise "all the special nutrition your puppy needs in a form he likes." In the latter case, you can offer a product that is three ways better than the one dry brand that's out there.

Now, how do you evaluate these two options? In this case, research was available that showed that 96 percent of puppy owners were feeding commercial dog food, 28 percent were feeding the other dry puppy food, 84 percent were using some kind of dry and canned food combined. Out of a list of five benefits, 87 percent chose "all the special nutrition your puppy needs in a form he likes," 53 percent chose "real meat," and 41 percent chose convenience for themselves. Obviously, in this case, strategy I wins hands down, since it offers more prospects, you have more to offer, and what you have to offer is liked by more of them.

This, in very abbreviated and simplified form, is how the Strategy Selection Outline works.

Other tools on which Y&R has offered training are the Competitive Advertising Summary, (Figure 2-11) and the perceptual map, (Figure 2-12).

All such aids contribute to the structuring of the Creative Work Plan for your creative people who want to "soar free." This way of planning—the groundwork for creativity—gives them a direction so their imaginations can really fly.

PRODUCT CATEGORY: DECAFFEINATED COFFEE

TIME FRAME: FISCAL YEAR 1976

	OUR BRAND: SANKA®	BRAND: TASTER'S CHOICE	BRAND: BRIM	BRAND: NESCAFE-D	RATIONALE FOR OUR RECOMMENDED STRATEGY IN THIS COMPETITIVE ENVIRONMENT.
PRODUCT CLASS DEFINITION	ALL COFFEES, CAFFEINATED AND DECAFFEINATED.	ALL COFFEES, CAFFEINATED AND DECAFFEINATED.	ALL COFFEES, CAFFEINATED AND DECAFFEINATED.	ALL COFFEES, CAFFEINATED AND DECAFFEINATED.	SANKA®'S RECOMMENDED STRATEGY IS UNIQUE WITHIN THE DECAFFEINATED PRODUCT CATEGORY, FOCUSING ON THE HEALTH BENEFITS OF COFFEE WITHOUT CAFFEIN. ALL OTHER BRANDS CONCENTRATE ON TASTE SATISFACTION. AS THE CATEGORY LEADER, THIS MARKET BUILDING STANCE IS APPROPRIATE TO SANKA®, AS IT ADVANCES DECAF BENEFITS VS. CAFFEINATED (I.E. LESS NERVOUS, FEEL BETTER) AND CONNOTES SUPERIOR HEALTH BENEFIT DELIVERY VS. DECAFFEINATED BRANDS. IT IS ALSO CONSISTENT WITH CONSUMERS' CURRENT PERCEPTIONS OF SANKA, WHICH ARE MORE HEALTH-RELATED THAN ARE THEIR PERCEPTIONS OF COMPETITIVE BRANDS.
TARGET GROUP	ADULTS OVER 50; PRIMARILY FEMALES, SECONDARILY, MALES. THEY ARE HEAVY USERS OF CAFFEINATED COFFEE, WHO ARE CONCERNED ABOUT THE SIDE EFFECTS FROM THE AMOUNT OF COFFEE THEY DRINK.	ADULT MALES AND FEMALES. NO SPECIAL AGE SKEW. THEY ARE TASTE-ORIENTED COFFEE DRINKERS, ESPECIALLY DRINKERS OF GROUND CAFFEINATED COFFEE.	ADULT MALES AND FEMALES, SKEWING YOUNGER (UNDER 45). THEY ARE CAFFEIN-CONCERNED DRINKERS OF REGULAR COFFEE, WITH NEGATIVE TASTE PERCEPTIONS OF DECAF. COFFEE.	ADULT MALES AND FEMALES. NO SPECIAL AGE SKEW. THEY ARE MODERATELY DEMANDING OF COFFEE FLAVOR, AND TEND TO USE THE INSTANT FORMS.	
MESSAGE ELEMENTS	ENJOY COFFEE WITHOUT THE ADVERSE EFFECTS OF TOO MUCH CAFFEIN.	FRESH-PERKED TASTE. THEME: THE FRESH-PERKED FLAVOR OF GROUND ROAST COFFEE.	MORE GREAT/FRESH GROUND FLAVOR (AND AROMA) IN A DECAFFEINATED COFFEE. THEME: THE (NEW) BRIM TWIST.	RICH/MORE COFFEE FLAVOR (THAT DOESN'T TASTE DECAFFEINATED) . . . SUPPORTED BY WORLDWIDE LEADERSHIP/STATUS/ HERITAGE. THEME: IF WE CAN PLEASE THE WHOLE WIDE WORLD, WE CAN SURE PLEASE YOU.	
EXECUTIONAL HIGHLIGHTS	NOT YET DETERMINED.	PERKING JAR MNEMONIC. NO PEOPLE; JAR/PRODUCT ONLY. DECAF TREATED IN A TAG OF REGULAR COMMERCIAL, WITH COMMON MESSAGE.	MUSICAL ENVIRONMENT, INCLUDING A SUNG THEME-LINE. VIGNETTE FORMAT. TWISTING LID MNEMONIC.	1. VIGNETTES OF PEOPLE AROUND THE WORLD ENJOYING NESCAFE. SUNG CHORUS OF THEME-LINE. DECAF TREATED IN TAG OF REGULAR COMM'L WITH COMMON MESSAGE. 2. DECAF ONLY COMM'L EMPLOYS MNEMONIC OF CRYSTAL GLOBE WHICH BECOMES A COFFEE CUP. NO PEOPLE.	EXECUTIONAL CONSIDERATIONS, IF ANY MNEMONICS ARE COMMON IN THIS PRODUCT CATEGORY, YET DO NOT DUPLICATE OR OVERLAP ONE ANOTHER. SOME GROW OUT OF STRATEGY, OTHERS OUT OF EXECUTION. SOME TENDENCY TOWARD THE VIGNETTE FORMAT . . . BUT THIS IS NOT OVERWHELMING.

MEDIA AND SPENDING HIGHLIGHTS	PROJECTED SPENDING FOR F'77
	
	9/20/76-4/3/77 $6MM
		TOTAL SPENDING
		(FY '76) $8.5MM (Regular and Decaf)
		
		NETWORK TV 76%
		PRINT 16%
		
		SOV: ALL COFFEE 11%
		     DECAF 29%
			TOTAL SPENDING
			(FY '76) $7.5MM
			
			NETWORK TV 67%
			SPOT TV 26%
			
			SOV: ALL COFFEE 10%
			     DECAF 25%
				TOTAL SPENDING
				(FY '76) $3.3MM (Regular and Decaf)
				
				(BEGINNING NAT'L EXPANSION)
				
				SPOT TV 86%
				
				SOV: ALL COFFEE 4%
				     DECAF 11%	

FIGURE 2-11

FIGURE 2-12

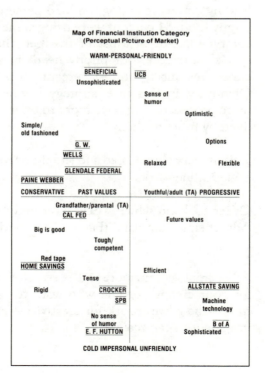

Map of Financial Institution Category
(Perceptual Picture of Market)

. . . .

CHAPTER CHECKLIST

. . . .

1. Seek a brilliant strategy and a surprising execution. Both derive from insight into the consumer.

2. Remember that the advertising strategy derives from the marketing strategy, which has one of four objectives: to accelerate or maintain growth, to hold share, to reenergize growth, or to introduce new products.

3. With the SSO (Strategy Selection Outline) and the CWP (Creative Work Plan), we examine options and focus on key issues.

4. The CWP is the groundwork for creativity. It has five components: the key fact; the consumer problem the advertising must solve; the advertising objective; and the creative strategy, which is based on the prospect definition, the principal competition, the consumer benefit, and the reason why; and the (if necessary) mandatories and policy limitations.

5. The SSO examines two or more strategies and gives a rationale for the one chosen. For each possible strategy, the SSO examines the product class definition, the target group selection, and the message element selection.

6. The key fact of the CWP is derived from a list of the biggest opportunities and the biggest obstacles, and the one chosen is that on which advertising can have the greatest leverage. The consumer problem, related to the key fact, is in terms of what the prospect needs, not what the brand needs. The stated objective is, specifically, how the advertising proposes to solve the consumer problem. In filling out the creative strategy, consider the prospect in terms of demographics or psychographics or how the product is used. The competition is based on the major competitive factors rather than simply on a list of brands. The consumer benefit should be in terms of the specific consumer targeted, should be as competitive as possible and a *consumer,* not a product attribute. The reason why should come out of the product's performance and be as competitive as possible.

7. For the SSO, the product class definition should be your product's area of competition, the target group selection—that product's consumer prospect, the message element selection what you would promise that specific prospect to surpass the competition.

. . . .

CHAPTER

3 How to Be More Creative

Howard Rieger,
former Y&R Associate
Creative Director

Andrew Wyeth said, never underestimate Jackson Pollock, he let every accident work for him. We were working on a battery for Sears. We talked about a car junkyard—"Where does a battery go when a car dies?" A writer said, it's like a diehard, it won't quit. The big idea was buried in the conversation. I said, wait a minute, it's a Diehard. That's how we found that idea.

To be a good chess player, you first have to understand the rules of the game. To be a good football player, you not only have to have natural talent, you have to understand what the game is all about.

But what is creativity all about? What are the rules of *this* game? Many people feel that there should be no rules. Creativity is a mystery which is better left alone. They fear meddling with the magic.

WHAT IS CREATIVITY?

We were committed, however, in our first traveling creative workshop, to teach and preach the *basics*. And since creativity was what the workshop was all about, we included a module called "The Basics of Creativity," which would attempt, at least in part, to explain the mystery.

We chose to begin at the beginning—with the etymology of the word to *create*:

To *create* comes from the Indo-European root *ker,* to *grow*. Its suffixed form was, in Latin, *Ceres,* the goddess of agriculture. Its extended form, *kre,* in Latin *creare,* meant *to bring forth,* to *cause to grow,* to *originate.*

So this is what we are trying to do when we are searching for ideas— we are seeking to *originate*, to cause something new and fresh to grow. We are looking for inventive, *original* ideas that invite participation, evoke reactions, and solve problems.

What are ideas? William James and the pragmatists defined an idea as "a plan for action," and since we are attempting to achieve action on the part of our consumers, that's an apt definition for us. We can also be guided in assessing our ideas by Jerome Bruner's definition that an idea is "an act that produces effective surprise." If we want to judge whether an idea is "creative," consider this criterion: Have we actually *originated* something that has never been seen or heard before? Is it based on a plan for action and is it effectively surprising?

Having defined what creativity *is*, the workshop went on to consider how to achieve it.

THE CREATIVE PROCESS

To understand the creative process, we can study the evidence of hearsay—the testimony of acknowledged creative geniuses throughout history who have attested to how they got their ideas. While their methods varied, there are commonalities that reveal a basic creative process.

Alex Osborn, the father of brainstorming, drawing on the testimony of those past creators, as well as his own and his colleagues' experience, codified the creative process as follows:

1. *Orientation*. Pointing up the problem.

2. *Preparation*. Gathering pertinent data.

3. *Analysis*. Breaking down the relevant material.

4. *Ideation*. Piling up alternatives by way of ideas.

5. *Incubation*. Letting up to invite illumination.

6. *Synthesis*. Putting the pieces together.

7. *Evaluation*. Judging the resultant ideas.

We have already discussed the first three steps in that process in the preceding chapter about the groundwork for creativity. These steps provide a direction, that is, a strategy. But why is a *direction* necessary? It's necessary because of the *nature* of creativity and our use of creativity to solve problems.

I once made a comprehensive survey of successful people in the advertising agency business, in preparation for my book, *The Compleat Copywriter* (McGraw-Hill, 1966). My question: "How do you get your ideas?" Almost to a man and a woman, they said, *through free association*. The accent is on the word *free*, and a person with imagination could start free-associating and go on forever. This may be enjoyable, but if you try to solve a problem without having a direction, a focus (i.e., a strategy), you could consume an infinite amount of time with no purpose.

This is why you shouldn't look for a creative idea without having a strategy. The strategy gives you a starting point from which to jump off into the unknown. You have something specific to free-associate *about*. If, in the course of your free association you discover an idea so compelling that it demands the revision of your Creative Work Plan, well and good. You would have been unlikely to have happened on that idea and to recognize its inspiration, if you had not been *coming from somewhere*—the strategy that set you on the free association path.

Once Set in Motion, Creativity Is Irresistible

S. I. Hayakawa, author of *Language in Thought and Action*, once described an idea as "the verbalization of a cerebral itch." Well, you know what a pleasurable sensation it is to scratch an itch. While you're thinking about it, consider all the other physical analogies you could make about the act of creation. This is how Mary O'Meara, a creative director at Young & Rubicam in the sixties, answered a letter from a high-school student who had written to the agency asking how creative people solved problems creatively (note that she concluded with that same point of reference as *itchiness*):

PROCESS →

There is the *sponge* part: when you soak up all the information you can discover (and a lot of misinformation).

There is the *shake* part: when you shake out the facts and question the problem itself and start to imagine all sorts of things.

There is the *squeeze* part: when you wring out the sponge and scribble down the most promising splashes and driblets.

There is the *bounce* part: when you and another concerned with the problem toss embryonic ideas back and forth until only the fittest survive.

There is the *scratch* part: like the above, but now you scratch brain against brain hoping to spark a *new* notion.

There is the *once-again-please* part: when you examine the survivors in the cold light of reason, abandon most, and incubate a few in the warm darkness of imagination.

There is the *dry* part: when you quit thinking about the damned problem and turn your mind to pleasure or routine. (You only think you've stopped thinking.)

There is the *yahoo* part: when things connect and an idea pops into your head that turns out to be the key to the solution. Often this happens when you least expect it and aren't even thinking about the big problem.

There is the *do* part: when you use your particular talents and learned skills and those of others concerned to shape and form the raw idea into a proper solution.

Then there is the *itch* part: which maybe should come first instead of last. The drive to solve problems creatively—with a new and original solution—stems from some chronic *itch*; dissatisfaction with all existing solutions. Even when the latest may be your own.

Encourage a Spirit of Playfulness   Having defined what creativity is and discussed the first part of its process, the workshop moved on to point 4 in Osborn's codification, which requires the free association of a great many ideas. This calls for a different frame of mind than that used to provide your strategy.

Albert Einstein described that frame of mind as "combinatory play," which "seems to be the essential feature in productive thought." Combinatory play: joining together two or more thoughts that have not been combined before, and doing so in an uninhibited spirit of playfulness.

If, then, the first steps in our process are to achieve a Creative Work Plan, this facet should be called a Creative Play Plan.

Playfulness is not as much a part of our adult nature as is the exercise of rational thought. Western society has always glorified the philosophy of Descartes: "I think, therefore I am." We have been conditioned to be logical and rational, to suppress our playful minds (except when we are children, and then society tells us to "put away our childish things" and to be serious about life).

The Hippie revolution attempted to swing the pendulum away from rationalism to irrationalism. Songwriter Neil Diamond summed up the Hippie philosophy with the words of his popular song, "Don't think, feel. Ain't no big deal. Make it real. And don't think, feel."

But the Hippies did not bother to have a focus, and we have a practical job to do. The ideal for us is to strike a balance between the rational groundwork of the Creative Work Plan and the intuitive mode of the Creative Play Plan.

Free-Associate a Huge Quantity of Ideas   Playfulness is essential for getting many, many ideas. We need to get many ideas to arrive at the one big idea. Even when we think that we have that big idea at the beginning, we ought to get more ideas, if only to test its validity. Ideas are our brainchildren, and when we are being creative, we fall in love with our brainchildren. If we get many, many ideas, it's easier for us to reject some of our brainchildren and to allow the strongest idea to emerge.

The goal of brainstorming, said Alex Osborn, is quantity: "Quantity! Quantity! and More Quantity! is the order of the day." And he added, "The more sights you take, the more likely you are to hit port." Osborn also found that when you are brainstorming a large quantity of ideas, the quality usually improves as the session gathers steam.

Ideas are our stock-in-trade, and it makes sense to have a large inventory. Said the writer Stendhal, "I require 3 or 4 cubic feet of ideas per day, as a steamboat requires coal."

When you are alone, seeking ideas, you have to encourage yourself to have a free flow of your own ideas. The researcher Daniel Starch offered some good advice for the solitary idea maker:

Recognize that your own imagination is your only source of original creativity. New ideas come out of something, something you have in your mind. They do not come out of a mental vacuum.

As a preparation for unleashing your creative powers, fill your mind with as much information about the problems you are working on as possible. These will start chains of ideas from which new ideas will arise.

At the start, give your imagination *complete* freedom to bring forth an *unhampered* chain of ideas and images.

To accomplish this free flow of ideas, put yourself into a completely relaxed attitude. Do not stop to be critical of your own flow of images, let them come as they will.

Try to Capture All Your Ideas   Starch then encouraged the *capturing* of *every* thought you have. Any one, or combination, may be the spring-board for the big idea, and if you don't capture them all, you may lose the ideal answer.

Our traveling workshop used an amalgam of methods, primarily my "Brown Paper Caper," which I'd hit upon 30 years before. I was brain-storming with a group, and became frustrated by the fact that so many of our thoughts were disappearing into thin air. Some of us were taking notes, to be sure, but there were so many thoughts happening so fast that there was every chance some might be lost. Furthermore, we don't get our best ideas in a linear fashion, one thought following another, and another following that, until we arrive at the best idea. Our minds free-associate back and forth, interconnecting ideas in a series of

FIGURE 3–1

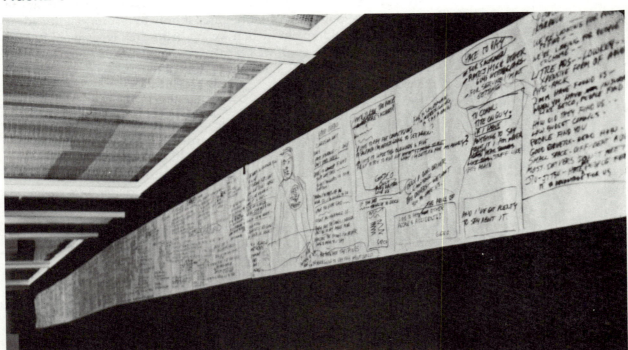

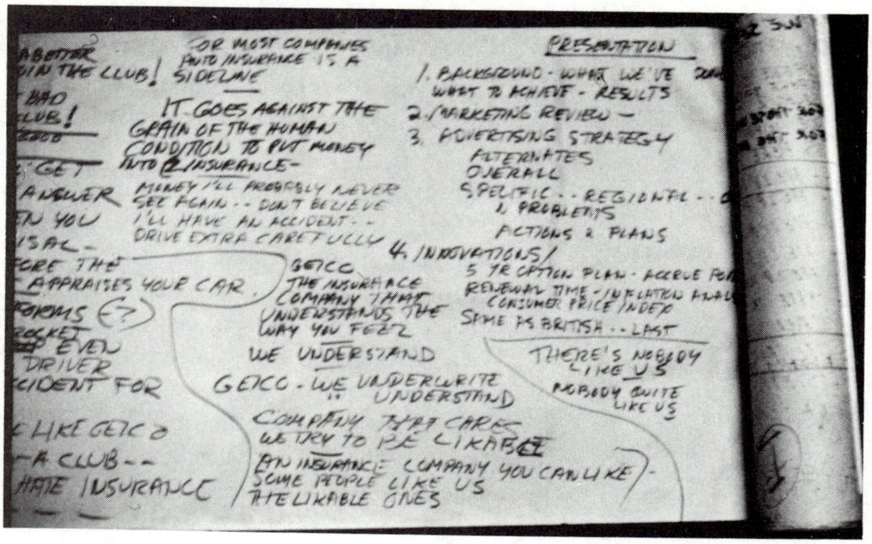

FIGURE 3–2

flashbacks and flashforwards. My inspiration was to cover the walls with long sheets of brown wrapping paper, and as the group free-associated ideas, to try to capture them all, with magic markers, on a kind of problem-solving mural (Figure 3–1). That way, the group could see a living picture of their evolving ideas, could interconnect them and allow any and every thought to trigger something else (Figure 3–2).

To supplement this brown paper display, I added tape-recorders and typewritten verbatims of our sessions, and more recently computers and high-speed printers that continually give the participants an inventory of ideas in real time.

Other creative directors have their own special methods of encouraging free association and capturing the ideas which occur. John Ferrell, Y&R's former creative director, hit on the idea of using 3-inch by 5-inch file cards for his display and interconnecting of ideas. As the group brainstorms, he letters key phrases on individual cards. Each card triggers thoughts on other cards, and they can be arranged and rearranged in the course of "combinatory play."

For our workshops, I have also borrowed from Synectics, which *Fortune* magazine called "the madness method of invention." The word *synectics* was coined from the Greek meaning "the joining together of different and apparently irrelevant elements" (another way of saying "combinatory play").

Trust Your Intuition Every so often, as our huge quantity of ideas emerges, something suddenly *feels* right. Everyone seizes on one individual's thought, and the intuition is shared by the many. Such an illumination has been called, variously, a gut-level feeling, the "Aha!" moment, the Eureka syndrome. Synectics people dubbed it "hedonic response," and I call it my "hackles method"—when the hackles on the back of my neck start to prickle and signal that we are on to something. This inspiration is the pleasure called *serendipity*, which is "the happy faculty of stumbling across something valuable accidentally."

Serendipity has only recently achieved respectability. In the late 1960s, *The Wall Street Journal* declared its value as news on the front page: "Sheer Luck," read the headline, "Is Largely Responsible for Major Inventions." The article cited how Charles Goodyear had accidentally dropped a glob of rubber and sulphur on a stove and thereby discovered vulcanization; how a DuPont chemist, trying to make an improved refrigerant, accidentally discovered the coating that would later become Teflon; how Ivory floating soap, better brakes for jetlines, artificial sweeteners, and puffed cereals, all happened serendipitously.

The best way to take advantage of serendipity is to cultivate an attitude—the attitude of openness, which enables us to recognize the lucky accident when it happens.

It is possible that this recognition is actually based on a physiological reaction. Brain researcher James Olds, in the 1950s, experimenting with animals, discovered specific "pleasure centers" in the brain, which when stimulated caused his animals to perform tasks for no other reward than the electrical stimulation to those centers. It may be these centers that are stimulated when we encounter a novelty, such as the punchline of a joke. Just so, when we are free-associating, we may be sending stimuli to these reward centers.

Serendipity: An Organic Rule

Perhaps the most telling evidence of the importance of serendipity is in a law of nature itself, which encourages so-called "sport buds," the essence of serendipity. Says Carl Sagan, in *The Dragons of Eden*, "The raw materials of evolution are mutations . . . in the gametes, the eggs, and sperm cells, which are the agents of sexual reproduction. Accidentally useful mutations provide the working material for biological evolution."

So you see, it's organically vital for us to be wide open for that original idea. I am convinced, from having conducted these sessions for many years, that *we* do not solve the problems. The solution to every problem is somewhere, up there in the air, and if we are sufficiently *open* to all the contexts, *we simply become the media through which the problem solves itself.* "That's why," said Bill Foley, when he read over my first draft of this chapter, "it's worth all the searching, patience, testing, and looking at many ideas. The BIG IDEA is already there!"

Or as William J. J. Gordon, the father of synectics, expressed it: "Reducing a concept to practice, the subject being constructed begins to have a life of its own. Successful invention depends on permitting the object to act with sufficient autonomy to guide the inventor."

Or, finally, from psychoanalyst C. J. Jung: *"It is not Goethe who creates Faust, it is Faust which creates Goethe."*

Get Ideas for Getting Ideas　　You can profit by inventing your own unique methods for stimulating ideas and by collecting and using other people's methods. At a Y&R creative directors' conference in San Francisco, the participants were asked to give instances of how they "broke out of the creative rut." Their answers were distributed to the agency. Here are some extracts from that report:

WARMING-UP

I'll type things on the typewriter, random thoughts. The act of typing does two things—it concentrates my thoughts—mind to hands to paper—and it helps me to get loose, the way a runner warms up before a race.

CHANGING THE ENVIRONMENT/CHANGING TOOLS

I do crazy stuff. Work at strange hours, sit on the floor, sit on the ceiling if I could, work in strange places. A teacher at art school once told me to tie my pencil to the end of a long stick, 20 inches long, and it makes the line more sensitive. My drawing process was too trained. By breaking down the training my hand had, there was more sensitivity in the line. Training can be an impedance.

START WITH "THE SAVE"

With a creative problem, we start with what we call "The Save"—a safe solution to the problem we know the client and account group can agree with. It's not necessarily noncreative, but it's safe. That takes a burden off our shoulders. Then we can let go and look for the big "aha," something that's never been done before.

WHAT HAPPENED TO THE "HOLY SHIT" ADS?

How many ads do you remember? How many ads are like those few outrageous ads that when you open a magazine, you say "Holy Shit! Who did that ad?" We took a blood brother oath that every ad we do will be a holy shit ad. We like to take accounts that no one else wants and make them visible.

GET RID OF THE FEAR OF FEAR

I've started limiting my group to two ideas, and when I look at those ideas, they know that they will not be rejected. Instead, I work with them to try to embellish the ideas, and in the course of that, something exciting often happens. Our fragile egos need praise. We need help to overcome ridicule, rejection, and compromise. Jack Tinker used to give an award for the most ridiculous idea. We need to try to do the ridiculous—the unattainable. Then our work will be fun again.

WHEN WE *FEEL* WHAT WE WRITE, WE KNOW WHO WE ARE AND WHY WE'RE HERE

We have to re-create universal values. Relevance has lost its meaning. We have to be relevant to the ways people *feel*—rather than to just analyze how they think. It's not a bank institution—it's the linty pocket of a kid, the chalky memories of a school teacher. It's not automotive engineering—it's the chill on the neck when you get a new car, the smell of new leather. It's not a public utility—it's someone giving us boundless power.

We're too incestuous. Instead of always meeting with each other, we should take a doctor to lunch, take a plumber to lunch, listen to people who *know* why people react as they do. We have to get out of ourselves and into people.

MAKE THE "PROBLEM" AN "OPPORTUNITY"

The word "problem" has always bothered me. Who said it was a problem in the first place? If someone had said to Edison, the problem is I don't have enough candles to light the room, and if Edison had been less of a man, he might have solved the problem by getting more candles or by putting reflectors on the candles. But if you said to Edison, here's an opportunity to light this room, what should we do, he would wind up inventing the light bulb.

THIS IDEA CAME OUT OF A LIFE EXPERIENCE

The Spic & Span campaign was a traditional slice of life, but it had a strong selling idea—"clean enough for a baby." We were new parents, and we were shocked to see our baby crawling on a dirty floor. The idea came out of a true life experience.

Play Idea-Multiplying Games   Game playing is a facile way to proliferate ideas. Here are a few of the games we have played in our workshops:

NONSTOP FREE-ASSOCIATION

This is a game in which the players are encouraged to let off steam by filling their papers with spontaneous thoughts about a subject.

You've heard of "automatic writing," and then there is the automatism, in some religious groups, of "speaking in tongues." What happens is that another self seems to take over and do the dictating. I suspect that it is a creative self which is an autonomous living force. In nonstop free association, we are attempting to impose a state of automatism that will free that living force.

The leader asks the players to place the tips of their pencils on their blank papers. The tip of the pencil must never leave the paper. The leader spends a little time explaining that the players will have a time limit, say 60 seconds or 2 minutes, and that they are about to have a race in which they must let their pencils, not their conscious minds, fill the paper. He purposely builds up the suspense before telling them the subject of their free association, and then he suddenly says, "Ready, set, go!" The players race against the clock, which forces them to bypass their usual judgmental minds. After the time limit is over, they read aloud from their papers, and are encouraged to hitchhike on one another's thoughts.

NONSTOP FREE ASSOCIATION, STARTING WITH THE WORDS "I WISH . . ."

You may be surprised at how these two words cause you to visualize and phantasize situations. Let's say that you are free-associating about the Eastern Airlines experiences mentioned in the previous chapter. If you start with the words "I wish . . . " your mind might prompt such thoughts as the following: "I wish that the moment winter starts, my family could rush to the airport and escape . . . I wish we could be snorkeling down through some crystal-clear grotto, where the fish have a thousand different colors and patterns . . . that we could sit in the sun under a beach umbrella, drinking a piña colada," and so on. The words "I wish" naturally evoke experiential visions, any one or combination of which could become advertising executions.

MAKING THE STRANGE FAMILIAR AND THE FAMILIAR STRANGE

This is a favorite synectics method of prompting original thoughts. Take any familiar subject and ask the players to describe it in an unfamiliar way. For example, the subject of "quality control" in the manufacture of automobiles was dramatized in an unfamiliar way in the famous Volkswagen ad with the headline "Lemon." Or take the strange topic and ask for a familiar expression of it. I like to use an example of an ad for the Berlitz school of languages. It showed a closeup of the face of a little Chinese girl and, underneath, the headline: "If she can speak fluent Chinese, why can't you?"

This handy little game is a discipline for getting "outside the circle" of hackneyed thoughts.

PASSALONG

This is a parlor game most of us have played, which can be put to our practical purpose. The first person in a group writes a phrase about a subject and passes his paper on to the next player, who adds to the phrase and passes the paper to the next player, and so forth, until all the players have finished writing. We usually play this game with competitive teams. Again, the free association has a time limit, to encourage spontaneity. The game is an excellent idea starter and ice-breaker because the teams are practicing how to hitchhike on one another's thoughts, and there is also the cohesion of an "essay" evolving.

LISTING ATTRIBUTES

This game provides many triggers for free association and feedback, because it disciplines the players to provide a catalog of the attributes having to do with the given subject. With this focus, one again is given to visualization. For example, if you were to list the attributes of any person, it is easy for you to go on for some time—about his physical presence and physiognomy, his personality attributes, his beliefs, his friends and relatives—the free association would easily and fluently proliferate. Just so, when brainstorming about a product or service, this game will easily proliferate hooks on which to hang your ideas.

THE SPACE RACE

In this game, we have teams competing to fill spaces with "ads." On long sheets of our brown wrapping paper, we draw dozens of blank rectangles. Each team is given, say, ten spaces, and at the word "go" they race to create headlines and/or pictures. The first team to fill all the spaces wins the game. The speed with which the spaces are filled guarantees spontaneity.

ANALOGIES

The entire Synectics system of brainstorming depended mainly on the use of metaphorical thinking. Don Fabun, in an early issue of the *Kaiser Aluminum News* ("You and Creativity"), summarized these methods as shown in Figure 3–3.

How to Make It Easy for the Group to Get Ideas

Here are three suggestions on how to be a sensitive and skillful group leader of a brainstorming activity.

1. *Don't lead; rather, encourage.* Some years after our first traveling creative workshop, I was asked by our county Mental Health Advisory

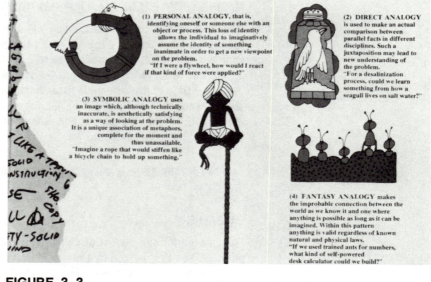

FIGURE 3–3

Board to act as the "facilitator" of an idea session. I had not at the time heard of the term "facilitator," and rather resented it as one of those pseudoscientific buzz words academics sometimes use to avoid common speech. As I thought about it, however, I realized that it was an excellent description of what a group leader should do—he or she should help to *ease* the act of self-expression to make it *facile*—easy—rather than to be a dictatorial leader or teacher.

I have never, in fact, liked the word "teacher" and prefer "educator" because it comes from the Latin word *educare*, which means "to draw out"—to lead someone to discover something. Sylvia Ashton-Warner highlighted the difference in her priceless little book, *Teacher*: "All [approaches to creative education] fail when they are too intentional, too self-consciously applied (the 'self' being the teacher). . . . The teacher must possess or cultivate 'negative capability'—listen, watch, and wait until the individual child's line of thought appears . . . ."

I believe that *all* people, not just a favored few, are potentially creative. Some of us simply have more facility expressing ourselves. For others, it is necessary for the "facilitator" to create an environment which gives them *permission* to be creative.

2. Go with the flow. To be an ideal leader requires a responsive attitude. The worst kind of leader is one who would impose his or her personality and ideas upon the group. The best is one who becomes a reflection of the group's thoughts and impressions. He or she is, in fact, the perfect reporter. At the same time, the leader *is* a kind of guide. For since such a huge quantity of ideas is emerging, and free association can go in so many different directions, the leader must be skillful in keeping the flow of ideas on the track of the original focus.

Occasionally, his instinct will tell him when it seems worthwhile to allow a detour. Subsequently, should the detour prove abortive, he can adroitly lead the group back on the track.

3. Encourage those ideas which are easy to multiply. A test of a good idea is how spontaneously it proliferates. The leader can tell, by the rising enthusiasm of a group, that they are "on to something."

The word "enthusiasm" comes from the Greek *enthousiasmos,* and that started with the word *entheos,* literally meaning "full of the god" or inspired or possessed. This kind of absorption is a practical tool. The group's god of the moment is the problem to be solved, which obsesses and possesses them. It carries them along on a wave, pushes them so intensely that they couldn't possibly stop to have negative thoughts that discourage free association.

When that contagious enthusiasm happens to a group, it's a profound emotional experience. A feeling of love occurs, of sheer joy in the game of getting ideas.

How to Sort Out the Ideas

Now we come to the last three points in Osborn's codification:

Incubation is that time when we relax and let our subconscious minds mull over the ideas we have had. The duration may be any length. In our traveling seminar, "The Basics of Creativity" was less than two hours long, so we did not expect that we would actually solve every problem. Yet many good solutions did occur, even in that brief time, so it's possible that the incubation period can occur in shorter takes when the atmosphere is just right.

As for the sixth and seventh steps—synthesis and evaluation—the workshop simply explained how to sort out and judge the enormous quantity of ideas. Here are the guides we gave:

1. First, inventory all the ideas, in the sequence in which they occurred.

2. Next, without any great effort of will, browse through the list. You may do this several times, to allow your subconscious mind to absorb the ideas. In the course of browsing, you will find that they begin to categorize themselves. You can then encode these categories and make a new list by categories.

A case in point might be a brainstorming session for a client of the Los Angeles office, Ralph's Supermarkets. The objective was to find a lot of ideas which could be used throughout the year to increase traffic in the stores. We had a list of some 1,500 ideas. We made our new list by categories of departments (meat, produce, deli, dairy, etc.), by incentives (contests and sweepstakes, coupon ideas, free offer ideas, etc.), by extra services to be added to the stores (valet parking, beauty shop, car wash, etc.).

3. The next step is to rearrange your lists by *concepts* and *techniques*. Some of the ideas may overlap, but for purposes of selection, you should arbitrarily separate them.

For example, in the Ralph's case, we thought of the idea of entertaining customers in some of the stores' usable spaces. That was a concept; the specific idea of having a bowling alley on the roof was a technique. In the case of an idea session for a special Lincoln-Mercury campaign, a concept was to offer "a sports car ride in a family car." Among the techniques for executing that concept was the notion of likening the driver's seat to the cockpit of an airplane. This triggered a suggestion to "bring back those jazzy early fliers' leather helmets" as premiums for the car promotion.

4. Having arrived at a manageable listing of the ideas, develop *criteria* for judging them. They should be *ideal* criteria, regardless of how impossible they might seem to be to fulfill. These criteria, of course, will vary according to the project and its objectives.

For example, in the case of Lincoln-Mercury, one criterion was that all the ideas should be of special appeal to Californians. In the case of an idea session for the Bekins Moving Company, whose goal was to increase the company's business activities, one criterion was that all the ideas should use the company's existing assets, either its trucks or its buildings.

There are three criteria that are applicable to every problem: relevance (to the facts surrounding the problem, as set forth in the briefing); originality (since creativity should result in effective surprise); and the intrinsic ability of the idea to grow and proliferate.

5. Use judgment *and* intuition to choose the best ideas. Using your criteria, you are able to evaluate the many ideas. You should not allow yourself to be wholly analytical during this procedure, for the selection is also a creative process. Our intuition is always at work and will tell us when an idea that does not seem to fulfill all the criteria, is nevertheless so powerful that it deserves to be selected.

The process I have just described is a kind of funneling activity. We funnel the huge quantity of ideas into the narrowest possible group of ideas, until, we hope, the one best idea emerges.

6. Schedule more brainstorming sessions, focusing on the few "best ideas" you have selected. Suppose, for example, you have inventoried several thousand ideas from your first session, categorized them into several hundred, winnowed those down to a dozen or so concepts and techniques, and applied your ideal criteria to a short list in order of preference. The next step would be to hold separate idea-multiplying sessions on, let us say, the first three preferred ideas.

Remember, I said that a good idea should have the intrinsic ability to grow and proliferate. By exposing those three ideas to the test of a thorough brainstorming exploration, they can further divide themselves until you feel confident in selecting just one. The truth will out. The best idea, by nature's law of natural selection, will *insist* on being heard and will, beyond all of the other ideas, survive.

CASE HISTORIES

A Nonstop Free-Association Game

This was the start-up game in a session at our San Francisco office to develop new product ideas for Heublein wines and liquors. The facts of the briefing covered 54 typewritten pages and a 30-foot brown paper section. Although I spent only 15 minutes reading all the facts aloud to the group, you would be surprised at how much was absorbed in that short time and how easily those facts triggered ideas during the free association.

The problem definition was to find new product ideas in as many as possible of eight previously selected directions. One way to solve the problem could have been to free-associate on the subject of each category separately. I opted not to do so because I felt that each would be too narrow a focus. I wanted our minds to range freely, in all directions at once, figuring (and rightly so, as it proved) that we could sort out our broad ideas into the narrow categories afterward.

The subject of the first nonstop game was "What I like in food and drink, free-associating about all five senses." As participants read their papers aloud, and the ideas were lettered on the brown paper, people shouted ideas triggered by the display. First entries included

Must be healthy

Old world

European-type flavor

Drinks associated with upscale life

Low in unsaturated fat

Heritage

Young

Adventurous

Bubbly

Tart

Sparkling

Icy

Shimmering

Fresh

Note how any one of these thoughts might refer back to possible categories of beverages and how any one could send the group on a particular line of thought. Thus, the following words, called out at various times, were probably triggered by the fourth phrase above, "drinks associated with upscale life":

Elegant

Opulent

Charisma

Glamorous

Sophisticated

Exotic

In that list, the word "exotic" triggered someone to say the word "tropical," while another said the word "mysterious," which, in turn, called to one player's mind the word "medieval," which would later lead the group to several lines of thought, including product names and package designs.

The following give-and-take shows how the leader nudges the group, encouraging them to hitchhike on one another's ideas. (In this, and later verbatims, I differentiate the group members' comments with a hyphen and mine without.):

Okay, keep going, fast!

—Refreshing

—Chewy

Chewy, that's an interesting word for a drink.

—Creamy

—Velvet

—Crisp

—Spicy

—Slurpy

Interesting. Why should we always be serious? We could have fun with something like Slurpy or Chewy or Crunchy. . . . Go ahead, go ahead.

—Sizzling

—Sizzling with a barbecue

Good.

—Spicy

Spicy again.

—Sparkling

—Icy

Anyone want to hitchhike on sparkling and icy?

Later, looking through the verbatims, one can see a virtual blueprint of how ideas came to be evoked. Take the word "charisma," for example, which later proved to be a popular idea. Here is how it happened:

—Color

—Coldness

—Less filling

Less filling—anyone want to make that familiar phrase strange?

—More filling (laughter)

—Slim

—Fattening

—Buttery

Good.

—Character

Anyone want to hitchhike on character?

—Complexity

Complexity. What do you call a person with character?

—Eccentric

—Unique

That's interesting—what's a person like who's unique?

—He has charisma

Charisma—that's terrific! Has anyone got a product named Charisma?

Worldwide Examples	If you were to conduct brainstorming sessions in any foreign countries, you will find that it's advisable for the participants to free-associate in their own language, even though they might be fluent in English. The need for speed requires that they think in their native tongue. We became experts, through our translators and sound systems, in synchronizing the ideas side by side.

FIGURE 3–4

Catching a Catchphrase

In Berne, Switzerland, the problem was to exploit Phillips video recorders. At that time, VCRs were little known, and the Berne office had the long-term assignment to make people aware of the advantages of Phillips video recorders while their TV receivers were being sold more aggressively.

In the course of brainstorming, one idea emerged predominant. It summed up the fact that people in the future would be able to build their own "libraries" of video entertainment and education. The German-Swiss word for a book library is *Bibliotheke*. Someone had the inspiration to call the Phillips VCR a *Videotheke*, and the group unanimously gravitated toward that simple and catchy idea (Figure 3–4).

A Quirk About Quark

In Amsterdam, we brainstormed about a French-made fresh dairy dessert called Mona Quark. Quark itself was a category of German origin, somewhat akin to yogurt, with health advantages in its protein content and lack of fat.

The major difficulty was that previous Quark products had not had wide acceptance because they tended to taste bitter. Consumer panel tests by the makers of Mona Quark had shown encouraging acceptance of their product's taste. The problem was to convince consumers, prejudiced against the Quark category, that Mona was different and better tasting, thereby winning a high degree of trial.

Our Amsterdam brainstormers went "all around the subject"—with ideas triggered by the Mona name, its French origin, and its fresh dairy and health appeals. Once again, one idea emerged from the many. It was a "lucky accident" that stemmed from thoughts about Mona Lisa, dairy products, good taste, and the proven success in America of a friendly spokeswoman, Elsie the Cow. The idea: "Mona Lisa Quark," a cow character with a Mona Lisa smile (Figure 3–5).

FIGURE 3–5

Capturing the Concept in Pictures	In Tokyo, we brainstormed about Old Spice Aftershave Lotion. The ideas gravitated toward its refreshment in the morning (i.e., "Wake Up with Old Spice"). Our Tokyo art directors had fun filling the space with visuals. (See Figure 3–6.)

Overcoming an Obstacle	In Madrid, the problem was to promote Balay, a Spanish-made dishwasher, surmounting the obstacle that German-made brands were thought to be more efficient. One popular idea was "Wash away your doubts about dishwashers," and the argument that Balay dishwashers were as efficient as imported brands, yet less expensive. (See Figure 3–7.)

Creating a Striking Visual Image	In Milan, our brown paper mural was about the launch of a new Cinzano Rose wine. Ideas gravitated to thoughts of freshness, rosy

FIGURE 3–6

FIGURE 3-7

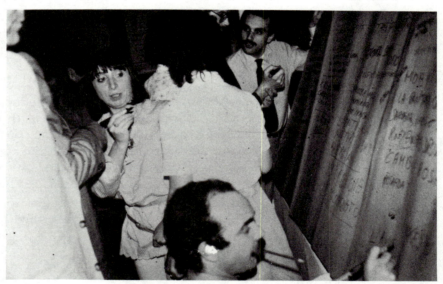

FIGURE 3-8

dawn, and the provocative slogan *Sapore di colore, colore di sapore* ("Tasteful color, colorful taste"). (See Figure 3–8.)

A "Buried" Idea That Made Itself Heard

In Copenhagen, we were brainstorming ideas for a new business presentation to a chain of Danish vacation resort hotels. The problem was that most Danish vacationers preferred to leave the country for resorts in sunny Spain or Portugal. The competitive concept of the Danish hotels was to offer pleasure and conveniences that would especially appeal to families, in some of Denmark's loveliest natural settings.

The Danish teams were unusually competitive and prolific, and the team members loudly proclaimed that their ideas were the best. The

FIGURE 3-9

ideas were so bright and original that it was difficult for the judges to choose among them. (See Figure 3-9.)

At that point, someone noticed a small copy line in one ad. It was not even the headline, but a footline modestly inserted under the logo. The line was *Himmel og Hav,* which was literally translated "heaven and sea," but was also a Danish slang expression similar to such an expression in English as "the living end!"

"That's a pretty good line," someone said, and then everyone started to climb aboard. The line would appeal to Danish chauvinism, they said; it could lead into and out of the catalog of the many advantages they felt should be stressed about the hotels. It also equated with the natural beauty of the settings, which they felt should be stressed.

Suddenly all the partisanship disappeared, and the one, hitherto buried, idea took over. They were off and running with variations on the one theme. This is a good example of the lesson expressed earlier—the need for unanimous openness to whatever the best idea may be.

A month later, back in New York, we received a cable that the Copenhagen office had won the account on the basis of their presentation— their elaboration on that one serendipitous idea.

The Power of Analogy

A happening similar to the one in Denmark occurred a few months later in our Hong Kong office, which was also about to make a new business presentation—this one for the Longines watch account.

The briefing explained that the popular watches in Hong Kong were those that could best be flaunted—either because of their appearance

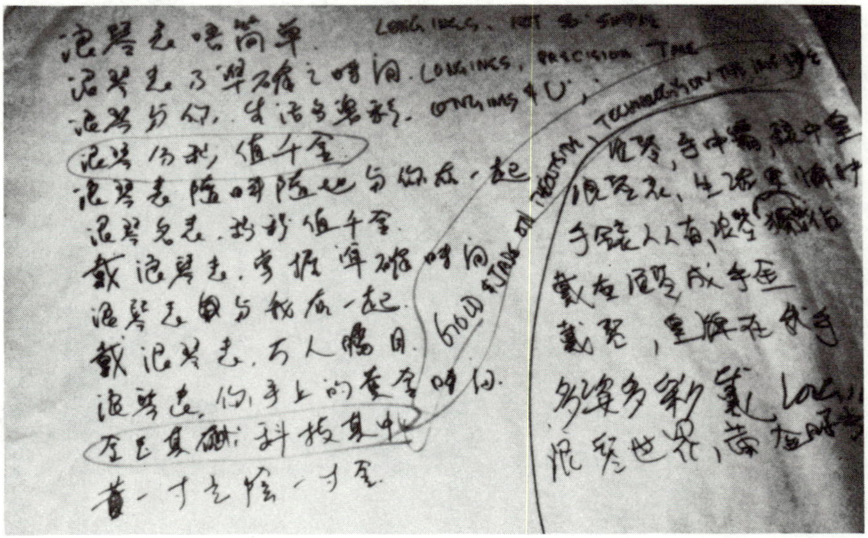

FIGURE 3-10

or because they had product names that were the vogue. On the other hand, the main advantage of the Longines watch was the quality of the Swiss workmanship.

The former appeal, in other words, was an emotional one, while the Longines major asset was a rational appeal. An exclusively rational appeal, said the briefers, would be less effective with Hong Kong consumers than it might be with people in other parts of the world.

In the course of free association, the concept arose of a combined appeal—that the Longines were stylish on the outside as well as superior on the inside: "Gold and jade on the outside, technology on the inside." (See Figure 3-10.)

This concept triggered an association, by one of the players, with a Chinese proverb about the need to guard against superficial appearances, that is, the story of the Mandarin orange, which appeared to be ripe and lovely on the outside, while it had, unfortunately, gone rotten on the inside. The players seized upon the one idea that had "a life of its own." It could be a "design for action" and would achieve "effective surprise." They began to sketch ads and TV storyboards and to plan displays featuring watches and oranges.

As in the case of the Danish hotels, a chanced-upon idea became the basis of the office's presentation and winning of the account.

CHAPTER CHECKLIST

1. Originality is the essential ingredient of creativity.

2. There is a definable process which can facilitate creativity. It involves the balancing of a Creative Work Plan and a Creative Play Plan.

3. A Creative Play Plan consists of getting and capturing a huge quantity of ideas, and for this there are definable methods, including
   a. Nonstop free association.
   b. Capturing *all* the ideas.
   c. Trusting your intuition.
   d. Getting ideas for getting ideas.
   e. Playing idea-multiplying games.

4. The best way to lead a group in its idea making is to be a facilitator: make the experience easy.

5. If we are open enough and trust our intuitions, the best idea will be recognizable.

6. But whether our intuition recognizes the best idea or not, there is a definable process for sorting and selecting ideas and enabling the best idea to emerge. This includes
   a. Inventorying the ideas.
   b. Separating them by categories.
   c. Separating them by concepts and techniques.
   d. Using "ideal criteria" for selection.
   e. Funneling the ideas to a favored few.
   f. Further brainstorming on the few ideas so that the one *best* idea prevails.

7. For inspiration, review the eight case histories, as examples of the various steps in the creative process.

CHAPTER 4

How to Create Better Print Advertising

Print is still the best place to learn what selling is all about. It's a tough, exacting disciplinarian—far more difficult to do well than TV in my opinion. Print is where capturing a prospect's attention is a supreme challenge, where holding the prospect and leading him to a sale takes enormous skill and craftsmanship. All this in one frame—not the 720 afforded in a 30-second spot . . .

Nick Rudd, Director of Management Services, Y&R, Inc.

If we do better print, I believe we'll be doing better advertising in every medium.

THREE GENERATIONS OF PRINT PRINCIPLES

Y&R's guides for doing better print have varied in number and terminology during the agency's 66-year history. Their character was influenced by the context of the times in which they occurred.

In 1938, there was a 38-point checklist, much of which would be still valid today. It had a detailed score sheet, with different values given to each component. Of course, Y&R did not intend then, nor does it intend now, with its latest guides, for clients, account managers, or creative staff to use their checklists for slavish adherence to rules. An ad, for example, whose sole objective would be to achieve high awareness for the name of a product might follow only one guide in a given checklist (capture the audience) while ignoring all the other guides. The main purposes of any lists, past and present, are to be stimuli, reminders, and triggers for discussion.

Nevertheless, such an exhaustive checklist was a reflection of the context of those days, when print was our dominant advertising medium, radio a novelty, and TV unheard of. Forty years later, when George Gribbin conducted the print section of our traveling creative workshop, the major context was a proliferating glut of media clutter, the major competitor being the far more glamorous TV. Another context was that Grib had only 90 minutes in which to deliver and hammer home his print-improving message. He condensed his principles for print into five yardsticks, in the form of five questions to ask oneself when creating or judging a print ad.

That same year, 1978, Alex Kroll gave a talk at a General Electric conference, entitled "Why Johnny Can't Read Your Ad," and discussed "the first totally tube-fed generation of *homo sapiens.*" Back at the agency, he noted that we had many young "tubies" who had never been properly schooled in the art and craft of print. We had been treating print as a second-class citizen, and he believed that an immediate print-training program was essential.

In 1980 that program was launched—and it was far more extensive than our workshop could be. This was a summary, which Bill Foley wrote for the benefit of the Y&R managers and creative directors who would later use the program for training their personnel:

THE PRINT PROGRAM

What it is. It looks like a two-day workshop about the outstanding execution of print advertising. But it is actually a one-year management program with goals set by management and the creative department before the workshop. And a strong follow-up after the workshop.

Why. Because we all need to go back to the basics of our craft. The print program ties in with the creative leadership goals of Y&R in setting new standards for an office or unit. It sharpens people's skills in creating print advertising.

Description. A three-step process: (1) manager and creative director set goals, including selecting target accounts; (2) two day workshop is conducted; (3) unit follow-up activities begin, for example, using program terminology in reviewing work, "Ad of the Month," quarterly reviews of print ads, and so on.

The print program began in September 1981, and the symbol the agency designed for it signified that by the following September the agency's print output would significantly improve. The results were encouraging, but they have never satisfied the agency's drive for excellence, and therefore the program has continued ever since.

Both Grib's 90-minute print session and the two-day print program consisted of three elements: a lecture about the principles, specific examples of good and bad practice, and participation by the workshop members—through critiquing ads and creating actual ads designed to solve advertising problems.

I shall now encapsulate these three Y&R generations of print principles. Although their contexts differed, I think that you can find useful guides from each of the three generations and can draw on them to heighten your awareness when you are creating print ads. They parallel and in some cases repeat one another, and none should be considered rigid rules—not if you would constantly "resist the usual." But the most original innovator, be he a Picasso, a James Joyce, or an Edison, has always been well grounded in the basic principles of his craft.

WHY WE NEED PERPETUAL TRAINING

The reason so many bad, ineffective ads appear is not because the ad-makers are all ignorant of these principles, but because they constantly forget or neglect them. Creative workshops are trenchant reminders in the course of our daily recurrent tasks.

Do we need these constant reminders? Just consider the shocking statistic Grib quoted at the beginning of his talk about print:

As a copywriter, I have known for a long time that most print ads don't get very much attention. But in a get-together with some of our top U.S. creative people this January I found out how bad the situation really is. At this meeting an executive of the Gallup & Robinson research organization showed us some figures on the performance of magazine advertising in the 1970s. . . . Gallup & Robinson finds that men and women—when interviewed the morning after they have read a magazine—can recall only 11 out of every 100 ads in the magazine. The shocking thing this statistic tells us is that the average ad is _not_ remembered by 89 out of 100 readers of a magazine.

So the idea is never to _create,_ never to _approve_ average ads. Your aim should be always to beat the average, always to do better than your competition.

Other statistics Grib reported: at the time of reading a magazine, an average of only 30 percent of the readers _note_ any given ad and less than 10 percent actually _read_ it. The conclusion, of course, is that if you can double the noting and reading of your ad, you are getting "twice the bang for your buck."

The 1938 Checklist

The 1938 38-point checklist consisted of questions to be asked regarding five major print elements. Here is a summary. (_Caution:_ Even as far back as 1938, such checklist entries were designed solely as _reminders_ for the print writers and art directors—not as rigid rules.) You should begin with a preliminary consideration of whether the ad advances the basic selling idea of the product and whether it fits the medium in which it appears. Then consider five print elements:

1. _Translation of the selling idea into reader self-interest._ Three questions, regarding consumer benefit, emotional pull, and clarity.

2. _The headline._ Four questions, namely, does the headline use the most appropriate type, does it compete in stopping power with editorial content, is it consumer and benefit oriented, and is it "mechanically" effective?

3. _The illustration._ Four questions, specifically, is it of research-proved interest, is it sales promoting, is it relevant to the product, and is it mechanically effective?

4. _The text._ Eighteen questions, regarding the copy's freshness, sequence, fluency, reader-orientation, benefit, conviction, support for claims, competitiveness, believability, and so on.

5. _The advertising as a whole._ Eight questions, probing whether the ad clearly describes the product, registers its name and logo, concentrates on the main selling idea, has a dramatic and accessible appearance, and so on.

It is interesting that so many more questions were devoted to text than to illustration. Those were the days when, despite many dramatic visuals, copy was king and the concept of the inseparable writer-artist team had not yet arrived. While the context of *our* times skews toward faster reading and dominantly visual ads, it would be well for us to profit from these lessons of the past, when the printed word was so respected.

The 1978 Print Workshop

We were lucky to have George Gribbin, fourth electee of the Copywriters' Hall of Fame, as our primary teacher of print principles. No one knew them better or took greater pleasure in presenting them. I can see him now, lean and immaculate, like the kind of copy he wrote, relishing the opportunity to influence the lives of the young people he liked so much. While he had been chairman of this huge agency, he came to this new task with a great deal of humility. He labored for endless hours, between each round of workshops, poring through foreign magazines, to select ads for his slides that were tailored to the language and experience of each office.

Grib's first basic principle was to "do ads that jolt the reader, that whet his curiosity, that keep him [or her] from turning the page."

Question 1: "*Is that ad of yours a stopper?*" Grib explained that to stop a lot of readers, you must put something unexpected into your ad that will arouse a prospect's interest the instant he or she glances at the ad.

To invite participation, he then showed a series of slides of both dull and stopper ads, asking for a show of hands as to which were which. By and large, there was general agreement and a discussion as to how the stopper ads worked. This kind of participatory analysis of ads would later become the single most important feature of the ongoing Y&R print program.

Grib would then play a game in which he showed a dozen or so ads in a category—in this case cigarette ads—where the names of the products and their package designs had been blanked out.

Participants would be asked to select those ads whose product names were identifiable from the originality and distinctiveness of the campaign. Usually only two or three of the campaigns were identified, and he then made the point that in any given category—cigarettes, automobiles, liquor, detergents—the "me too" school of copy and visuals prevailed. "This is copycat advertising and it should be avoided like the plague."

Question 2: "*Is the product the hero of your ad?*" and Grib noted, "You rarely see a Young & Rubicam ad today in which the product is *not* the hero of the ad. Our development and widespread use of the Creative Work Plan really guarantees that the product and the principal benefit it brings to the user are front and center in every ad."

The trick, then, is to present your hero in a fresh and exciting way, and Grib would present a series of slides in which the product was "neither a pasteboard hero nor a trite one."

Question 3: "Is your ad completely believable?" He emphasized that this is a vitally important question, for if the answer isn't yes, you not only haven't helped your product, you have hurt it.

I have been asked, as was Grib occasionally, whether such a guide might be out of date, when many ads today use exaggeration, fantasy, and outlandish humor to make their point. All I can answer is that a technique should be *right* for the right strategy and for the true personality of a product, and if that is so, it will still have the ring of "believability." In recent years, we and our clients have paid more and more attention to characterizing a product with a "brand personality" statement in advance of the preparation of advertising—one that is so truthfully germane to the product that its proper communication would never ring false.

Again, Grib showed slides of ads, examples where the promise made or the benefit offered was, to his mind, believable, and again followed a stimulating discussion.

Question 4: "Is your ad a likable person?" Apropos of brand personality, this is a question which today is commonly asked by advertisers but which at one time was a concept Grib originated:

The simple truth is that people, although they seldom realize it, judge ads the way they judge people. Quickly. Without mercy. They like them or they don't.

So it pays to do ads that your prospects will immediately like.

Who likes people who shout at you? Nobody. So why create ads that shout at the reader? Like this one.

Who likes stuffed shirts? Very few of us. So why do stuffy or pompous ads?

Do you like dull people? Not much. You avoid them whenever you can. But dull ads are legion. There are many more dull ads than bright ones.

Grib went on to characterize and show ads that were like people in various ways—people who have something interesting to say, people who are amusing to be with, people who care for others, who want to help them: "Wherever we go and put on a workshop, we always leave this message with our writers: Read that ad of yours over one last time to be sure—if the ad were a man or woman—you would really like him or her. . . . If you wouldn't, start your ad over again."

Question 5: "Is the theme one that will last?" This final question is the one most often honored in the breach. "Great advertising should have consistency and continuity over a long span of time. By positioning the product in the same way in each advertisement month after month, year after year, you can create a definite personality for it, and it is the only way I know that you can create such a personality." Grib then showed examples of advertising that had strong continuity in visual terms and/or in terms of a slogan and/or a personality representing the product.

The print module of the first traveling creative workshop concluded, as did every part of the workshop, with enjoyable game-playing, ad-making discussion and debate—all prompted by the use of Grib's scoresheet as we viewed the local office's ads and those of their competitors. A score of 1 is given for a positive answer to each of the five questions, and 5 is a perfect score.

The idea of scoring ads in this fashion is a good training device, primarily because it makes for a lively discussion. It is not intended to be used for judging ads on the job. And we always pointed out that you are free to make deliberate exceptions to any of these given guides if there is a good reason. For example, as I touched on before, if the main purpose of an ad is to create the highest possible *awareness*, say, in the case of a "teaser" ad, one might opt for "stopperability" and let the other attributes go by the board. In that case, in the scoring game, you could score "5" for that space only and argue for that decision in the discussion that followed. (See Figure 4–1.)

THE ONGOING PRINT PROGRAM

The ensuing print program started with the publication of a strikingly designed booklet, which expanded on Grib's five questions. (Excerpts from this booklet are shown in Figure 4–2.)

The program began in the United States with a series of regional seminars, conducted by key New York creative executives. These missionaries fanned out in teams and conducted a workshop of four modules:

1. Page personality

2. Simplification

3. Stopping power

4. Craft

SCORE SHEET FOR PRINT

ADVERTISER	STOPPER	HERO	BELIEVABLE	LIKABLE	LASTING	TOTAL
1.						
2.						
3.						
4.						
5.						
6.						
7.						
8.						
9.						
10.						
11.						
12.						

FIGURE 4-1

FIGURE 4-2

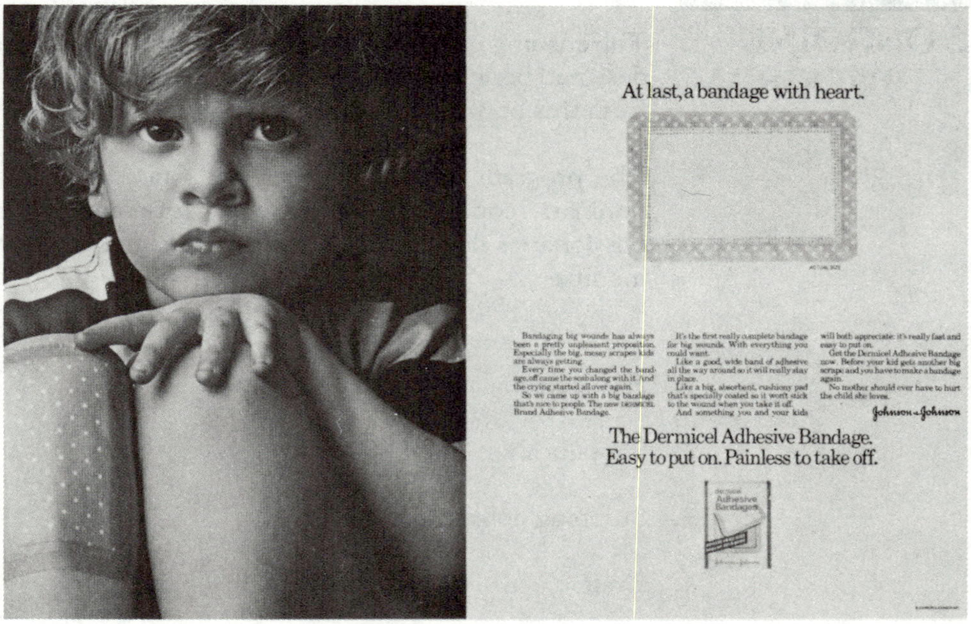

FIGURE 4–2 *(continued)*

A comprehensive explanation and examples of all these modules entails a text as long as this entire book. For this chapter, therefore, I shall simply touch on some of the details.

Each seminar began with this preamble:

QUESTIONS TO CONSIDER
WHEN YOU CONSIDER PRINT

Overall

1. Does ad arrest the reader's attention?
   a. Does it have a strong focal point?
   b. Is it a stopper?

2. Is stopper relevant to prospect?

3. Is ad based on concept clearly related to the selling premise?

4. Does stopping power generate additional investigation?

5. Does ad have continuing campaign potential?
   a. Unique page personality?
   b. Distinctive in its category?
   c. Visual or verbal equity maintained from ad to ad?

6. Does ad create positive feeling about product and advertiser?

Layout

1. Is ad arranged to facilitate readership?
   a. Headline clear and readable?
   b. Body text open, easy to follow, digestible?

Illustration

1. Does illustration stop, intrigue, and involve the reader?

2. Does illustration dramatize selling premise with a visual idea?

3. Does reader see the picture or see himself in the picture?

4. Does visual take advantage of demonstrable product benefit?

Headline

1. Does headline work with illustration to stop, intrigue, and involve reader?

2. Does headline offer promise or benefit relevant to selling idea?

3. Does headline surprise reader or involve him or her emotionally?

4. Does headline encourage readership of body copy?

Text

1. Does copy persuade by leading the reader through a single-minded argument?

2. Does copy advance the argument with clear, concise, well-staged prose?
   a. Is it factual and informative rather than puffery?
   b. Is it vivid and memorable, making use of examples and quotes?

3. Does it carry the reader from interest to conviction?

4. Does copy close the argument with a call for action?

The Page Personality Module	Page personality is the effect or impression created by a combination of elements (graphics, words, size, and shape) that gives the page distinctiveness. It must be a proper reflection of the brand personality.

One example is the ad for the Jamaica Tourist Board campaign (see Figure 4–3, color insert).

"They're stunning in their unique and elegant projection of a distinct brand personality. And it was done in a category choked with skin divers, sunfish, tropical fruit, sunsets, bikinied maids, plantation punch, thatched huts, gaming wheels, and wet t-shirts—all thrown onto a page with yards of copy."

"And boy, did it stand out. It was impossible to mistake this advertising. All it took was a glance. It was Jamaica and you knew it immediately."

Ads for *People Magazine* and its promotion campaign that ran for years: "It's one of the finest examples of page character that I know of." (See Figure 4–4.) "Everything comes into play—outrageous headlines, pun and fun pushed to the limit—lively and inventive text with the use of editorial art, all blending together into an airy soufflé that is indeed a personification of the magazine itself."

Page personality is dictated by the personality which has been determined for the product, and that, said the presenter, is a strategic issue because "a product's relationship to other products in the same category is a vital marketing and advertising consideration."

FIGURE 4-4

A product, he would explain, is seen by the consumer in three ways: physically, functionally, and emotionally. The *physical* is merely what a product looks like. Today, many products look alike. All peas are green, all bourbons brown, all coffees black. And some products, like gasoline, you never really even see.

The *functional* is what a product does. Within their categories, many products *do* the same thing. All green peas fill your stomach, all brown bourbons achieve the same net effect, and all gasolines function more or less equally.

Product positions are often so close to one another that there fails to be a distinction between them. That is why a brand's personality is often a key component in the strategy-making process. And the execution of the ad can reveal whether it is tough, old-fashioned, natural, romantic, friendly, dependable, motherly. For the brand to be successful, it must offer the public a clear, quickly identifiable, and consistent personality.

The elements of an ad that contribute to the communication of the brand's personality include the use of graphics—photography versus illustration, color versus black and white—and the *tonality* of words and pictures.

The Simplification Module

This module is easier to understand, yet too often honored in the breach.

The famous Hunt's Catsup and Volkswagen ads of the '50s set the style—where the visuals and designs said more about food and car quality than a thousand words would have said.

The Simplification Module pointed out the simple directness of commonplace signs like "No Smoking," "School Crossing," political campaign buttons, and so on.

The Stopping Power Module

"It's no news that you have to stop your prospect before you can make a sale. . . . Perdue Chickens stopped them with a surprising fact"; "*People* did it with an invitation to overhear gossip"; "Volkswagen went to extremes"; "While Volvo simply stated the obvious."

During this module, participants played a game in which they identified stoppers. The group was divided into teams, and each team was given copies of the same 30 ads and a scoresheet. Each group marked the number of their team below the ads they judged were stoppers. The ads were judged and ranked, and the teams' selections compared. If there was a similarity in scoring, the chairperson would say: "There does seem to be a definite trend here. The _____ ad, the _____ ad, the _____ ad, the _____ ad, and the _____ ad seem to be clear winners. And this means something else is very clear. We all agree on what a stopper is." If there is no similarity in the choices of the teams, the leader would continue a discussion and/or debate on what makes an ad a stopper.

The module summarized seven principles which go into making an ad a stopper, and showed examples for each:

1. That it "attracts beyond the prospect group"—has intrinsic drama with everyone;

2. That it demands participation;

3. That it forces an emotional response by touching on a basic human want or need;

4. That it creates a desire to know more;

5. That it surprises the reader;

6. That it exposes expected information in an unexpected way;

7. That it breaks with the personality and rules of the category.

Among the stimulating techniques by which these principles were executed were open-ended narrative, ironic twists on ordinary behavior, plays on words, and incongruity of visual elements and/or words.

The Craft Module

"Craftsmanship moves an ad from an edge that's merely serviceable to an ad of grace and elegance. . . ." How many ads fail to realize their promise simply because their authors failed to go the distance?

Type, art, visual, pace, balance, and design were all considerations. The art director who is a craftsperson spends many hours trying and revising and trying again before achieving that particular vision.

Observation on the whole ad. How does the whole thing work at first glance? *Does the whole ad communicate what you want it to communicate?* Is there one word in the headline which, when added or deleted, makes the whole ad better? Is there a better visual technique than what you've first used? If you like the ad today, will you like it tomorrow?

Observations on the headline. Does it touch a basic human emotion? Does it invite participation? Does it provide new information or something of value?

Observations on the body copy. Does the body copy flow from the headline? Does the first paragraph entice you to read the second, the second the third? And does the copy march inevitably to its conclusion? Is the body copy selling its subject or the copywriter? Is there a better headline buried in the body copy?

Observations on the visual. Do you have a visual *idea* or just a picture? Does the headline gain strength from the picture, and vice versa? Is the visual totally appropriate for the ad, the technique appropriate to the subject?

Similarly searching questions were asked regarding layout and typography, with pro and con examples illustrating the points made.

The Other Language

Speaking of visuals, in 1979 John Rindlaub, a former Y&R creative director and agency manager (now Y&R director of corporate relations) joined our traveling workshop and added a module about visualization in advertising. This proved to be one of the most popular and effective of our presentations and has been used by the Resource Center since.

While this module discussed visuals in TV as well as print, its principles were especially important for the refurbishing of Y&R's print program. Here are some of the points John made:

Long before man could write, he drew pictures. As a matter of fact, in some of the oldest languages, the words *are* pictures. Long before you could read, you could see. Long before you could write, you could visualize. You may think in words, but you *dream in pictures* . . . .

Gallup & Robinson has found that ads in which the visual *works hard* are remembered by 32 percent more people than the average ad . . . .

So . . . I hope you will remember just one thing from this presentation. And it's this: Say it with pictures.

To help you "say it with pictures," there are three questions you might ask about the visuals in your ads:

1. Is your picture *interesting?*
2. Does your picture help to identify the *brand?*
3. Does your picture help to convey the *message?*

Interesting? Brand? Message? There's an easy way to remember these three questions, but I'm a little embarrassed by what it is: I.B.M. . . .

It is possible to communicate without words, using nothing but the other language. . . . You don't need a headline to understand the depths of this woman's grief (Figure 4–5).

You don't have to hear words to know what this man is saying (Figure 4–6). . . . Here's a picture you've seen before, every May Day (Figure 4–7). And here's a set of words, "The Pepsi Generation" that's also familiar. . . . Put them together (Figure 4–8) and the combination is explosive. The picture doesn't simply illustrate the headline—it enlarges it, magnifies it.

Surprising combinations of pictures and words are the stuff of most great print advertising. Art Director Roger Mader describes the day he was putting the finishing touches on an ad for the Chrysler Imperial. He pasted down the headline: "It must pass 392 checks for perfection before it becomes an Imperial." He handed the mechanical to a traffic man and opened up the latest copy of *Life* magazine to the Volkswagen "Lemon" ad.

The surprising combination of a simple, black-and-white picture and a single five letter word said more—and said it more provocatively, more memorably, more believably than our four-color spread with its long headline.

Surprising combinations of headlines and pictures. It's hard to find them. But don't settle for less. Whatever the problem, there's a surprising, explosive

FIGURE 4–5

FIGURE 4–6

FIGURE 4–7

ONLY IN FORTUNE

FIGURE 4–8

picture-headline combination out there waiting to be born to those who labor hard enough.

There's a simple test you can try on your own print ads to see how well you are saying it with pictures. Take away the words, and ask yourself the three I.B.M. questions—Are the pictures *interesting?* Do they help identify *the brand?* Do they help convey *the message?*

For participation, John would show five pairs of Y&R print ads, with and without words, and encourage a discussion and critique. Participants then divided into groups, each group was given a written concept, and their assignment was to make a picture-headline combination poster on each.

There followed a discussion of techniques that help to make pictures interesting, among them:

People are interested in people, show interesting pictures of people

People are interested in news, show pictures that dramatize news

Use pictures that tell stories

Next, John discussed ways to dramatize the message, including *anthropomorphism* (making an inanimate product a person), and showing a dramatic demonstration. Finally, he discussed personifying the product, remarkable product shots, and other techniques for registering the brand visually.

THE ART DIRECTOR: CHANGING ROLE

"Registering the brand visually" is, of course, the special talent of an art director. He or she may do this through the layout, typography, the selection of art or photography, and influence on a great many activities in the production process, much of which is discussed in the next chapter.

The role of the art director, however, has changed radically during a number of decades, owing primarily to the closer teamwork of art directors and copywriters, and the changing technology that aids the art director's craft and relieves him of some of his earlier functions.

Art Harris, one of Y&R's veteran art directors (who this year celebrates 40 years with the agency), characterizes the various eras:

When I first came to Y&R, you were an assistant to The Art Director and you sat in the same office with The Art Director. It was really the old apprenticeship of the master and the student.

Your title was "layout artist." The copywriter would write the copy and the way you would get it was that they would slip it under the door with a work order, and you'd look at the copy, often without even talking to the copywriter, and you would *lay out* the page—almost like the layout man of a newspaper lays out the story.

It wasn't until the sixties that you really started to work with the copywriter, and that started with the Doyle, Dane, Bernbach agency, where the copywriter and the art director became an inseparable team.

Art is a fine example of one who has "paid his tithe to the agency business" by teaching his trade—not only within Y&R, but at the same time for 15 years at the School for Visual Arts and for the past 20 years at Pratt Institute. When asked the difference between what he originally taught and what he teaches now, he said:

Thirty-five years ago, my class was called "Rendering," and the most important thing to be an art director was to put it down in a simple, clean way that people could understand, and it was sort of half way between a rough sketch and an illustration. A layout is only a means to an end, and there's a certain art to doing a layout—it's not a copywriter's rough and it's not an illustration, it's somewhere in between. And it's knowing what to leave out.

You almost have to know everything before you can edit something, and so you have to know how to draw and compose and color, and then you have to edit down to the simple form. So that's what I was teaching.

Now, mainly, I'm teaching concepts or ideas or how to solve problems, not giving as much attention to the craft. Most of my students today just get by, in that craft. I just saw the portfolio of a girl to whom I gave an "A," and she's one of the best students in my class. She's pretty sloppy, in a way, but her ideas are so exciting and so fresh and so original, somebody would say, "Oh, fine, we can get somebody to clean up your stuff, but we want that kind of freshness and that kind of originality.

When I was at Art Center, we would spend hours and hours just to get watercolor to lay down beautifully. Now that would be almost like teaching a car mechanic to shoe a horse—it would have almost no relationship to what we do now.

A recent Y&R panel discussion, entitled "What Is an Art Director?" highlighted the contemporary art director attitudes.

The seminar was hosted by John Eighmey, former senior vice president and manager of creative services, and by Bill Taubin, senior art director and member of the Art Directors' Hall of Fame. Taubin had earned his qualifications for the Hall of Fame at Doyle, Dane, Bernbach, and had then retired. Y&R brought him out of retirement to help train and inspire a new generation of art directors.

Members of the panel were Bob Czernysz, vice president and senior art director, and Clark Frankel and Gary Goldstein, both senior vice presidents and associate creative directors. Here are some excerpts from this discussion:

Frankel: An idea "comes about," and an art director "puts it down," whether it's a printed page or a film design. He creates an *environment* for the idea.

Taubin: But, Clark, that sounds like . . .

Frankel: The layout man?

Taubin: Yes. It sounds like somebody who comes in afterward. That does not sound like the art director is very much a part of the origination of the idea.

Frankel: When the art director and the writer work out an idea.

Taubin: Yes.

Frankel: Well, the writer has to go off and type out the body copy or the headline. And the art director has to go off and give the idea an environment. That's not the conceptual portion of the process, it's the art *direction* portion.

Taubin: In the way I've always worked, both the art director and the writer are equally responsible for the words and equally responsible for the visuals.

Goldstein: I've always thought that "art director" is the wrong name for the job. It's really "arts director." You're overseeing illustration and typography, or in the case of TV the film-making, editing, taping, performances.

Taubin: As is the copywriter.

Goldstein: As is the copywriter.

Czernysz: I'd like to go a little further than that. Obviously, art director and copywriter make up a creative team. And sometimes their roles are interchangeable. But I think the copywriter's and art director's real functions come before the technical aspects are applied—you know, the craft aspects. Their real functions are to be able to translate a selling proposition, or a strategy, or whatever is necessary, into human terms. That is what they are experts in. They can put their finger on human nature, somehow, and express it as it relates to a product. They translate a strategy into human terms and make it exciting, and dramatic, and appealing to other human beings.

THE COPYWRITER: BASIC GUIDES

Vital as is the inspiration and craft of the visualization of ideas, we still need to be reminded of the fundamentals of the printed word. For this section, I draw on my 22-year-old book, *The Compleat Copywriter* (McGraw-Hill, 1966). Most of what I wrote in that book I had learned from the daily "workshops" I had absorbed from my mentors during my previous 15 years with Y&R as well as from peers in the business. I believe that these fundamentals are timeless and still relevant today.[1]

Writing Headlines

Stop the most possible readers by telling them the most interesting news, but do not tell them so much that they need not read the rest of your ad. Leave enough unsaid and intrigue them so adroitly that they *will* read on—but say enough so that those who *are* only noters, who *refuse* to read your body copy, will carry away a memorable message. "Avoid blind headlines," cautions David Ogilvy, "the kind which mean nothing unless you read the body copy underneath them; most people don't."

Good and bad headlines are quite recognizable. . . . Here is an ad for Tender Leaf Tea with a picture of a loving wife feeding her husband a cup of tea. The headline: "It's all in the family!" Could that possibly be a good headline? Does it fulfill any of our definitions of "communication"? Does it "impart knowledge" . . . further "an interchange of thoughts"?

Here, on the other hand, are headlines that do express one big thought, that impart knowledge, that select their audience, that promise a benefit, that involve the reader—that do all those magic things that add up to communication, to making a connection:

"World's only dog food that *makes its own gravy.*"

"Now! Color only the gray without changing your natural hair color!"

"General Electric introduces P-7, the oven that cleans itself."

"Now a beer bottle you can open with your bare hands!"

---

[1] The following discussion is taken from *The Compleat Copywriter* by Hanley Norins. Published by McGraw-Hill Book Company in 1966. Reprinted with permission.

At the time my book appeared, all those product benefits were new to the categories.

Those headlines make you want to read more. You want to know how those benefits are possible. You find the promise worth reading about. But even if you do not read more, you have the gist of the message. In the case of the oven, the advertiser's name is propitiously in the headline, but in the other three cases the logos were equally prominent for the noter.

No wonder headlines like those were read and noted (the researcher's term for "remembered") and the one of Tender Leaf Tea was missed by most of the readers.

But, you say, all four of those products had important product news to impart. How do we write headlines for benefits that are not new?

We cudgel our brains harder. Instead of writing about a perfume in the same old way, one writer says, "Wear Crepe de Chine at 80 throbs a minute"—the lead-in for a picture of a girl applying the heady stuff to the pulse of her wrist. Instead of the usual clichés about beer, another writer comes up with this inspired snobbery: "If they run out of Loewenbrau, order champagne."

Writing Subheads

We ought to write subheads as we write headlines—only a little more so. They should, as Mr. Ogilvy puts it, "heighten the reader's appetite for the feast to come." The best training for writing subheads, this writer has found, is constantly studying those that appear in *The Reader's Digest*. See how they develop the ideas in the headlines, yet lead the reader into the body copy.

At that point, I quote some of the intriguing subheads in the magazine. Which brings up an important point—the clues we can derive from going to school to the best magazine editorial content.

Learning from the Content Surrounding Our Ads

The year before Alex Kroll's ambitious print program began, he held a creative directors' conference, hosted by Y&R Santo Domingo. Each creative director was given one facet of many print subjects to discuss, and I believe that I got the plum—"Editorial Clues to Better Print Advertising." For the assignment, I studied the history of successful magazines and interviewed the editors and art directors of some of the leading contemporary magazines. Among the tips I learned and presented at the conference were these:

From the history of the old *Saturday Evening Post:* "Find a need and fill it." . . . The key to that magazine's success was the rare ability to give readers what they wanted. As George d'Hassy, editor of *Cosmopolitan,* told me, "Give it to them regularly!" A clue for us and our clients—more continuity, more lasting campaigns that stand for something consumers want most.

From Clay Felker, then editor of *Esquire,* formerly of *New York* Magazine: "'Bitiness'—lots of tiny ½-column pictures with involving captions. Adding those to *New York* raised our readership 20%."

From Milton Glaser, inventor of "The Glaser Grid": "When I designed *New York,* I did it with the proposition to make that magazine totally comprehensible in ten minutes, at a time when people's time span was determined by television and the capacity to pay attention was more limited than ever before. You had to provide a series of clues so that reading a magazine would be a very easy experience. So we used subheads on every page, dramatically, small pictures with captions, and the headline, all to make it possible to understand the magazine within minutes."

From Arthur Hettick, editor of *Family Circle,* the biggest selling service magazine: "Instead of trying to be clever, we try to be very specific. We try to say exactly what it is the reader will get. We also try to give the reader an idea of how much she will get. We know that numbers—'110 Gifts to Make'—are better than 'Gifts to Make.'"

From John Mack Carter, editor of *Good Housekeeping,* the most trusted service magazine, given a list of general communication principles that I cited to him, which would he select as the most important: "Relevance. How does the editorial content—in your case the ad copy—relate to the interests and needs of the reader? After that originality, how that relevance is expressed."

From Hal Silverman, editor of our leading San Francisco Sunday supplement, for which I had been writing feature articles: "The ad campaign that gets out ahead of the editorial product gets out of the general level of editorial-speak, is the kind of campaign that's going to work. So the advertiser who's going to be ahead will be ahead of the editorial environment he's in."

And that last clue summed up, to me, the most important goal for creating better print advertising. Advertising is the only form of communication which does not have a voluntary, ready-made audience. Politicians, preachers, authors, and teachers, all are speaking directly to somebody who is directly there to listen. But we are in a borrowed medium, when our ads appear in a magazine or newspaper. So what greater goal than to be even *more provocative*—to write *stronger headlines,* use *more powerful pictures,* write *more interesting copy* than is even in the best magazine itself!

- -
CHAPTER CHECKLIST
- -

1. Learning to do better print can improve our creativity in all media.

2. We tend to forget or neglect the basic principles; therefore we should constantly review and be aware of them.

3. The average ad is not remembered by 89 out of 100 magazine readers.

4. To improve memorability and effectiveness, Y&R training has, historically, provided three "checklists" about the basics.

5. The 1938 38-point checklist concerned five print elements:

   a. Translation of the selling idea into reader self-interest

   b. The headline

   c. The illustration

   d. The text

   e. The advertisement as a whole

6. Both the first traveling creative workshop and the print program had three elements: a lecture, case histories,

and participation by the seminar attendants.

7. The five questions of the first traveling creative workshop:
   a. Is the ad a "stopper"?
   b. Is the product the "hero"?
   c. Is the ad believable?
   d. Is the ad "a likable person"?
   e. Is the theme one that will last?

8. Y&R's ongoing print program considers the elements of
   a. The ad as a whole
   b. The layout
   c. The illustration
   d. The headline

9. The program provides the following general guides to print creativity:
   a. Create a "page personality" that distinctively reflects the brand.
   b. Strive for simplicity.
   c. Create stopping power by "resisting the usual."
   d. Cultivate craftsmanship in all the elements of the ad.

10. Visuals are "the other language." Ask yourself three questions:
    a. Is the picture interesting?
    b. Does it help identify the brand?
    c. Does it convey your essential message?

11. In the early days there was more emphasis on the art director's *craft*; more recent emphasis has been on the art director and copywriter collaboration to execute strategy in provocative ways.

12. Guides to improved copywriting include:
    a. Write headlines that stop and intrigue.
    b. Write subheads that heighten the reader's appetite to read on.
    c. Write body copy that fulfills the promise of the headline and/or the subheads.

13. Study exciting and interesting editorial content and strive to make your ads *even more exciting and interesting*.

· ·

CHAPTER

5 Creativity in Print Production

Andre Desmarais,
Print Production Manager,
Young & Rubicam, Montreal

The 17th Y&R Print Production Seminar proved to be somewhat of a revelation. Here were individuals, all specialists in their own right, willing to step forward to make presentations on a variety of subjects, in order to make us better informed and better equipped to deal with the daily demands of our jobs. Individuals whose only motivation appeared to be genuine desire to share their knowledge and experience with fellow members of the Young & Rubicam family.

SHARING IS WHAT TRAINING IS ALL ABOUT

Nowhere at Y&R has there been a greater desire to share knowledge with their peers than among the staff members of the New York print production department. Their traveling creative workshops existed ten years before the general one that we first conducted in 1978.

During the 18 seminars that have taken place in the past 20 years, the New York production specialists traveled to outlying offices in Los Angeles, San Francisco, Cedar Rapids, Kansas City, Toronto, Chicago, Houston, and so on, with the latest seminar taking place in Puerto Rico. At each location, there were guest speakers, and during the three-day seminars some time was allotted for field trips to suppliers.

It is fitting that Y&R print production pioneered the habit of planning and staging formal training seminars because, of all advertising disciplines, production is the most technical and specialized. Specialists in any field can become parochial and insulated from the environment outside. Yet the state of the art changes so greatly, so constantly and swiftly that it's essential for these specialists to share their knowledge with one another, if only to keep current in this changing high-tech world.

The seminar in 1969, in Los Angeles, for example, covered the same production subjects of photoplatemaking, typography, and printing as did later seminars, but at the seventeenth seminar in Montreal there were discussions about "smart scanners" and "electronic retouching and pagination," while at the eighteenth seminar in Puerto Rico they shared their experience with computer graphics and the Quantel Paintbox, Y&R's electronic artists' palette.

Most of the knowledge shared at these seminars has been far too technical and detailed for those of us who are generalists.

However, it is useful to understand, in broad strokes, the areas covered. And whatever your interest in the subjects of this book, it is worthwhile to examine at least an overview of these production processes.

WHAT PRINT PRODUCTION IS ALL ABOUT

An excellent summary about print production is that by Klaus F. Schmidt, senior vice president and manager of Production Services at Y&R, Inc., and author of *"What Every Account Executive Should Know About Print Production,"* [1] a little booklet published by the Four A's (the American Association of Advertising Agencies) for the benefit of account executives.

Says the introduction to that publication:

While you, as an account executive, need not become an expert in the myriad technical details surrounding the type-setting, color separation, and printing areas, you should understand at least the basics of graphic arts technology and also the procedural steps that are necessary to move a print advertisement through the production process.

Only if you possess this working knowledge can you expect to communicate successfully about print advertising with your client and with staff in the areas of your agency involved in its creation, research, and media planning and buying, as well as trafficking and production.

The booklet then outlines four aspects of print production:

1. Who the print producers are and their functions

2. Their tools and procedures

3. Production suppliers and the account managers' role in production

4. A chronological glossary of production terms

Who the Print Producers Are and What They Do

Print Services at Y&R New York include

- □ **art buyers, who are versed in various forms of photographic/illustrative techniques. They know the available talent and make all business arrangements with photographers, illustrators, manual and electronic retouchers, photo labs, etc., in close cooperation with art directors and print producers.**

- □ **type directors, trained in the creative as well as technical aspects of typography. Working with the art directors, they select, specify, mark up, and purchase all typesetting.**

- □ **printing buyers, who specialize in the production planning and buying of outdoor and transit advertising, newspaper and magazine inserts, and collateral printed material from brochures to elaborately die-cut mail pieces. While a**

[1] The following discussion is taken from "What Every Account Executive Should Know About Print Production," by Klaus F. Schmidt. © 1988, American Association of Advertising Agencies, New York. Reprinted with permission.

print producer usually purchases only the image carriers necessary to have an advertisement printed by a publication, a printing buyer's knowledge reaches into properties of paper and ink, and into the capabilities of printing, binding, and finishing equipment.

Tools and Procedures

The 4A's booklet describes four basic steps that take place during the production of a print ad.

The first is planning, estimating, and scheduling:

So that creative and production steps for a print ad may be executed with precision, a time schedule must be planned at the outset. It should work backwards from the closing date when all printing material must arrive at the publication. For a color advertisement, scheduled to appear in several magazines closing on August 1, such a plan might look like the following sample. (Note that not all calendar days are working days.)

> **Shipping date of duplicate materials**
> **July 28**
>
> **Duplicate material order date**
> **July 24**
>
> **Final separator's proof**
> **July 21**
>
> **First separator's proof**
> **July 11**
>
> **Color separation order date**
> **June 29**
>
> **Retouched artwork and mechanical finish date**
> **June 26**
>
> **Typesetting order date**
> **June 20**
>
> **Artwork finish date**
> **June 19**
>
> **Artwork order date**
> **June 19**
>
> **Layout and copy approval date**
> **June 8**
>
> **Start of creative work**
> **May 28**

Art directors and producers work as a team in the estimating, bidding, scheduling, and ordering of photographic or illustrative artwork and its preparation for reproduction:

Close cooperation . . . is obligatory at this stage to ensure that the artwork gives the best possible printing result in the publication and that the most cost-saving approach is employed, especially with today's electronic color pagination and retouching equipment.

Decisions on the type of retouching (manual or electronic) and whether photocomposing of photographs is executed by a color lab or by the color separator on electronic pagination equipment are but two examples of how the cooperation (or the lack of it) between your art and production group can influence print advertising cost effectiveness.

The second tool and procedure is the typographer's work in selecting and ordering the appropriate style and size of type, and administering the typesetting, fitting of the type and provision of photo repros to be pasted-up into camera-ready mechanicals or keylines.

There are thousands of typefaces available for today's advertising, but they generally have four classifications: roman (with serifs); sans serif (without serifs); square serif (blackletter or Old English); and scripts/ decoratives. ("Serifs" are the little "feet" at the end of the strokes of a letter.)

As Klaus explains:

Typesetting for print advertising is done by digital or photographic composition. While in the past ads were usually set on metal composition machines, today digital and phototypesetting, aided by advances in electronics and computer technology, have become dominant in advertising typography. These methods are faster and qualitatively superior to metal typesetting.

A third activity is evaluation by the art director, art buyer, print producer, and supplier of the photographs and/or renderings—as to sharpness, color rendition, and other printability factors: "This evaluation, as well as the subsequent viewing of the color proofs against the artwork, takes place under standard lighting conditions with transparency viewers and overhead lights of 5000 Kelvin color temperature—a measurement of the warmth/coolness of light."

Finally, a fourth activity is production of the image carriers:

The bulk of publication and of commercial (collateral) printing is done by one of two major processes: offset lithography or rotogravure.

These two major printing processes can be utilized on sheet-feed or web-feed presses, although sheet-feed gravure printing is very rare nowadays. There are also minor printing processes like screen printing (formerly called silkscreen), flexography, photogelatin printing, and others. . . .

One basic principle is common to the major printing processes: a photograph or painting consists of a continuous blend of numerous tones. Both are therefore called continuous-tone pictures. These tones must be converted into printable form by breaking them up—by means of a screen—into halftone dots. These dots in halftone or screened pictures are large or small, depending on the tone value of the specific picture area.

Four-color printing is based on photographing or "separating" the original full-color artwork through filters, creating films for each of the primary printing colors: yellow, magenta (red), and cyan (blue). To these a fourth color, black, is added for printing the type and adding depth to the shadow areas of the picture. This separation process can be accomplished on a graphic arts camera or an electronic scanner.

A printing plate is produced from each of these four separation films. When these plates are inked in the four process colors and printed onto paper, a full-color picture results. Your print producer receives "progressive proofs" of these plates, showing all colors singly and in combinations. Such proofs serve for evaluation and are subsequently transmitted, along with the films, to the publication printer.

While the production of black and white printing image carriers is relatively speedy, the making of color separations, plates, and films is a longer and considerably more expensive process. The print producer on your account will frequently use competitive bidding among several suppliers. . . . He or she is a focal person in the planning, ordering, quality control, and follow-up concerning the production of printing image carriers. Work with your print producer and listen to his or her advice!

Being Creative All Along the Line

So far, we've been discussing the mechanics of print production. Each step of the process is an opportunity to be creative, "to resist the usual," to provide production values that validate, enhance, or even essentially create "the big idea" of your ad.

Like special effects in movie-making, the art of retouching and its new high-tech aids enable art directors and print producers to create all manner of magic, and creativity in the selection and placement of type are especially forceful when the art director chooses typography as the major design element.

Here are some examples of both techniques, as explained by their print producers:

This stopper was created from two pieces of Polaroid film, one for the base of the shoe and one for the sole of the foot. The two elements were combined in a photo-composed transparency and yellow added to the "torsion bar." (See Figure 5–1, color insert.)

All of this work was done on a CEP (color electronic prepress) system. We started with two shots of the can splashing in water. One was of the can splashing, which had water sheeting over the label, and the other was a straight shot of the can, sprayed down with water droplets. Since there is diffraction when shooting through the surface of water, we moved the bottom of the can—that portion under water—over to line up with the rest of the can. In order to see the label without the water sheeting over it, we stripped the label from the second shot on to the original. Then we picked up droplets and bits of the splash from other chromes, in order to create this masterpiece. (See Figure 5–2, color insert.)

This was a daylight shot that had to be reworked to portray a night scene. A dye transfer was made, with a color shift to darken the scene, and was retouched to portray a night crossing. (See Figure 5–3, color insert.)

For practical reasons, and for cost efficiency, each of the models at the computer terminal was shot separately. The photographer also shot the background devoid of any people. All the elements were stripped together with a color electronic pagination system, blending the background, extending the background on the two ends, cropping the rear end of the third person from the left to create room for the gutter of the spread, and doing the same to the second person from the right to separate him from the desk. (See Figure 5–4, color insert.)

Each of the storm elements was shot separately—the snow blowing, the snow on the ground, the sunset, the rain, the cloud, and the water squirting up from the tire. Then all the elements were combined on a CEP system. (See Figure 5–5, color insert.)

Rather than having to travel to Mexico to shoot this ad, it was shot in a studio in Manhattan, using a model to create a dry lake bed and pyramid. A stock shot of mountains and a sky were stripped into the shot, on a dye transfer, and retouched. (See Figure 5–6, color insert.)

Typography

The big display word "IN" is hand lettered to fit the page area proportionately, following the art director's layout, in the same style letter as set in the headline. Note the use of color in the headline to echo the big word "IN." This theme has been carried out in the whole advertising campaign. The short text is set in a clean sans serif to balance off the base of the page and so as not to intrude on the graphics above. (See Figure 5–7, color insert.)

The headline was set and illustrated to complement the illustration and carry through the Father's Day theme. The stick-up initial in the first paragraph of the text is designed to draw the reader's attention to the message, and the body text is set in a large point size for quick, easy reading. (See Figure 5–8, color insert.)

The illustration dominates the page, but the art director wanted a vertical feel to the type to balance the layout and not to take away from the illustration. The text was selected first, and set in an ITC Cheltenham Book Condensed type, carefully broken and sized to leave plenty of white space above the text area to provide the illustration as much area attention as possible. The headline, set in the same face as the text, was sized to draw the reader's attention, but again so as not to detract from the illustration. (See Figure 5–9, color insert.)

This spread probably breaks more type legibility rules than any ad we've turned out this year. But the theme of the ad, and who is reading it, had a direct influence on the type selection. The ad is for kids, and it's trying to replicate a cartoon spread in a comic book style. The text is all caps and italic. Hard to read, but kids are used to seeing this kind of type setting, which invites their participation. Hand-lettering with shadow, and on different angles, adds to the fun of the layout and helps complete the theme of a kid's board game. Overall, the type solves the graphic problem of faithfully conveying the concept of a kid's game taken from a comic book. (See Figure 5–10, color insert.)

Innovation   Seek to be innovative. As in all the subjects of this book, Y&R print production experts are encouraged to *Resist the Usual.* Here are just a few of the landmarks in Y&R production that benefited the industry at large:

☐ Y&R pioneered preprinted full-color, magazine-quality inserts for newspapers. These were preprinted color ads (dubbed "Hi-Fi"), with a repeat pattern of illustration and text which could be fed into a rotary newspaper press and would be backed up by a regular black and white newspaper page. They represented a complete advertising message regardless of the page cutoff.

To prepare these ads required a new imaginative method for creating ads—wallpaperlike art and copy. This idea evolved, within four years, into the SpectaColor principle—ads with a controlled cutoff by an electronic insetting device.

☐ Also in the newspaper field, Y&R introduced fragrant printing inks, so that run-of-press (r.o.p.) color ads would smell of coffee, oranges, and so on.

☐ Y&R was the first to develop technical means to insert product samples, like bandages, coffee, lotion, and so on, in magazine ads. Earlier the agency had used varnished inks in major publications to give a rich gloss to clients' packaging.

☐ Y&R was the first agency to use electronic scanning in ad work for four-color separations.

☐ Y&R was the first agency to mandate, and to announce, that all typesetting would henceforth be done by means of photographic composition.

CHAPTER CHECKLIST

1. Sharing of knowledge is especially important for creativity in print production because the state of the art changes so rapidly.

2. Print production includes art buying, type directing, planning and buying printing materials for the various media, purchasing, and overseeing the many needs of the commercial and publication printers.

3. There are four basic steps in print production:

   a. Planning, estimating, and scheduling.

   b. Selecting and ordering typography and preparing mechanicals, or keylines.

   c. Development and evaluation of the photographs and art renderings and preparing them for reproduction.

   d. Production of the image carriers, entailing, for the most part, offset lithography or rotogravure, and involving such techniques as retouching, type selection, color separation, and color correcting.

4. For inspiration, review the case histories in this chapter—the whole

process in the Dr Pepper ad; retouching devices for adidas, Sanka, the U.S. Army, NYNEX, Mercury, and Cuervo; the clever and technically ingenious typography devices for Heublein, Express Mail, *Time,* and Colgate.

5. Always attempt to be creative in each step of production, that is, to validate and enhance the idea of the ad. In some cases, your big idea may be in the production itself.

· ·

6 How to Create Better TV and Radio Advertising

Y&R Broadcast
Programme, Europe

We must always remember that ordinary viewers do not have the skill or the interest to search through a piece of advertising for the idea. For them, the idea is immediately clear or it's not there at all.

COMMERCIALS THAT PEOPLE WANT TO WATCH

On October 7, 1988, The Museum of Broadcasting in New York City began a three-month exhibit: "*Y&R and Broadcasting*—GROWING UP TOGETHER." It was a signal honor for Y&R to be chosen for the Museum's first exhibit of the advertising of sponsors who had supported broadcasting for so many years.

During those months an extensive series of screenings and seminars revealed the work of the agency to the public. Here is how the Museum introduced its exhibition schedule:

Young & Rubicam's history as an advertising agency parallels the growth of broadcasting. The Museum's exhibition . . . reviews the agency's numerous contributions as a producer of commercials as well as a radio and television packager. The exhibition screenings focus on the evolution of commercial styles and trends over six decades. During the course of the exhibition, more than 500 commercials are being shown in a series of thematically related screening packages supplemented by special features. These special features range from Y&R radio and television shows such as "The Jack Benny Program" (sponsored by Jell-O Gelatin) and "The Goldbergs" (sponsored by Sanka Brand Decaffeinated Coffee) to Y&R documentaries, in-house instructional tapes, and behind-the-scenes recording sessions which offer insight into the commercial production process.

The Museum charged admission for these events. And a catalog ($7), in addition to a listing of exhibits, featured articles by, among others, a professor of American Studies at *Brandeis University* and a Pulitzer Prize–winning author who discussed the sociological implications of the advertising commercial.

For people to *pay* for the privilege of watching commercials is a new phenomenon. In Paris, France, reported *The Wall Street Journal* that same year, 2,850 people "gladly shelled out 150 French francs ($26) for the privilege of staying up all night" to watch seven hours of TV commercials at the premiere of an annual theater event. "It sounds like some kind of media-age torture," commented the *Journal;* but those commercials "aren't designed just to sell products; they're a product unto themselves, to be admired for their humor and inventiveness."

In America, whose television programming is, by and large, more entertaining than the average French TV fare, I'm not sure that such an event would be a successful commercial enterprise. However, during the New York Museum's three-month exhibit, more than 6,000 people did pay admission to view the Y&R efforts. So you might say that with that exhibit the advertising commercial came of age.

How can commercials be worth viewing in and of themselves, rather than be an intrusion into the program content which, with today's technology, can be zapped by the viewer before it is seen? Growing up with the broadcasting industry as it has, Y&R has learned the lessons which make for commercials that are worthwhile viewing. This chapter summarizes some of the lessons we have learned.

THE NATURE OF EARLY BROADCASTING

Y&R's history of training in the broadcast media, just as with print advertising, was influenced by the context of the times. The heyday of radio in the United States occurred during the 1930s, 1940s, and early 1950s. Radio was a foreground medium, with a big Atwater Kent console as the home entertainment center and good old familiars like "Amos and Andy," "Fibber McGee and Molly" and the soap operas "Young Doctor Malone" and "The Romance of Helen Trent." These shows were often identified with one sponsor and produced by the advertising agency itself. Y&R, with such dominant sponsors as General Foods, Bristol-Myers, and General Electric, pioneered, among other techniques, the commercial integrated into the content of the show, and our commercial writers and producers were trained in the school of show business.

When the fledgling television medium came along, we all had to learn by doing. We were the blind leading the blind into a medium where eyesight was paramount, and we learned from our mistakes. That was the era, in the early 1950s, of the live commercial, when Betty Furness watched with horrified fascination as her G.E. garbage disposal suddenly reversed itself and when a commercial announcer was unable to open a refrigerator door. Curiously, what few viewers were watching responded to such gaffes with empathetic loyalty.

Commercial writing was easier, and in some ways perhaps better, than it is today, because we were having so much fun with our new toy. I have described, in Chapter Three, how playfulness makes for better ideas. Our TV ideas were, for the most part, fresh and uninhibited by a body of do's and don'ts. We did, however, learn some basic principles that still apply today.

THE Y&R PRINCIPLES

One of the first principles Grib had for print was the attractive notion that we should think of our advertising as a person. The fact was that so many ads *were* a person; for example, Texaco gas was Uncle Miltie, Jell-O was Jack Benny, Lipton Tea was Arthur Godfrey. They bestowed their powerful personalities on their sponsoring products.

Another principle for writing an effective commercial was to "keep it simple." This should always be a must, for all times, but in those pioneer days, our limitations mandated simplicity. That's why so many of the commercials we created hold up so well today. We had no fancy videotape technology. Our "opticals" in live commercials consisted of cue cards for the presenters and "telops" or "balops," which were simply title cards and still photographs inserted at intervals into a "standup" presenter's salesmanship. We did create film commercials, but they were in black and white, and we did not have large budgets for them because our clients had much smaller TV audiences.

It didn't take us long to realize that television was the next best thing to a door-to-door salesman, and what does a salesman do? He demonstrates his product. Furthermore, demonstration was the ideal way to achieve simplicity. So we demonstrated our products in action.

The first characteristic we had noticed about our new magic peep show was its intimacy. Television was a very small space compared with a larger than life movie screen. We took advantage of this intimacy by concentrating on close-up shots, and as competition grew keener, our close-up demonstrations became more original: the J & J bandaid fishing an egg out of boiling water, the Remington electric shaver shaving the fuzz off a peach and the bristles off a brush.

Simplicity and the power of TV demonstration were among the basics emphasized in our first traveling creative workshop and in the five-day Broadcast Programme which the European creative directors developed a few years later. While the principles we presented were guides, rather than rules, there was one inviolate rule we insisted upon. Important as that rule was then, it is even more important today, with all of TV's new permutations.

The One Inviolate Rule

The hour-long TV module of the traveling workshop emphasized the need for the one unbreakable rule through a comparison between the TV medium and the other media we dealt with.

Print is a comparatively permanent, tangible medium. You can hold a magazine in your hands, can leaf back and forth through the pages, and refer back to an ad whenever you wish.

Newspapers are an immediate action medium. They come out every day. They are utilitarian. The reader can *use* a newspaper, to get information and shop for bargains.

Radio is potentially the most involving of all the media, since it concentrates only on the audio and encourages the prospect to involve her other senses as she participates with her imagination.

But television is transient. In my book on copywriting, *The Compleat Copywriter* (McGraw-Hill, 1966), I had called it "The Fast, Fast Medium."

Its messages speed by, never to be recaptured. And unlike radio, television, with its sight, sound, motion, and color, overloads and saturates the senses, which is why McLuhan called it the cool medium.[1]

At the beginning of this module, I showed a videotape of some two hours of prime-time television programming, interspersed with the lead-ins to a great number of commercials. It was all telescoped into an edited tape only 10 minutes long. This tape dramatized the competitive clutter we were up against with our brief commercials.

After showing the tape, I discussed what it illustrated and from this lesson, and the research done on TV commercials for many years, concluded with the one inviolate rule, namely *A.Q.R.I.—Arouse Quick Related Interest.*

That one rule simply means that the first few seconds of your TV commercial are crucial.

Important point: **You must seize and hold the viewer's attention in those first few seconds or his or her mind and attention will wander away. You must *arouse quick interest,* which means that those first few seconds should be *interest-provoking.***

But why should it be *related* interest? First, because the client is paying a great deal of money for a very small period of time. Doesn't it stand to reason that every second should count, in relation to his or her product and its benefits?

The second reason why the message should be related to the product is a psychological one. It is important for the viewer's mind to be traveling on the track you want her to pursue. Considering the transient nature of the TV medium, it is an imposition to ask the viewer to switch her mind to another track in midcommercial.

My old mentor, Ed Barnes, advised me to follow the dictum of the Southern preacher: "Tell 'em what you're gonna tell 'em, then tell 'em, then tell 'em what you told 'em."

This period of explanation consumed a deliberate interval after I had shown the 10-minute "clutter" videotape without editorial comment. (This was a severely edited video, compressing 3 hours of prime-time TV into 10 minutes.) At that point, I referred back to the tape and asked the group to write down the subjects, products, and/or sales messages they could remember having seen. I then asked for a show of hands as to how many commercials they remembered. The conclusion drawn from this exercise always provided a convincing punctuation to the presentation of our one inviolate rule:

Note[1]We should constantly be aware of the fleeting overload nature of TV. With that awareness, we can more easily create effective TV commercials and all members of the product group, whatever their specialties, can more skillfully judge them.

There were 33 commercial lead-ins on that tape, and the average number re-membered—by you and consistently by workshops all around the world—was only four. And mind you, these sessions have a captive audience, just a few minutes after the tape (not "day after" as in a Burke recall test), and with profes-sional people already interested in the subject of advertising. Certainly this demonstration emphasizes the need to "A.Q.R.I."

We are an agency which does not slavishly follow rules. But as in art and sci-ence, one has to know the rules to have the right to break them. "A.Q.R.I." is the one rule we are citing today. Break it at your own risk.

The Workshop's Five Guides

The rest of the TV module of the workshop was devoted to five guides for creating effective commercial ideas and four guides for preparing to produce them. I used a carefully selected reel of ten commercials, which unmistakably drove home these creative guidelines. Most of these commercials also illustrated more than one of the principles, of which there are five.

Simplicity   A good TV commercial is not a beginning, a middle, and an end, but a unified whole. It should be one powerful, simple entity.

Example: A good way to judge whether you have a strong, simple idea is if you can describe it in one sentence—"Hey, I've got a good idea for Frito-Lay potato chips! 'Bet you can't eat just one.' I'll have a commer-cial where the guy is trying to resist the temptation to eat more than one Frito-Lay."

Obviously, that's not a commercial with a beginning, a middle, and an end. It's one concept, one powerful, simple entity—one big idea.

Example: The European Broadcast Programme dramatized this "single-sentence" concept by handing out blank telegraph forms to the partici-pants and showing them a selection of ten commercials, both good and bad. They were then asked to send a telegram, of 20 words or less, to Alex Kroll, explaining what each commercial was all about. It was obvious, with this exercise, which commercials had a strong, single-minded idea. By having to communicate the essentials of these com-mercials, the participants learned by themselves, without having to be "instructed," what a big idea really is. Figure 6-1, a commercial from Melbourne, Australia, illustrates this principle.

Credibility   The five principles were not mutually exclusive. A Glad Pack comparative commercial was both simple and highly credible, because its stop motion concentrated on a single, locked camera so the viewer knew that the demonstration could not have been faked or doctored. Even more powerful in its credibility was a Union Carbide commercial that started with a short panning shot and then held for almost a minute on the single-minded demonstration. (See Figure 6-2.)

WATCH DOG FLEA COLLAR   AUSTRALIA   30 SECONDS

MAN: Imagine you were your dog.

You'd have to put up with fleas or messy washes or dusty

powders or smelly collars.

Give your dog a break. Announcing Watch Dog. New

Watch Dog works every time your dog moves because it releases

tiny flea killing specks that work their way through all the

coat all the time without odor, without trouble. If you

were a dog, you'd want to be a Watch Dog.

FIGURE 6-1

The quiet voice-over of the narrator, during that impressive demonstration, piled one explicit fact on to another, information about insulation that kept a chick alive and comfortable. And, finally, the priceless, credible line: "If you don't think it's as good as we say it is, watch the birdie."

Do simplicity and credibility have to be achieved with a single scene, holding on your product? Not at all. A Levi's jean commercial, from Tokyo, achieved its credibility with dozens of quick-cut scenes, to the beat of catchy contemporary music. Its appeal was unassailable to its youthful target—especially when you consider the translation of the last words in the commercial: "The only way to have more fun with Levi's jeans is to take them off"! (See Figure 6-3, color insert.)

So far, the commercials emphasize demonstration: TV is the next best thing to actually sampling your product.

There are many ways to demonstrate, including the use of humor and animation. The definition of the word "to demonstrate" is "to make something evident." In that sense, all good commercials, no matter what technique, are a form of demonstration.

Important point: As we judge ideas, we should ask ourselves, do they clearly and simply make very evident the copy strategy we've agreed upon, the nature and benefit of the product?

Originality   This is a must for all advertising. However, in the fast, fast medium of television, it's especially vital. We are seeking that

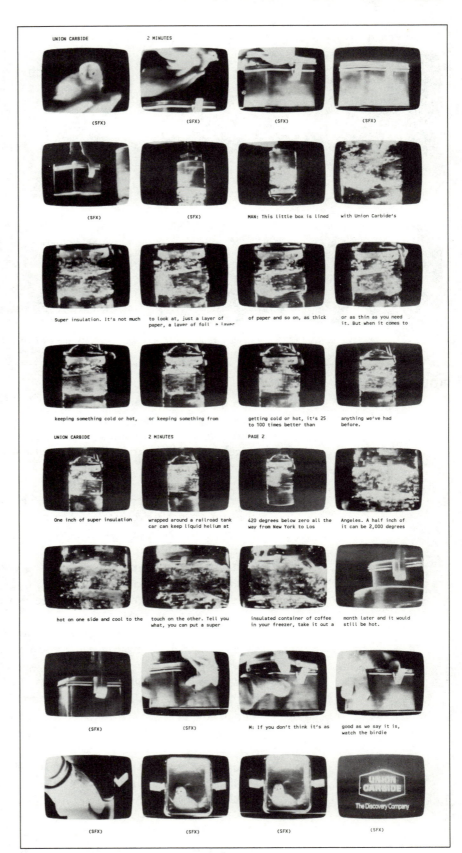

FIGURE 6-2

element of surprise that will catch the viewer's attention in a split second—what David Ogilvy called "a burr that will stick in the viewer's mind."

As we conceive ideas, let's keep asking ourselves, "How can I show and tell this idea in a way that has never been seen or heard before?"

For this principle, I showed a commercial for a snowmobile from Y&R Montreal. How would you normally show a snowmobile? In the snow. Not so for this commercial's creators. They showed it performing *without* snow. A simple idea, but they were the first to think of it. It dramatized better than any other way the durability of the product, a primary benefit because in Canada their customers gave this product very tough wear. (See Figure 6–4.)

Relevance   Never let anyone tell you that your product has no difference from anybody else's, that it's a "parity product."

Important point: All products have some innate difference from all others. We have to study them enough, and be imaginative enough, to be able to dramatize their uniqueness, and their unique benefit to our prospects.

Here, for example, is a commercial for a Gaines dog food made with eggs whose strategy led to an original, entertaining commercial that aroused quick related interest and was totally, single-mindedly relevant, as the dog chases the chicken, in hopes of catching an egg. (See Figure 6–5.)

Finally, the last of the five principles, and perhaps the one most difficult to agree upon, is this:

Empathy   Empathy means "the capacity for participation in another's feelings or ideas." In our case, it should be participation in what the product has to say about itself, and how it is said.

This is a difficult principle to interpret because we are dealing with the elusive emotions of human beings. But if people are not emotionally involved with our commercial, they are probably not involved at all.

If we have the right creative strategy, it is an empathic strategy—one that feeds directly to our potential consumers' feelings and desires. In the execution of that strategy, we must try to put ourselves on the other side of the set, so the viewer, in turn, will have the same kind of empathy with our message as we have in transmitting it to him.

We can learn a lot from the verbatim comments of focus groups as to whether our commercials have empathy—by the quality, involvement, and richness of the group's verbatims.

Example: The workshop showed a commercial from Y&R Puerto Rico which achieved that most elusive of the five principles in a courageous

FIGURE 6–4

way. It was one of a series that had been running for several years for Don Q Rum. Don Q had been made by the Serrales family for a hundred years and a 100 percent of the Puerto Rican population knew the brand name and the family that made it. An upstart competitor came along, with more years of aging and a higher alcoholic content, and was eating into Don Q's share of market. (See Figure 6–6, color insert.)

Instead of trying to vie with the competitor's claims, the agency chose to solve the problem in a bold, assumptive way. They hired historians,

GAINES DOG FOOD   30 SECONDS

MAN: Eggs, the best natural | source of complete protein. Everybody loves them including | dogs. So it's no wonder a dog will do most anything to get | an egg for himself. But there's an easier way,

Gaines Burgers Dog Food with egg, the moist, meaty taste | dogs love plus a quarter of a real egg in every burger. So | why not give your dog a taste of your love and all the | goodness of real egg. Give him Gaines Burgers with real egg.

FIGURE 6–5

experts on Puerto Rican customs around the turn of the century, and produced storyline commercials that showed the old-time festive family life. Their strategy was to convince viewers that "the old traditions are the best traditions" and therefore that they should be loyal to the quality and family tradition of Don Q Rum.

A highly evocative music track added to the emotional appeal of the involving story.

Little did the people responsible for the campaign anticipate what a rich vein of empathy they had tapped into. People came in from the fields and the other rooms in the house to watch the commercials when they were aired. Y&R Puerto Rico became famous because of those commercials. And best of all, Don Q held and even increased its share of market.

The reason for the power of such a campaign: Puerto Rican pride. No one had thought, until that time, to dramatize the roots of the Puerto Rican past. In the United States every school child knows about his or her heritage. But in Puerto Rico, the subject had never been fully emphasized.

This rich source of involvement, of pride and nostalgia for the good old days was so powerful that our Puerto Rican office used a similar technique successfully for its bank client—with a print campaign that illustrated great moments in Puerto Rican history. Hundreds of thousands of reprints were distributed to customers and schools by the bank, and the campaign garnered enormous goodwill.

Scoring the Commercials

One rule and five principles. The rule: A.Q.R.I.—Arouse Quick Related Interest. As for the principles, they are easy to remember, for their first letters together form an acronym that can be quickly used to assess commercials as they are created:

S.C.O.R.E.

S for Simplicity

C for Credibility

O for Originality

R for Relevance

E for Empathy

The common course was to score 1 for each principle evidenced in a given commercial, and 5 would be a perfect score:

FIGURE 6–7

TELEVISION COMMERCIAL	If it does not A.Q.R.I. (Arouse Quick Related Interest) SCORE ZERO	S Score 1 for Simplicity	C Score 1 for Credibility	O Score 1 for Originality	R Score 1 for Relevance	E Score 1 for Empathy	TOTAL A Score of 5 is perfect

As we played the game, we pointed out that exceptions would be made where one or more principles should dominate while others might not apply. For example, when your goal is primarily to achieve the highest possible awareness, the principle of Originality might play a dominant role. With such a strategy, one might score 5 for that principle alone. An example of a strong appeal to empathy is the experiential campaign for Eastern Airlines cited in Chapter Two.

The simple, mnemonic scoring game proved to be consistently useful, primarily as a vehicle for stimulating discussion and debate—the same kind of discussion and debate which you should encourage, in your daily activities, to hone and improve your output and to avoid settling for second-best.

FOUR BASIC PRINCIPLES FOR CREATIVE EXECUTION

In our traveling creative workshop, I discussed these four basic guides for the preproduction of TV ideas:

Start with a Crystal-Clear Script

A beautifully written script presents the audio and the video in a way that a child, unfamiliar with TV production—or a client totally new to the medium—would understand exactly what you have in mind. Audio means "I hear" and video means "I see." What precisely *do* you hear and see and how clearly can you express it? The author Leo Rosten said that the best writer is one who can "make himself clear to himself first."

Writing clear audio and video instructions is as much an art as playing the piano with two hands. Or, to draw an analogy from the ballet, it should be a graceful *pas de deux* of the mind, hearing and seeing at once. The writing of clear scripts, unfortunately, is a neglected art, and unclear written or verbal production instructions have been the cause of many a poor, fuzzy commercial.

Be Creative About Presentation . . .

. . . as creative as all your work in developing your commercial and the details of its execution. In our business, one usually presents ideas through a number of echelons. It is important to anticipate the mind-set of all these audiences before the actual prospect finally gets to see the commercial. The principles of S.C.O.R.E. apply, in fact, to *these* audiences too.

Example: I have seen Creative Director John Ferrell coaching a copy supervisor in the best physical way to present a storyboard consisting of single, blown-up frames—to overlap them in such a way as to provide a margin for the fingers to flip them, in sequence, without awkward interruptions—a seemingly niggling precaution, but one that could make a difference in the idea's acceptance.

Clients differ in their reaction to different presentation techniques. Some prefer the informal work session, others a more buttoned-up presentation. I discovered that one client, when seeing a storyboard, always said, "Move that first scene down to the middle, and add a second scene at the end." It did not matter whether the timings of each sequence would not fit the rearrangements, or the logical flow would not apply. For this client, I improvised a new kind of giant storyboard, with the audio lettered as large as the pictures and large timings in each frame—again a seemingly petty foresight, but one that solved that particular presentation problem.

Important point: **Whether you use a key frame, an animatic, giant boards, or a combination of presentation methods, your decisions can vitally affect the eventual success or failure of your commercial.**

Be Creative About the Preproduction

"I hear" and "I see" will now come to life in every facet and should be clarified as cleanly as when you wrote your first fluent script. This process included, at Y&R, the often-neglected, but eminently helpful, second-by-second preproduction board.

Does a finite preproduction board inhibit the creative agency producer or production company director? Not in the least. In a meticulous preproduction meeting, every party to the commercial—contact, copy, art, production—are agreeing on the preconception of the finished film or tape. If changes are later made, they occur for practical or creative reasons, but everyone is ideally party to them, and they happen against the backdrop of this carefully thought-out matrix.

Know What's Going on "Out There"

The fourth step in the process of execution is to be aware of the changing world of television and cinema techniques. Keep an audiovisual tickler file. What are the exciting things that are new or improved?

At the time of our workshop, technical advances included such devices as the Steadycam, which eliminated the need for dolly tracks; a new airplane rig, which provided superior aerial shots; the improved quality of 16mm film; new computerized animation techniques; and the 3-D effects of the "slit-scan" method developed by Bob Abel.

We talked about the increasing importance of sound in television. The fast, fast medium had already begun to go the way radio had gone, to become more of a background than a foreground medium. Said Dick Low, then head of TV programming: "We need to bear in mind that people watch television with varying degrees of activeness and passivity. But the sound is always reaching them. And if you can find devices—attention-getting devices that will pick a person up through the ear—you then will get them to look on the screen."

Of course, no changes would affect TV commercials more than "the changing video environment." Y&R had discovered a rule of thumb that had applied to radio, and then to TV, and would now apply to cable and the use of home videorecorders: when each advance achieves one-third coverage of American homes, the momentum becomes a breakthrough, and the new medium may be said to have arrived.

So it was then, and of course now, when even the sponsorship of videocassettes may prove to be an important new medium.

This module of our workshop ended with the following resolution:

The new video environment will add to our challenges. It will mean, among other things, more commercials in more media with shorter lengths. In such a world, of communication overload, of a greater variety of choice, the Fast, Fast Medium will require *more* simplicity, not less, *more* clarity, *more* originality, *more* relevance, and above all, more, much more, empathy. We are potentially the most skillful of all communicators, because we work in a borrowed medium, with abbreviated time and space, and under the obligation of commercial accountability. If we are to be the most creative agency worldwide, we must hone these skills to razor sharpness and tune our minds to people's needs.

HOW TO ENCOURAGE CREATIVITY IN RADIO

Shirley Simkin, who undertook the radio module in our traveling creative workshop, acknowledged that while radio should be an exciting medium for creativity, it is one of the least appreciated. There was no doubt that it was little appreciated then, and to tell you the truth, it is still neglected today, even at Y&R.

I have speculated as to why this is so, and here is one theory: we do not value radio as much as the other two major media because it does not seem to us to be as "rich" an experience. While print can fill the eye and TV overload most of the senses, radio does not literally *fill* any space. Sound has become so multilayered around us, and our ears are so used to screening out the manifold layers, that we tend to hear with a relatively crippled part of our sense of sound.

Example: In the chapter on radio in my book on copywriting, I cited the experience of the hero of Georges Simenon's novel *The Bells of Bicetre*, who was confined to a hospital bed, and who gradually became sensitive to the wealth of omnipresent sounds. Day after day, isolated and immobile, while passively looking at the monotonous walls of his room, the man's ears became subtly attuned to, and fascinated by, the infinite world of sounds. For the first time, he was a totally sensate hearing creature.

In that chapter, I had not set forth many rules or principles for writing radio commercials, but rather attempted to provide a kind of *smorgasbord* of sound techniques which might inspire the tastes of my readers. Just so, some ten years later, Shirley found herself presenting a similar solution for training Y&R copywriters in the art of writing effective radio commercials.

The objective we both attempted to accomplish was this: to attempt to *open up the participants' conscious minds to ever more sensitive auditory inspirations.* There are principles, of course, for writing better radio, such as the same admonition to A.Q.R.I. as for TV. But, first, we need to *like* the medium more and *to be wide open to its endless possibilities.*

Variety Is the Word for Radio

In my 1966 edition of *The Compleat Copywriter*, I had remarked on the metamorphosis of radio, after the glamorous new kid had arrived:

Radio, in the context of television, could never be the same and survive. It had to adapt to the changing times. And the medium adapted in the most radical way. It did not change imperceptibly, as newspapers and magazines have been doing. It changed overnight. And it changed *completely.* Radio became the exact *opposite* of what it had been. As it had been stationary, it became mobile. As it had been large, it became small: one massive console became several small transistorized sets per family. And as radio had been centralized, with relatively few stations controlled by a few national networks, it now became segmented—many stations, more localized than national, and deliberately specialized in their programming appeals.

Today, at this writing, radio has more individual outlets than any other consumer medium. There are almost 5,000 radio stations, compared with about 1,700 newspapers, 500 TV stations, and less than 700 magazines. More families own more radio sets than they do any other means of communication—more than 225 million, an average of about four sets per home . . . more than 55 million car radios that go with us to work, to school, and away on vacation . . .

Since these words were written, more than 20 years ago, the number of radio stations has quintupled, and while the number of radio sets has multiplied at a slower rate, many of them have been transformed into components in the new technology's trend to home communication centers featuring many media at once.

In short, the medium itself has become as commonplace as lighting and heating. It's a utility with endless uses, outlets, and purposes. Its variety of occurrence and uses, the techniques of programming, and partnership with other media, all add up to making it among the most neglected media for creativity, and therefore one of the greatest opportunities for standout, original advertising.

Consider the Possibilities

Having pointed out what a stepchild radio had become to TV, Shirley said, in her opening remarks:

The challenge of radio to me is that there are so many, many techniques that you can use to do successful radio commercials, and I think that very often an office or a country or a group of people, through laziness and sheer me-tooism, get lost in one or two ways of doing it. When we visited Santo Domingo, for instance, we found that everything was music, and practically all the music was the same. All the commercials were sung and if you weren't paying attention, they all sounded exactly the same . . .

We're pretty much that guilty at Y&R in New York, and all over the world, and so are the other agencies. So what I'm going to do, instead of setting out rules and principles, is just to play you a variety of types of effective radio commercials, with some short comments in between—to open your minds to some of the fascinating things you can do with radio that you can't do with TV or print.

Then Shirley would dim the lights and urge people to settle back in their chairs and, as the sound effect of a creaking door was heard, to close their eyes and to "enter the mysterious and wonderful world of radio." She underscored the most powerful factor of all, the total *participation* that radio requires of its listeners:

Each of you must enter alone and each will enter a different world, for radio is not TV without pictures or a piece of print copy being read at you. Radio is a magic potion of sound which, properly used, will cause each listener to see scenes more vivid and more moving than any photographer could capture or any painter portray . . . because they will be *your* scenes evoked from *your* experience and imagination.

It is impossible, of course, with the printed page of this chapter, for you to experience what the workshop's participants did. I shall simply include a few printed extracts from Shirley's smorgasbord, so as to illustrate the variety.

How You Can Do It

The best way for you to duplicate the experience, for *your* workshop, would be to get in the habit of collecting reels of prize-winning commercials, in all categories and of all techniques, perhaps obtained from the Radio Advertising Bureau, and periodically to hold listening sessions. Keep yourself *current* with the variety of techniques others are using, open your ears, and condition yourself to be constantly approaching radio with "a fresh earpoint."

Some Selections from Radio Techniques

Announcer: It's 5:12 A.M., April 18, 1906 . . . San Francisco began to tremble . . .

[An ominous rumbling sound effect, as Shirley's listeners, each in his or her own way, picture, in their minds' eyes, the experience of many, many years ago. This SFX goes on for a good long number of seconds.]

Announcer: By 5:13 there was no San Francisco. Only fire destroyed most of everything left. When it was all over, 28,000 buildings had been destroyed and 500 people were dead. Total property loss, four hundred million dollars . . .

Of all the insurance companies covering claims, only a few paid in full. Insurance Company of North America was one of them, and if it happened again today we'd still pay in full.

Said Shirley, "Good radio *makes* you participate visually and emotionally. Good radio can also take you on journeys where no visual medium would dare to venture."

[SFX: Car ignition turning over, but car failing to start.]

Announcer: Want to know what makes your car so hard to start on a cold morning? Come inside the engine and see for yourself.

[Echo effect.]

Announcer: Down here cold makes your motor oil [voice gradually gets thicker and thicker and thicker] get thicker . . . and thicker . . . and thicker . . . 'til every moving part [thicker still, until it grinds to a halt] can hardly move . . . so your car . . . won't . . . start . . .

[Appropriate pleasant music under announcer's voice]: But now Gulf has developed a motor oil that solves the problem—New Gulfpride Super G Synthetic motor oil.

[Appropriate SFX as car starts and goes.]

This amazing lubricant doesn't thicken in cold like conventional oil—in fact it still flows and protects at fifty degrees below zero. And Gulf Super G Synthetic gives you more than a cold weather start. It actually saves you gas because it reduces resistance better than conventional oil. Change to Gulfpride Super G Synthetic, the super oil. Better cold weather starts, better gas mileage—only from Gulf.

(Shirley:) "My next example—dialogue commercials. The trick in doing good dialogue is to set up the situation fully and clearly in the first two lines, so you know who's talking, where you are, the whole setup."

[SFX: Brakes squealing as a car stops.]

Voice of Police Officer: Pardon me, sir, would you step over here to the patrol car, please.

Nervous Man: Oh—oh—h-hello, officer.

Officer: Do you have business in this neighborhood, sir?

Man: Yes, I live f-four blocks from here. It's the brick colonial with the crack in the driveway.

Officer: What are you doing out this time of night, sir?

Man: Well, I got all ready for bed, see, and darned if I didn't forget to pick up a copy of *Time* Magazine at the newsstand today.

Officer: What kind of coat would you call that, sir?

Man: This—this is a h-housecoat. See, I spilled cocoa on mine and I just grabbed my wife's—guess the puffy sleeves look a little silly [laughs awkwardly].

Officer: Do you want to get in the car, sir . . .

Man [Speaking faster, very nervous]: In the car? . . . See, I just don't go to bed without a *Time* movie review or something from the Modern Living section . . .

Officer: Yes, sir.

Man: I tried reading something else, but there isn't anything like *Time.*

Officer: No.

Man: Do you know, officer, how many editorial awards *Time* has won?

Officer: No, sir.

Man: Time is so respected. I'm a firm believer, along with Winston Churchill, that you are—uh—what you read.

Officer: Mmhmm.

Man [Almost hysterical]: Don't send me up the river just for wearing puffy sleeves!

Officer: You're home, sir.

Man: Oh—oh—thank—oh—okay—g'bye . . .

Announcer: Time makes everything more interesting . . . including you.

Shirley then played three openings in the *Time* series, all of which illustrated the point she had made. She followed with an example of the use of a documentary technique in radio commercials: "*Real people,* identified by name, also make great personalities for radio. In fact, even company presidents are quite convincing. Here's one." (There followed the extraordinary voice of Frank Perdue in the now-famous series.)

Perdue: You'll notice when you go to the store, my chickens always stand out from the crowd. Perdue Chickens have a healthy golden yellow color instead of that pale white look. That's because I have them on a rigid diet consisting mainly of golden yellow corn, soy bean meal, and marigold petals.

(Shirley:) "If you're going to use actors instead of real people to deliver your message, it pays to cast voices the way you cast people. There are fat voices and thin voices, angry voices and soothing voices, and young and old and funny and straight. And there are as many different kinds of voices as there are people. Listen to one simple one here—you'll recognize it."

The Distinctive Voice of Titus Moody: Pepperidge Farms' very thin sliced white bread . . . because Pepperidge Farm remembers.

(Shirley:) "That voice has been their trademark for years. Here's another . . .". Shirley then played a commercial for Eastern Airlines, with the voice of Orson Welles. Could anybody have mistaken that uniquely rich voice for anyone else's? An excellent way to give a special personality to the product he described.

(Shirley:) "Now, there are two primary techniques for gaining awareness on radio. One is humor. Here is one of a series that has become a classic."

Announcer: Stiller and Meara.

Meara's Voice: Say, aren't you Sancho Margoles, the tennis pro here?

Stiller's Voice: Yes, I am.

Meara: I couldn't help but admire your racket.

Stiller: Thank you. It's a Wilcox 500.

Meara: No, I mean teaching beautiful girls tennis all day. Now, that's what I call a racket.

Stiller: Well, it has its faults.

Meara: Haha.

Stiller: Say, you've got a lovely forehand.

Meara: Oh, thank you. Most people notice my eyes first.

Stiller: Maybe we can discuss your form over lunch.

Meara: Love to. I'll start with the Wimbledon fruitcup and then I'll have the King crab.

Stiller: And I'll have the Mixed Doubles salad and the Singles steak. And perhaps we could share a bottle of wine.

Meara: Aces.

Stiller: I'll have a little Blue Nun sent over.

Meara: Oh, I thought everyone had to wear regulation white.

Stiller: No, no. Blue Nun is a wine—a delicate white wine.

Meara: Oh, you can't have white wine with meat.

Stiller: Blue Nun is the white wine that's correct with any dish. It goes as well with meat as it does with fish.

Meara: Sancho, you really do things with class.

Stiller: Like I always say, what good is a tennis pro who can't serve well?

Meara: Hmph. Sancho, you got a little gravy on your sweatband . . .

Announcer: Blue Nun. The delicious white wine that's correct with any dish. Another Fischel wine imported by Schieffelin Company, New York.

(Shirley:) "In relation to humor, one small reminder. It's a good idea to make sure it is humor and not just jokes. One-liners can wear out pretty quickly, but if you really use humor and if it's product related, it has a good chance of doing very well on radio. Here is an example, from our Houston office."

Announcer: You get fast results in *Chronicle* classified.

[SFX: Telephone ring.]

Girl's Voice: Miss Classified. Can I help you?

Man: Oh, yeah, sure thing. I ran an ad in the *Chronicle* to sell my horn. I lost my lip, y'know.

Girl: Oh, gee, I'm sorry.

Man: Oh, that's okay. I sold my horn the first day. I got the pipe organ. You want to hear it?

Girl: No, that's all right. What can I do for you?

Man: I need to run another ad—find a new apartment—some place where the neighbors appreciate good music—y'know what I mean.

Announcer: Call Miss Classified at 224 6868, and get fast results."

(Shirley:) "A very, very successful campaign. They also ran humor on TV and the *Chronicle* just passed any other newspaper in the country in the number of lines of classified ads. That includes the L.A. and *The New York Times.*

"That also makes the point that when you use humor, it's better to integrate the sell, if you possibly can, than to isolate it.

"Of course, you're well aware that the second major device to provide awareness is music."

Shirley then described the differences between "jingles" in the old days and the relatively lush varieties of spots, effects, and backgrounds in commercial music today. Contemporary commercial music, in both radio and TV, is a complex art, and Y&R, with its music specialists, does not, per se, provide training to creative personnel at large.

The major goal: In a medium so saturated with music of every kind, the goal is to aspire, as with the print medium, to rival the editorial environment that surrounds your commercials.

CHAPTER CHECKLIST

1. The principles of creativity in broadcast media have been influenced by historic context.

2. In the early days, radio was a foreground medium, the most popular programs closely identified with their sponsors, and commercials were often integrated.

3. Early television also relied heavily on personality programming and advertising.

CREATIVITY IN TV

4. Three major early TV principles still worth considering are
   a. Simplicity.
   b. The power of demonstration.
   c. Emphasis on closeups to take advantage of the small screen intimacy.

5. The first traveling creative workshop stressed one rule and five guides. The rule is A.Q.R.I. (Arouse Quick Related Interest). The guides, or principles, are:
   a. *S*implicity
   b. *C*redibility
   c. *O*riginality
   d. *R*elevance
   e. *E*mpathy

   adding up to the acronym *S.C.O.R.E.* and a "score sheet" with which to assess your TV ideas and executions.

6. Four principles of creative TV *execution* are
   a. Develop a crystal-clear script.
   b. Practice as much creativity for your presentation as in conceiving the idea.
   c. Be thorough and conscientious in preproduction.
   d. Remain aware of the new communication developments—for ideas and inspiration.

7. Use sound and music as an important tool (because people can avoid the picture, but the sound follows them).

CREATIVITY IN RADIO

8. Variety is the word for today's radio. Constantly listen, to achieve "a fresh earpoint."

9. Radio is potentially the most participatory medium. Involve the listener visually and emotionally.

10. For dialogue commercials, cast voices the way you cast people. Set up situation fully and clearly in first two lines.

11. Two major ways to assure awareness in radio: humor and music. But use humor prudently ("one-liners wear out quickly"). And explore the endless possibilities of relevant use of music.

12. As with print, constantly strive to rival the programming environment.

CHAPTER

7 Creativity in TV Production

Manny Perez,
Senior Vice President–
Worldwide Creative Projects

The trick is to keep everything and everyone in line, on one single track, so that no matter what the hell happens, no matter what differences occur, or what the compromises are, or the technical problems, one person always knows he's getting what he needs on film . . . and that the film actually works!

WHAT PRODUCERS PRODUCE

There are four kinds of TV commercial productions:

1. The finished, complete filmed and/or videotaped commercial with all necessary production refinements, ready for airing.

2. Filmed and/or taped live action with minimum production refinements.

3. The "animatic," which is a filmed version of the commercial with limited artwork and optical effects (also called "steal-a-matic" or video "swipes" from existing film or video material).

4. The "photomatic," which is a sequence of filmed and/or taped still photographs, with limited optical effects to simulate motion.

The last three forms of production are for presentation and/or research test purposes. Other, more primitive forms of commercials are also used for presenting and testing, such as concept statements, concept cards, the original storyboards themselves, drawn or photographed flip cards of the individual frames of a storyboard, and so on. The advertising agency and its client may use any or all of them, as well as on-the-air posttesting with the finished commercial, depending on the attitude and policy of each product group, client, and account. But a well-rounded production department should be knowledgeable and creative in all these regards. At Y&R New York, there is a separate Test Production Unit, and entry-level producers often serve first in this unit, which is an ideal training ground for finished productions to come.

The following comments are extracted from Y&R seminars and guides for creative production.

The Goal of TV Production

Excellent production cannot make a basically weak commercial effective, but it can make a basically good commercial *more* effective. Weak production, unless it involves an extreme goof, seldom totally negates the effectiveness of a strong commercial—the truth will out and a powerful strategy and concept will still register, but weak production, even without a big goof, can prevent a strong idea from becoming outstanding.

Remember, however, that if a commercial really bombs, the reasons are usually far deeper than production negatives, that is, wrong strategy, bad executional concept, a poorly structured storyboard, or lack of message credibility or relevance or rapport.

Important point: Above all, the essential element of a commercial *must* be an *idea.*

Don Egensteiner, executive vice president and director of production services, has explained that imperative in the seminar he conducted for the public during the Museum of Broadcasting exhibit of Y&R's work. He began by showing two commercials, both with excellent production, but one with and the other without an *idea:*

During this discussion you'll see a number of commercials—some good, some great—and you'll notice that most of them, certainly the great ones, contain without exception that one central and essential ingredient: an idea.

But just exactly what *is* an idea? Well, we have a clue in the way we all commonly talk about advertising we admire. We tend to say things like "What a great idea!" or "What a clever idea!" which is not the same as saying "What a beautifully shot commercial" or "What a powerful graphic design!" or "What great film editing!" In fact, if a commercial generates *only* reactions like that, then, chances are, it *lacks* an idea.

An advertising idea is something that connects the product and the prospect in a way no one ever did before.

In further illustration, Don showed two commercials for Lay's potato chips. They were produced 20 years apart (one of which follows), but both interpreted the same *idea*—that Lay's potato chips taste so good.[1] (See Figure 7–1.)

The Role of the TV Producer

In his Museum seminar, which was entitled "Production Power," Don explained that the TV producer should, ideally, be in on the early preparation of a commercial because the idea and the execution of it should be inextricably linked:

In the advertising business we have a risky tendency to employ interchangeable labels for many of the tools of our trade. You'll hear some people talk about execution, by which they mean how a basic idea is presented or developed on a script or storyboard, you'll hear others talk about execution, by which they mean how a given storyboard is produced on film or tape.

To me, neither of these definitions gives execution its proper scope; I think they tend to disjoin what is really *a continuing process.* I believe that execution is the action of taking a concept or idea on an unbroken journey—starting out from someone's brain, then to paper, then on to storyboard and casting and set design and cinematography and directing, and so forth, straight through until it reaches its final form.

---

[1]Copyright Frito Lay. Reprinted with permission.

FRITO LAY   "DIVER"   30 SECONDS

MAN: Lays Potato Chips are

so thin, so crisp, so

light, no one can eat

just one. WOMAN: They're

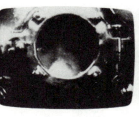

good. MAN: Yeah, I um,
(MAN MUMBLING)

(SFX)

(SFX)

MAN: Look, there's
somebody in here.

FIGURE 7–1

> I see execution as a continuum of creative endeavor, so that the copywriter, the actors, the grips, the musicians, the cameramen—all the myriad talents involved—are all part of the executional team.

The Production Process

In 1986, Laurie Kahn, executive vice president and director of television commercial production in New York, gave a tutorial on TV production to print production personnel at the seventeenth Y&R Print Production Seminar in Montreal. Her talk was an excellent overview of the *continuum* Don Egensteiner champions:

> I think the TV producer is the team captain. I don't think the producer is the quarterback. The producer's supposed to analyze and size up a variety of situations, orchestrate the environment in which a group of disparate people come together, and create a special moment: the day of the shoot.
>
> The producers are in charge of organizing the production, controlling it, and knowing all the facets of it, and orchestrating the environment where the specialists can come in and create a tender, fresh, unique interpretation of the creative idea. . . . We don't think up the pictures. But we're conduits and interpreters so that a lot of people who speak a very different language, can speak to each other. Account people, art directors, writers—that's just the agency side. Then there are all the specialists from the production companies or the crew side, the people we hire on a per job basis. They have names like cinematographer or cameraman,

gaffers, the grip who moves everything (he's the big guy whose neck looks like my thigh). We're dealing with all these people and trying to coordinate the puzzle.

Laurie went on to explain that the producer must, in the first place, understand the creative strategy, so the commercial becomes a translation of the storyboard that interprets those elements. Hence the producer, who evaluates the best way to tell the story, is a storyteller with business acumen.

The producer's job begins with the *production* storyboard, which is not the 8-frame summary board you usually see, but a second-by-second 30- or 60-frame outline of each second in the commercial. (See Figure 7–2.)

With such a board, there's no such excuse as "I didn't know *that* was going to happen."

From the outset, the business side of the two-headed producer takes over, with detailed schedule and budgetary forms.

Y&R now has in-house production units in a few of its agencies. However, for the most part, all of some 500 commercials a year, produced for the New York office, continue to be subcontracted to outside production companies. "One of the producer's key responsibilities," says Laurie, "is to choose the right suppliers."

Producers spend a lot of time screening directors' reels. And it's a creative judgment selecting the companies whose directors are right for a specific job: "For example, there are directors whose specialty might be tabletop photography or others might specialize in dialogue, or special effects, or fashion. It's important to know who will be the best 'translator' of the given storyboard."

The producer is responsible for writing an articulate set of specifications for the production companies, so they can determine the cost of the commercial. Bids from at least three different companies are called for. Precise specs are also a blend of the creative and the businesswise:

In the old days, in the 1960s, even Young & Rubicam used to operate a little more randomly. . . . It used to be a little bit like Johnny Carson's Karnak—"Six days in Acapulco—$210,000," and they'd be at the airport. Now there's much more analysis. Every dollar has to be accounted for: Do we really need to build that three-wall kitchen on the stage in Los Angeles? Isn't there a kitchen in Westchester County? Somewhere else? . . . These questions are answered in the specs, from which the budgets are rendered.

After the numbers come in and the job is awarded, come the preproduction meetings:

This is where everybody sits around a table and we review a multitude of details—everything from the selection of wallpaper, to the talent's makeup, to

FIGURE 7-2

drawings or pictures of location. Every imaginable aspect is discussed, because on the shooting, we're talking about somewhere in the neighborhood of $7,500 an hour.

Casting, of course, is a vital part of the process, and you want to have sensitive and knowledgeable people in charge of it. Y&R New York interviews between 13,000 and 15,000 actors and actresses a year, so they have extensive cross-files and videotapes. Y&R agencies around the world interview and cross-file many, many more.

Like the TV producer, the casting director must combine creativity with practicality—in the latter case, for example, avoiding liabilities to the agency caused by nonadherence to the SAG, SEG, and AFTRA codes, and in both respects, maintaining good relationships with all members of the talent field.

All such preliminaries considered, next comes the shoot. Current technology has made that somewhat easier for the producer to control:

At a shoot in the old days, everybody—the client, the producer, the art director, and the writer—would line up to look through the camera to approve the shot. Now, fortunately, they have through-the-camera video, so everything that goes on in the camera can be seen on the video monitor. So when the director says, "Got it" and you say, "wait a second, you couldn't read the toothpaste label because it wasn't being held upright to the camera," now you can play it back, and sure enough, everyone can see if the shot was okay or not. You don't have to wait until dailies to see if the shot was okay.

Next, you move directly to dailies where you screen everything you shot and review all the film with your editor:

He's the person who can make you look smart. For a 30-second commercial, we shoot about 3,500 feet of film a day. Hollywood shoots 2 or 3 to 1: for every scene, they shoot two or three different takes. But we shoot about 20 to 1! Each of the scenes is screened and the best take of each scene is selected and cut together at the editorial sessions. The first screening after you've edited it together is called the rough cut or the work print—at this point the color hasn't been corrected, and the sound tracks are not yet mixed.

The work print is shown to everybody, "and that's when all the agency people stand up and cheer and say 'what a wonderful job . . . but I just have a few issues.' Unfortunately, the issues are usually things like, 'Is that the best take'?"

So then you do the refinements, and then the client's screening. Traditionally we've shown the clients the work on a large screen and it's a very emotional experience. But clients now say, "Let me see it the way it's going to be on television." So we're screening on little TV sets and it's just not as overwhelming.

Finally, the music is scored, the voice-over recordings where the announcer comes in and they mix all the sound tracks together:

This way, the music is not overwhelming the announcer, and the announcer is not so loud that you can't hear the music. And then we're almost done. In postproduction, there are no more opticals—everything now is finished on videotape. We're shooting most spots on film for texture and lighting sensitivity, but everything now is finished with electronics. And while it used to take 12 weeks to go through the process I've just described, we've cut that down to about five weeks. And sometimes—say, for a new business pitch—we can do it in less!

Judging Production Values

There is virtually no way to isolate and to measure a commercial's production effectiveness, although a module in our first traveling workshop (as described in the next chapter) demonstrated how modest production changes in commercials can improve research test scores.

In his Museum seminar, Don Egensteiner emphasized three fundamental elements which make for "Production Power": (1) the power of pictures, (2) the power of sound, and (3) the power of time and movement. The last of the three is a little difficult to understand unless one considers that film is a composite of still pictures:

We all know that film is an illusion. We think we see movement because our sense of sight can't discriminate between still images following each other at 24 or 30 pictures a second.

Since this movement is actually artificial, then time, as we *perceive* it, can be made to stand still, to be reversed, slowed down, or speeded up.

We can identify five basic ways of dealing with time in the film medium: real time, compressed time, expanded time, fantasy time, and parallel time.

He went on to explain each of these methods, with examples, as follows:

Real Time: the portrayal of an event on film in such a way that the event *appears* to occupy the exact time frame it would in real life.

Compressed Time: A 30-second commercial can present action that would take hours, days, even years in real life.

Expanded Time: Presenting details of an action that happens too fast for the human eye to record in real life.

Fantasy Time: We fantasize along with the film maker—letting him take us back to the past with a flashback or into the future with a flashforward.

Parallel Time: A cluster of actions or events that are meant to occur simultaneously rather than consecutively. . . . Film has no tenses, so we can utilize parallel time to move the story along as seen from various vantage points.

Time and movement have a significant relationship in three ways: movement within the frame, where the camera serves as the eye of an observer; movement of the frame itself, by moving the camera, which makes the camera a part of the narrative; and movement frame to frame, through editing, which organizes all types of motion into a rhythm or pace.

Within the three basic ingredients of the power of production (the power of pictures, of sound, and of time and movement), there are numerous techniques, or values, on which we concentrate so as to make our point. These are techniques such as casting, demonstration, music, and sound effects. The most fruitful way to learn how production values, used creatively, can add to commercial effectiveness is to accentuate the positive. We can look at commercials that are known to have been successful and see how specific production factors have contributed to their effectiveness.

The major part of Y&R training is teaching by *example*. To be sure, each problem is a unique one, and no case history is directly applicable. But we learn through the *inspiration* of case histories.

The following commercials are Y&R examples of production values that have accentuated the positive.

Casting

Without just the right kid this commercial could lose much of its credibility and all of its charm—and be unintelligible besides. (See Figure 7–3, color insert.)

Sensitive casting for a sentimental spot. Performed with the kind of restraint that touched the emotions without being syrupy. (See Figure 7–4, color insert.)

Demonstration   Good use of candid camera technique allowed for "prepared" dirt which would otherwise arouse a suspicion of a rigged demonstration. This production idea, therefore, was the key to that priceless ingredient I cited in the previous chapter, commercial credibility. The device of the two-headed mop not only saved demonstration time, but verified equal amounts of liquid, pressure, strokes—all important to the conviction of any staged demonstration. (See Figure 7–5.)

The famous award-winning demonstration shown in Figure 7–6 had implicit credibility, and it also had great empathy, because the viewers, as they described their reactions, felt the tire's own punishment in the pits of their stomachs!

Lighting, Editing, Pacing   Here is a case where it would have been difficult for poor production to have ruined the suspense and power of a superb idea. But the sensitive production accentuated the positive. The lighting. The whispers. The buildup of suspense. Change of pace with sudden music. Shadows through the window. Porch light. Sound effects, including dog's bark. All a good gag, so well done you look forward to seeing the commercial again and again, even though you

SPIC & SPAN   "CUSTODIANS"   60 SECONDS

(MUSIC)

(MUSIC)

(MUSIC)

(MUSIC)

(MUSIC)   (MUSIC)   (MUSIC)   (MUSIC)

(MUSIC)   (MUSIC)   (MUSIC)   (MUSIC)

(MUSIC)   (MUSIC)   MAN: Spic & Span, the big job cleaner, gets the   dirt liquid cleaners leave behind.

FIGURE 7–5

MAN: This is sharp, merciless steel.

(SFX)

M: This is the new Good

Year Double Eagle Poly Steel Tire, the long

wearing tire with the smoothness of polyester

and the protection of

steel. Watch as we match steel against steel.

(MUSIC)

M: To soak up the shocks, a body of tough, flexible

polyester cord. And to resist penetration, double

belts strong protective steel cord.

(MUSIC)

M: The long wearing Good

Year Double Eagle Poly Steel Tire, polyester for

smoothness, steel for

protection. Poly Steel only from Good Year.

FIGURE 7–6

DR. PEPPER   "FRONT PORCH"   30 SECONDS

MAN: Come on, Mary

Màrgaret. WOMAN: Well, I
don't know. M: How do you

know if you don't try it?
W: My mother and father.

M: So what, come on. W:
All right, but just a

little. CHORUS: Dr.
Pepper, so misunderstood.

W: I love it. AN: With a
name like Dr. Pepper, it

isn't easy to get people
to try us. But once they

taste our blend of 23
flavorings, they love us.

FIGURE 7–7

already know the punchline. If it *had* been poorly produced you might not have enjoyed repeated showings, which could happen because the commercial proved to have effective longevity. (See Figure 7–7.)

Spokesperson

Great appeal to target males, and a good way to introduce the unique idea of deodorant for men—keep it masculine. You're surprised to see *her* in the pool hall. But she can carry it off. Attracting but not distracting. (See Figure 7–8, color insert.)

Music and Sound Effects   Alas, a printed book has its inadequacies, but perhaps you can, at least in a mood sense, recall the impact of the music you heard (and felt) in commercials.

In 1985, Hunter Murtaugh, Y&R New York's music director, and Sid Hecker, of the Consumer Insights Department, prepared a videocassette for the Resource Center. It gives some excellent tips about music production. Here are some of the points it makes:

- Music is one of the creative person's most effective tools, because you can only do so much with words and pictures.

- Music adds another dimension. Sometimes it sets the right tone for a commercial, sometimes makes a complex idea more human, and acts as the glue to hold unrelated ideas together.

☐ Above all, music gives the viewer an emotional connector to identify with, so that he or she relates to our commercials. Whether the mood is tension, sweetness, frivolity, majesty—we don't have to be told, because through music we can feel that emotion immediately. Which is why music is the one universal language which everybody, all over the world, understands and responds to.

How do you know when to use music? There are no rules, but you should use it when it feels right to do so, whenever it will help the goals of a commercial. But *don't* use it if it serves no function.

There are, of course, so many advantages to music that it is used more often than not. An exception might be the closer one gets to documentary reality, when music might seem to be an unbelievable stylistic addition.

The major flaw occurs when music is "stuck on" to a commercial as an afterthought. Instead it should be carefully preplanned, so that it will appropriately add to the excitement or emotion that will keep viewers from walking out on the message.

During their presentation, Hunter and Sid demonstrated the effect of music in feature films—clips from such movies as the early Keystone Cops, *Patton, Apocalypse Now, Psycho, Chariots of Fire,* and so on. Each sound track evoked a different but equally powerful emotion.

The cassette inventoried, among the values that can be developed from music, the following:

Attention

Background

Excitement

Relaxation

Empathy

News

Imagery

Communication of a product's attributes and benefits

Important point: Which value should take precedence depends on the objective of your commercial.

This presentation moved on from the "what" of music to the "how," which Hunter summarized as follows:

A lot of writers and art directors, even TV producers, feel insecure about using music. But if you follow a few simple procedures, you can't go wrong.

a. First you have to decide exactly what you want to achieve—tension, nostalgia, sex appeal, whatever. Later, a composer can interpret your directions.

Let's say you want music to run under your announcer track, to set a mood for the commercial. That's what we call an "underscore," sometimes a "rug." It's a kind of emotional adhesive that holds the film together.

Consider these examples:

☐ The episode from *Patton* in which the general, standing at the site of an ancient battlefield, feels a sense of *déjà vu:* "I was here . . . two thousand years ago." The mood is heightened by the evocative music, with its faint trumpets in an echo effect.

☐ The scene from *Chariots of Fire*, where the runners pound up the beach, paced by the tympanic music.

☐ An episode from the "Marlboro Man" campaign, when cigarette advertising was allowed on TV. As we watched a thundering herd of wild horses, we simply couldn't get that powerful mnemonic music out of our heads.

b. The next step is to choose the composer. Here's where a lot of people get lazy. I hate to tell you this, but there's no substitute for sitting down and listening to a lot of sample tapes. It's hours and hours of work, but worth every minute, to find the composer whose work in the past strongly suggests the kind of mood and melody you have in *your* mind.

c. Next, sit down with the composer, and his rep, and discuss *everything*—about the product, the schedule, the objective of the music. Mention, if you have found it, anything on his reel that's similar to what you have in mind.

d. Next, make the decision to proceed or not. Assuming you will proceed, discuss *in detail* the role the music will play. Show the script, the storyboard, explain the agency point of view, get the composer's point of view. Discuss the size and type of orchestra he might use.

e. At the next meeting, when the composer plays his demo, he'll explain the overall tone, structure, melody, rhythm. You may not be able to visualize the finished result, but you can pick out the melody and feel the general tone.

Cost   Their presentation went on with details about costs. They cited that in New York, at that time, the going price for a simple piano and voice demo was $500 to $750, for a piano and group vocal (possibly with some extra keyboards and drums), $1,000 to $2,000, for a deluxe kind of demo that you might prefer for the client presentation, $2,000 to $4,000.

Musical Techniques   The cassette then enlisted an on-camera well-known composer, Jake Horn, whose credits included the Dr Pepper,

7-Up, and Kentucky Fried Chicken songs. Along with his informal vamping on the piano, they illustrated techniques, each of which segued into the finished versions of the music in postproduction. Those techniques are as varied and individual as the number of examples shown.

Sound Effects   This tape also discussed ways and means for using sound effects and dealt with the subject of economical use of stock music and sound:

[After showing a complex sound-and-music scene from *Star Wars*]   Sound effects have come a long way in the last few years. They're no longer a stepchild of the business but a real art form on their own. Again, the best way to use them is with the same kind of careful preplanning we have discussed for music. Imaginatively planned and mixed, with the sophisticated new electronic devices available, sound effects can emotionally knock viewers right out of their seats!

The five production values I have listed, plus other relevant values like

- The effective choice of locations

- The use of special effects and camera techniques, such as slow motion, animation, and three dimensions

is what the work of creative producers and directors is all about. (See Figures 7–9 and 7–10, color insert.)

***Important point:* How they best learn their craft depends on their innate qualities and their daily attention to detail and the sheer pleasure they derive from their trade.**

Low-Cost TV Production

You might assume, from all of the foregoing, that TV production has to cost an arm and a leg. Not so, if you have a strong, simple idea and the TV producer uses ingenuity to come in on budget, even when modest. In a Resource Center videocassette on low-cost production techniques, Manny Perez showed 20 commercials, all very effective, that cost a fraction of comparably effective, more costly commercials.

The techniques used

Simple location

Close-up presentation

Still pictures

Simple demonstration

Tabletop photography

Limited animation

Dramatic casting, concentrating on a product shot

A simple optical device

Pickup footage (stock or library)

Figures 7-11 (see color insert), 7-12, and 7-13 are all examples of ads that are implicitly economical, but each with a powerful, simple idea.

FIGURE 7-12

HUNTS CATSUP "CLAPPING HAMBURGERS" 60 SECONDS

MAN: Hamburgers of the

world, attention. Great
news from Hunts. Now

catsup comes in flavors.

Now there's a hickory
flavored catsup, and a

pizza flavored catsup.

MAN: Hunts new hickory
flavored catsup, the

instant barbeque, a touch

of hickory smoked flavor

in a rich tomato catsup.

And Hunts new pizza fla-
vored catsup, an

Italian accent. For
hamburgers, hot dogs,

french fries, you name
it. M: Yes, hamburgers,

catsup now comes in
flavors, new hickory

flavored catsup and new
pizza flavored catsup both

from Hunts, the catsup
with the big tomato
taste.

(HAMBURGERS CHEERING)

DRANO   "TALKING WRENCHES"   60 SECONDS

WRENCH: Hey buddy, where you been? I have not seen | you around the old joints. WRENCH: Have not you | heard? This old girl has wised up. She is using | Drano in all the drains. W: You are kidding. She

is using it in the kitchen and the laundry? W: True. | W: And the bathroom? W: Also. W: Even in the tub? | W: You have named it. W: Hm, we is out of work. | MAN: Sorry fellows, but once in every week Drano

in every drain keeps all drains clean, free running | and sanitary. It just takes a second. A tablespoon of Drano down the | drain, then cold water. Drano's churning, boil- | ing, bubbling action eats away at that greasy mess.

Drano wipes out all the muck that clogs your | drains, even hair in bathroom drains, leaves them clean, free running | and sanitary. And these new easy pour top cans | make once in every week, Drano in every drain, a snap. W: I am speechless.

FIGURE 7-13

Y&R PRODUCERS TALK ABOUT THEIR WORK

I have described the teachings of our peripatetic workshop and of the Resource Center in the years that followed. Even more important training is the metaphorical traveling workshop that happens every day at Y&R. In 1980, *Back Stage* magazine devoted an entire issue to "The Creative World of Young & Rubicam's Television Commercial Department." They queried 33 of our producers about their work, asking questions about their function as producers, their greatest problems, their roles as collaborators, how they chose and worked with production companies, their opinions of copy testing and awards, and what their production philosophy was.

I have selected, at random, a number of the responses, to give you a firsthand feel for the ways and works of producers—what they bring to the game and what they learn in the process:

The Producer's Function

I wish I could say (only) "the multi-million dollar package we shot in Europe or in the Caribbean or Hawaii with a small talented group of people, a great director, and a dynamite board"; but really how many people are that lucky? The work of the producer is usually an everyday "bid this," "cast that," "remix this," "revise this," or "get a cassette to the client now!" Yet to be very honest, every board offers a rewarding experience. With every job comes new challenges, new opportunities to learn and grow. Whether the job is a simple one-scene West Side stage tape job or a job that takes you to the Coast to produce a "cast of thousands," there is always something new to learn, something new to be challenged by, some unique problems to solve and some new and wonderfully talented people to meet, work with, and become friends with. As long as each job offers opportunities, then each job is a rewarding experience.

Problems

Tighter budgets, increased testing, shorter schedules, the trend toward commercials by committee, all create pressure to reduce our job to the art of compromise, instead of making it the art of the possible. *How to resist these pressures to satisfy only the lowest common denominator is the most serious challenge we face.*

One of the major problems is rushed production: Cost control can get out of control, and one of the reasons is that with rushed production, you don't have time to make many of the decisions beforehand. The articles in *Back Stage* the last two weeks about the rising cost of film point to some of the problems. But if we allow the time to rehearse and to discuss camera angles and different alternatives in the way we want to go, and different direction and casting, we'd have just the time to do it—and that alone would save a lot of money. But we don't always have the proper preproduction time.

It would be very tempting to single out tight production budgets and prohibitively cost-conscious clients as the major problems faced by producers today. That would be an easy out, though. . . . Up until the client signs that piece of paper that says I can call the production company and book them, *there is no more important function for the agency producer than making sure the client understands what he's buying, why it's needed, and that we're not running wildly out of control, spending his money indiscriminately.* In most cases the account group is inadequately prepared for this job. It will probably do more harm than good for them to "fake their way through it" rather than let the producer sit down with the client. If a producer cannot make a client understand why an agency recommends what it does in the area of commercial production, then he doesn't belong in the business of communication. The outcome isn't always what we hope it will be, but even the most unyielding client will gain some respect for the agency that not only strives for creative excellence in its production, but will take the time to explain how they propose to achieve it.

Collaboration

Ideally, production is a collaborative process. The trick is to control the process so that a single, clear approach to the execution can be extracted from all the ideas that each member of the group contributes; to be flexible enough to take advantage of a new thought or a good suggestion when it comes along. . . . A producer is in a unique position to put everything in perspective for the group, from making sure the execution is consistent with the advertising's strategy, to knowing how one scene will play against another.

Testing

Working in the Test [Production] Unit, I have to stick within the rules of test production. *To get across the idea of a commercial is what we're after.* Budgets are low and time is very short. There isn't time for frills. It's sometimes hard, because I'd like to do more, but that isn't the way test production works. It's like walking a tightrope. I always feel I'm balancing between the basic idea of a spot and putting in more production than it needs—overproduction. It's a hard balance to keep. But it's important, because if we don't keep it, it's not test production anymore. . . . Production details can add a lot to an idea. But a good, clear idea is the most important thing of all. Production should complement it. *The most important thing is to have a great idea and start from there.*

Awards

Awards are important to the industry. *They create a uniform standard of excellence by which to judge ads. They're also an incentive to add that something extra.* Awards also build confidence and credibility, which are important in a largely subjective business.

I know there's competition among us all in a sense. *It makes you think harder to try to top someone.* I think you'll find the best spots are the ones that won Clios . . . Also, it is very exciting to win a Clio—it still has the old showbiz ring of excitement. It's not an ego trip, it's a fun thing and maybe it's some measure of a good commercial.

A "WORKSHOP" FOR CLIENTS

We have all had the experience of sitting in a screening room, viewing an answer print, and asking one another "What went wrong?" What often goes wrong is a production by committee—not to be mistaken with a production by close collaboration. Often, between the conception and the final execution, committee afterthoughts and decisions obscure your first simple, clear idea.

Some clients, like Procter & Gamble, have their own knowledgeable production experts who are given a lot of autonomy. With other clients, there are looser lines of responsibility. Among the guidelines Y&R has developed is a courteous, but firm list of do's and don'ts regarding the client role in TV production. The following are some typical entries.

General Y&R Guidelines	1. *Be a realist about production.* Keep reminding yourself that this is not show business, it's real business. It's not an entertainment extravaganza that's being produced. It's a minute or half-minute selling message. Concentrate on helping it work.

2. *Have your "decision maker" involved*—not people who spend time "second-guessing" the decision maker.

3. *Concentrate on the broad strokes.* Don't worry too much about the color of the buttons on the talent's jacket. Is the concept right? Is the advertising working?

4. *Try to reduce alternates.* They cost shooting time and editorial time. Decide in the preproduction meeting what you want; then do it. You can only air one version.

Preliminaries

1. *Storyboard approval.* Make a firm commitment: to major visuals, exact words. Don't figure on shoehorning in another product point later, or a legal qualifier, or an extra package shot. Be sure it has cleared all necessary levels.

2. *Production house approval.* Do it as quickly as possible so that the house doesn't make other commitments that block you out. If the agency recommends low bid, be sure you know what you're getting and what you're not. If agency recommends middle or high bid, understand why. If you don't go along, be sure you know what may be sacrificed.

3. *Casting approval.* Do not attend casting sessions unless there is some unusual reason. Too many spectators can distract talent, especially children. If there are any special client requirements (ethnic, manner, age, looks), make them known *in advance*. Screen videocassettes of selected talent and listen to selected announcer audition(s). Or attend callbacks. If other members of your company must approve, arrange for them to see/hear sufficient material to make an educated judgment.

If you are going to pay overscale for special talent or celebrity, understand the contract (duration, escalation clauses, options to renew, etc.). If you might want to use the person also in print, sales promotion, sales meetings, or similar activities, request that this be part of the original negotiation. (You can really get held up if you don't ask until after a successful commercial is on the air.)

4. *Package correction.* Be sure to deliver sufficient packages of correct sizes to agency well in advance of shooting date so they can be color corrected and cleaned up. Figure on spares for safety. Be clear about what package(s) must be included. In which color(s). And what modifications can be made so they will "read" better.

Preproduction

1. *Attendance.* Go to the meetings! Have any other client people there who are crucial to decisions.

2. *Ask questions.* Now, not later. Leave as much latitude as possible for the human side of the action to "play" when the cameras are rolling. But if you have reservations about whether a demo will work in the allotted time, or whether there's enough package identity, and so on, raise them now. And reach agreements.

3. *Alternate shots.* If it is necessary or desirable to try filming certain sections more than one way, these alternates should be included at the end of the shooting board. Discuss any requests you have. But keep them to a minimum. Don't figure on adding more "cover" shots on location, unless you come up with a much better way to do a scene that is not working well.

On the Set or on Location

1. *Attendance.* Go if you are the "responsible" client. And get there on time. Be able to make on-the-spot decisions or get very fast answers on any changes that come up. Arrange to have any of your specialists there who are really necessary (home economist, technician to set up or verify demo, etc.). But don't take a whole gang. There's enough distraction. And don't put in a token appearance and then disappear for several hours—*if* your approval is necessary for certain shots or if you want to check out certain things. The cameras won't wait.

2. *Attitude.* Be positive. Be enthusiastic. Be patient. Don't be alarmed if the first shot isn't taken for several hours. There's a lot of final prepping, lighting, makeup, and so on to be done in the morning. Have faith.

3. *Protocol.* Be there when you're needed. Keep out of the way of the crew and the wires. When you have questions or suggestions, try to channel them through one person, usually the agency producer—don't bug the director or cameraman or talent or art director individually.

4. *On-the-spot changes.* Give a definite answer. Or get one fast. If a shot obviously isn't working, try to help. If something magical starts to happen, let it happen. If you think a recommended change could be controversial, ask that the shot be covered as boarded, also. Don't suggest new alternates just for whim. The schedule is usually tight.

5. *The overtime question.* Help avoid overtime by not causing delays or creating indecision. If toward the end of the day a terrific new way to do a shot arises, decide whether it's worth the overtime. If so approve, and accept the responsibility.

   In the rare cases where overtime is necessary due to unforeseen snags, don't panic and rant. Stay calm. It will help get the job wrapped without added turmoil. And that's what everyone is trying to do.

Next Steps

1. *Editing.* In most cases it is not necessary to look at the dailies or get involved in editing. And usually it is better not to. You can then be objective when you see the first cut.

2. *Recording and mix.* Same advice as for editing.

3. *Work print screening.* Attendance mandatory. This is the time to make any requests for reediting or refining. And, when this is done, to give go-ahead-to-finish approval.

4. *Answer print.* You, of course, must be present because it is the moment of final approval: this is the way the production will really look and sound.

. . . .
CHAPTER CHECKLIST
. . . .

1. TV producers produce four kinds of commercials—the finished production for on-the-air plus three kinds for testing and/or presentation.

2. Their goal: to enhance the strategy and the executional idea.

3. The ideal producer is both a creative collaborator and a sound business manager. His or her functions are to understand the strategy, to collaborate clearly with all concerned, to "spec" commercials, to budget and schedule them, to know suppliers and their commercial directors' capabilities, to be a conduit for communication with production people of varying specialties, to interpret production values to clients, to obtain supplier bids and recommend choice, and to oversee all stages of the production process.

4. The production process entails development of the second-by-second production board; casting; preproduction details and step-by-step meetings; overseeing the shoot; editing for work prints; and overseeing music, voice-overs, the sound mix, and postproduction details.

5. The power of production includes the power of pictures, sound, and time and motion.

6. Five production values are: casting; demonstration; lighting, editing, and pacing; use of spokesperson; and music and sound effects.

7. Use of music and sound effects provide mood, continuity, and emotional involvement. They can achieve greater attention, excitement, empathy, newsworthiness, and emphasis on a product's attributes and benefits. The producer oversees selection of the appropriate composer, orchestration, budget considerations.

8. Client participation includes approving storyboards, production house, and casting; attending necessary pre- and postproduction meetings; providing necessary product expertise and packaging; making on-the-set client decisions; dealing directly with the producer; attending work print and answer print screening; offering encouragement and decisive approvals.

. . . .

8 How to Use Research More Creatively

Albert Szent-Gyorgyi,
biochemist,
Nobel Prize winner

Research is to see what everybody else has seen, and to think what nobody else has thought.

What advertising and marketing research should you use for your communication efforts, and how can you use it more creatively?

Y&R is perhaps the most qualified source for answering those questions because of its extensive experience with research and because of the single-minded objective Y&R research has always had. Since Ray Rubicam hired George Gallup in 1932, and during every research director's tenure since then, the agency's main objective has been to *Resist the Usual.* When you have that goal, research must always be the handmaiden of creativity.

This chapter discusses some of the lessons we have learned about research that you may also apply.

WHAT YOU NEED TO KNOW

The prerequisite for research is to have a specific goal and the knowledge to pursue it. This was the thrust of a seminar entitled "Developing a Knowledge Base" that Sid Hecker, then vice president of the Y&R New York Research Department (a.k.a. The Consumer Insights Department) conducted for an Advertising Skills Workshop.

The following are the goals you might have: four for the short term—awareness, attitude, enhancement, and sales increase—and five for the long term—total market awareness, image establishment and enhancement, brand loyalty, a larger share of market, and expansion of the product line.

The answer to achievement of these goals, said Hecker, lies in the interpretation of the marketing concept—the 4Ps: product, price, place, and promotion.

We must have the right product, supported by the right message, to the right market, via the right channels, in the right amounts, at the right time. And all those are accomplished through the marketing techniques of advertising, sales promotion, market research, salesmanship, merchandising (the form utility—color, shape, size, etc.), and publicity.

In order to implement these policies, we need a solid grounding of information, market intelligence. I don't mean to imply that we cannot make a move along any of these marketing dimensions without a bunch of numbers in front of us. Some of our best moves will be made on judgment. But where you know that market or consumer intelligence would help, consider these possibilities for developing your

knowledge base, and be aware that there are people to help conduct all of this research, within the Y&R system or at competent research companies.

Sid then asked the participants what kind of real, day-to-day situations trigger the need for information: "The client calls, the creatives need to know something. Why did he call? What does he need to know?" A summary of responses revealed the need for knowledge about such subjects as these:

1. *New product.* What's the potential market, demographically and psychographically?

2. *New parity product.* How best to position it, to preempt a position, to develop a "USP" (unique selling proposition)?

3. *Advertising.* What to *say* in a new campaign, how to say it, with regard to product attributes? benefits? for emotional involvement?

4. *How well are specific ads or commercials communicating their intended messages?* Are they building bridges between the personality of the product and the personality of the consumer?

5. *Is the entire campaign having the desired effect over time?* Re consumer attitude (brand loyalty), sales (campaign tracking).

6. *How best to market the product.* Through retail stores? direct marketing? other?

Where to Get the Knowledge

Considering all such subjects, the workshop examined the different kinds of research that are possible for the product group to *get* or to *do* for themselves to use research creatively to arrive at the best strategies and executions of the given goals.

1. *Product research.* Sources of actionable data for product selection and improvement include
    a. The company's own records on successful and unsuccessful product lines, including profitability analyses.
    b. Home use testing of products—placement and callback.
    c. Laboratory test markets, such as *Yankelovich* and *Assessor*.

    These are, in effect, miniature models of actual markets, to help predict what will happen to products in the real marketplace. They include use tests, repeat purchase, attitude tests.

2. *Message research.* Start with upfront research (e.g., focus groups) on habits, attitudes, and initial reactions to rough messages. Then we move on to lab studies of prefinished advertising in markets or homes, with learning, it is hoped, taking place for improving the finished ad or commercial. An example is the *Viewer Reward Profile,* which helps us to understand advertising in terms of entertainment value,

consumer empathy or rapport, news value and good taste. And delivery of the message is the province of *Media Research*, which helps guide placement of the message in programs, magazines and newspapers.

3. *Campaign tracking.* Over time, our campaign should result in changes in attitude, and ultimately sales. Tracking attitudes can be accomplished with simple or sophisticated telephone surveys. Sales are assessed by factory, warehouse, or retail movement tracking methods (including the relatively new computer use of the Universal Product Code scanners).

4. *Market research.* This is the broadest information base, and it studies the potential market in terms of age, income, education, life-styles, and attitudes. A separate comprehensive workshop presents the ways and means in detail.

5. *Channels of distribution.* They range from mass media, such as TV, to specialized forms of direct marketing, highly focused and often zeroing in on a narrow market segment, such as with a mail campaign to farmers who have a particular need for specialized insecticides. The purpose of these studies is to uncover the most efficient and profitable channel, or combination of channels, and the studies are therefore highly customized.

CHOOSING YOUR RESEARCH METHODS

Among the many research tools you might be considering are development and diagnosis of advertising, evaluation, campaign tracking, and "psychotechnology." There are methods for measuring the recall of TV, radio, and print advertising; for measuring the effects of the nonverbal, music, commercial lengths, comparative advertising, ethnic audience measurements; and so on; and so on. The assessments don't make sense unless you have first determined your research objectives and then have tried to select the best methods for answering them. For example, Y&R New York provides its product groups with an inventory of outside suppliers' activities for measuring advertising effectiveness, with explanations of each method and the pros and cons of each clearly set forth. Using such an inventory and knowing your objective you can make your selection more productive.

Training for creative use of research had been going on at Y&R long before our first traveling creative workshop and the first Creative Leadership program. For one thing, the Research Department, for almost 30 years, has issued hundreds of research evaluations and bulletins on every communications research method imaginable.

From the standpoint of consumer research, the methods assessed fall generally into four categories:

1. The attitudes and behavior of the target consumers.

2. Idea development.

3. Ads and commercials effectiveness/potential.

4. The impact of the executed advertising program.

Moreover, the kinds of research used are both quantitative and qualitative, and the ideal would be a balance of these two approaches, since advertising should be both a science and an art, and one can no more assess its directions and their success through head counts than through the ever-elusive aspects of motivation.

The determination of what research methods to use depends on many factors—individual judgment, the product group's agreement, client requests and biases, and, let's face it, the accepted research biases of a given time. When you approach an advertising problem, your own applied research can be of great value. As Alex Kroll put it, "We are the audience. We in advertising are not immune to the things that are going on in the rest of the culture." He tells how, when he became a copywriter at Y&R, he would constantly check on his own instincts by visiting shopping malls, armed with a tape recorder, doing his own research on people's habits, likes and dislikes, and getting an intimate feel for the individual consumers he would be writing for:

Advertising people often become insulated from the people they are trying to communicate with—it's more comfortable to sit in an office, reading predigested statistics, and drawing our pat conclusions. The best of both worlds is both quantitative research *and* qualitative, and much of that we need to do personally. They're both valuable, and they're like two stones we ought to grind together. The creative imagination can't work sufficiently without the inspirations of "tactile encounters."

It was that kind of attitude which led Y&R, in 1987, to change the name of its Research Department to Consumer Insights. Since we are in the business of influencing people, all our research, it was felt, should be based, first and foremost, on the understanding of our fellow human beings.

Qualitative Creative Research

However valuable your own first thoughts may be, you can be misled by pure subjectivity. To probe farther, there is the kind of qualitative research of Y&R's own "creative research" division. This was first called The Answer Lab, then The Discussion Lab, and now Creative Research because it is there for the express use of the creative people. Here there are living-rooms, with one-way glass viewing booths, and trained, empathetic interviewers. With such an intimate aid to creative development, you have an ongoing, organic workshop that constantly hones the creative person's communication skills.

I asked Stephanie Kugelman, in charge of the group, to discuss their work, and here are some of her comments:

This research can be focus groups or in-depth individual interviews, or it can be what we call "ethnographic" interviews, which are on-site, whether in a home or a

gym or at a hotel talking to business travelers. It's especially valuable when you're getting your feet wet with a product or a product category. You've got respondents who use the products, who can speak about them firsthand. It's revealing and stimulating for the creative people to hear and see those people and to understand their connection with the product.

Say it's canned pasta—you wouldn't necessarily choose to eat it, but you see people who use it and like it and position it in a certain way. You develop a new respect for the product, a new understanding of what it's all about. At the same time you can get energized and want to write to this prospect and about this product. That's so much better than using some stereotype you really don't know.

The second area is to start to develop concepts. If the strategy's not clear to you yet, you've at least got the glimmer of an idea, and groups are interviewed for playback, to make sure that you're starting to define the right area.

The next thing, after the concept, would be to start to create advertising—whether it's a rough storyboard or a line or a couple of key visuals and a line, or a paragraph with one visual—something that starts to be a semblance of the idea you intend to express. This first concept is the most critical stage in copy development because it's before there's a whole big storyboard, before it's necessary to present to the client, before there are perhaps a lot of politics surrounding it, or personal agendas. This is when you can see a beginning that you're comfortable with and can nurture the idea. It's not a threatening situation. You're using consumers' response, trying to understand what motivates them best, and how your concept can be even more motivating.

Another way to use this research is when you've got a storyboard or animatic or a couple of key frames with either a sound track or some kind of voice-over, and you can present it to the consumers, and if you've explained it to them, they can use their imagination and imagine it like a finished TV commercial. So you get a preliminary feedback on the execution you intended, and while some of the aspects are rough, you can get enough of what the idea is like and how they're motivated. You can do this right up until it's a finished commercial.

Quite often we're used when you are looking at competitive advertising, or at your finished commercial—something you've just shot and you've gotten a low score and you don't quite understand why. Maybe you could see it got a flat response or a highly emotional one, but you're not sure what triggered it. Then you can use our laboratory diagnostically as the groups talk about the commercial. It's done in a certain way that they're not there to be experts. They are consumers and can respond to the pros and cons in a fresh way.

So you see, we can be helpful all along the whole creative development process, while there's lots of other research that should be done as well.

How Qualitative Research Was Used: Two Case Histories   An excellent example, in my experience, of the creative use of this kind of research was when I was working with Y&R's Direct Marketing agency, Wunderman Worldwide, on a presentation for the Geico Insurance Company. This company specialized in auto insurance for drivers with safe driving records, and the premiums were lower because of the drivers' reliability. We had conceived a campaign with the theme line, "For all the good things you've done" and had prepared some rough ads. They had what we thought were compelling positive headlines, such as "If you're a good driver, you can pay less for car insurance." We showed the ads to focus groups of people who were in our (preselected) product category. To our surprise, their verbatim responses were bland or adverse: "Well, all companies say that" . . . "I'm cynical about offers like that."

We were discouraged by that first go-round and were almost ready to abandon our concept. But we executed some more ads, and among them were a few with so-called negative headlines—an approach which copy books in the past have often discouraged—such a thought as "Why should good drivers pay for bad drivers' accidents?" We held another focus group and those were the ads that hit the target. They won strong positive emotional response from our panelists, as well as a rich variety of verbatim discussion: "That's right! Why *should* I pay for bad drivers' accidents! It's a damned shame to have to pay the same amount as drivers who aren't as careful as I am."

Obviously, we would never have been confident enough to recommend our approach if we had not had that encouraging feedback. And we buttressed our confidence, in our presentation to the client, with actual recordings and a videotape of the contrast in response to our first and our revised ads.

Another case in point was Y&R's research for the Kentucky Fried Chicken fast-food chain. Our qualitative, motivational findings were largely responsible for Y&R's winning the account, after many months, from a field of some 23 agencies. For years, Kentucky Fried Chicken had enjoyed a smashing success with its "finger-lickin' good" campaign. But competition became keener when McDonald's, and other hamburger outlets, entered the fast-growing fast-food business. Y&R's focus group research revealed a "hot button": the fact that consumers had serious doubts about the nutritional value of fast food. Changing times bring changing needs, and research should be sensitive to the needs of change. With a higher awareness of nutrition in America, poultry was already making inroads into the consumption of beef. Y&R's research, at that time, sensed the wave to come, and the recommended campaign was designed to reassure mothers who felt guilty about feeding take-out chicken meals to their families. The strategy was to position Kentucky Fried Chicken, implicitly, against fast-food hamburger. The theme: "It's so nice to feel so good about a meal."

The *execution* of that strategy was also a crucial element in its success. The catchy, emotion-stirring theme song made an enormous contribution: "It's so nice, nice to feel . . . So good about a meal . . . So good about Kentucky Fried Chicken." The entertaining storytelling commercials were also a contributing factor, because they invited "closure"—i.e., participation by the viewer. The music and storyline techniques were also researched, both qualitatively, with in-depth focus groups, and quantitatively, with pre- and posttesting.

But again, times change and the needs change, and research must keep pace. After 33 months of sales gains, there was a major new competitive climate. Rising beef prices, and the obvious success of KFC's strategy prompted Burger King and McDonald's to introduce chicken entries. The number of fast-food restaurants specializing in fried chicken increased by more than a thousand. So there was a need for a campaign change. And, again, judgment was buttressed by research. The theme of the new $60 million campaign in the 1980s took advantage of the strong image franchise KFC had won for so many years. It was competitive against other chicken outlets: "We do chicken right." And the new strategy—that "all chicken isn't created equal"—again won the day.

Quantitative Research: Uses and Abuses of Measuring Recall

I mentioned that the use of certain kinds of research may occur due to biases, and one example has been the tendency for some clients to use the single scoring measure of D.A.R. (day-after recall).

One of the reasons day-after recall has been so popular with advertisers is that it draws simple, forthright conclusions: What do people remember having seen on the air 24 hours before? Another reason for the popularity of the method is that it has been used for so long that there are well-established norms, in every product category, against which to measure *your* advertising.

With day-after recall, it's easy to measure one factor: if a commercial scores poorly, it failed to register the message you set out to communicate. That alone is not sufficient reason to kill the commercial because some great advertising requires multiple exposure to communicate and whether or not the message to be communicated is the best one "deponent sayeth naught."

Another possible fallacy in this method rests in the very fact that it is simplistic to a fault. Said Frazier Purdy, then creative director of Y&R, in one of the training sessions:

In the Burke day-after recall system, what counts toward the score is *related* recall.

This can be specific audio elements, such as "It was new and it contained an ironing ingredient called Super Glide," or specific video elements, such as "There was a lady ironing and the Colossal Genie appeared out of her steam iron." or general, nonspecific elements (when no specifically incorrect element is mentioned), such as "They said it was good for clothes and made ironing easier."

This is one of the chief disadvantages of the system. You can achieve a good score, even an outstanding one, without having communicated the selling promise.

You must (therefore) carefully examine the richness of the verbatims in order to determine if the selling message is coming across. It often makes sense to run a spot with a lower score because of better verbatims related to the selling idea. Smarter clients will do that. Most will not.

Good Use of Recall Measurement: A Case History   The typical print ad corollary of day-after commercial recall is the measurement of "Noted" and "Read Most" scores by such methods as Starch and Y&R's own "Canada Today." Ads are printed or tipped into magazines and respondents, after a time lapse, are questioned as to which ads they noted and read.

Again, finite scores alone are not a totally fair method of copy research, and intuitive judgment beyond the mere numbers can often make a crucial difference. Here is where a combination of quantitative and qualitative research can work best.

A powerful case in point is the "No Man Around" campaign for Goodyear tires, with which I was intimately associated. The campaign was the result, you might say, of a series of lucky "accidents," plus the intuition and courage of the Goodyear advertising director, John Kelley.

It was in the early 1960s when I gave a new woman copywriter, Dee Mansfield, the assignment of coming up with a print campaign idea targeted toward women in women's magazines. It was for the expensive, top-of-the-line Goodyear Double Eagle, which had a special "inner spare" that could keep the tire going, after a blowout, until you could reach a service station for repair. I had long wanted Goodyear to advertise to women, but since, at that time, women were a small percentage of the tire-buying decision makers, management had shown little interest.

Dee said that she really couldn't think of an idea, because tires to her were just big black ugly doughnuts, something to be ignored. Except, she said (being a recent divorcee, with two small children), all she could imagine was what would happen to her "if a tire had a blowout when I'm on a deserted road and there's no man around."

My ears pricked up and I sensed the power of that "throwaway" line. We were soon brainstorming an entire campaign for that one specialized tire.

The Double Eagle, however, was not the subject of our main assignment, since it was only 1 percent of Goodyear's tire sales. Furthermore, when I showed our idea to Goodyear management, after presenting our main campaign, the president complimented us on our initiative, but rejected the effort: "Keep your eye on the main chance. Women are too small a market."

After the meeting, John Kelley's intuition came to the fore, and he said, "I still like that campaign. Let's test its appeal to men." We had previously run a test ad in the women's issue of the Gallup & Robinson test magazine. The recall scores and verbatims were no great shakes. But when we tried the same ad in a men's issue, the scores were higher, and, best of all, the verbatim comments were exceedingly rich. The men played back such comments as these: "I pictured my wife with a flat tire, on a lonely road, where she could be accosted." "I felt guilty when I thought of the situation my wife could be in if I weren't around."

The rest is a long but happy story. Suffice to say that, on the basis of that research, and a gut feeling on his part, John Kelley determined to recommend the "No Man Around" campaign for Goodyear's entire line of tires and for the mainstream campaign. To their great credit, Goodyear's management agreed, and the campaign ran, in both print and TV, for several years with great success. (See Figure 8–1.)

While the sales of the Double Eagle top-of-the-line tire only tripled (from 1 percent to 3 percent of sales), the next-in-the-line premium tire sales increased by 30 percent, and the campaign set a precedent for the company to adopt "best foot forward" advertising from then on.

Improving the Day-After Recall Scores

Despite doctrinaire abuses of recall scores (such as making them the sole criterion for a go/no-go decision), they do have their merits and you can usually get a high TV commercial score if you create your commercial to A.Q.R.I. (Arouse Quick Related Interest), and if it is also simple, original, and relevant. Furthermore, it is possible to "save" an expensively produced commercial before it is killed because of a low score.

In a module of our first traveling creative workshop, Shirley Simkin presented a series of pairs of commercials, each pair consisting of a commercial that had received a low recall score and the same commercial that was pretested, after a production revision, and received a higher recall score. To encourage participation and discussion, Shirley played a guessing game. She showed each pair without identifying which of the two was the low scorer and which the high.

How to Measure the Immeasurable

A major criticism of recall research is that it does not take into account such elusive-to-research factors as *empathy* and *entertainment*— emotional, nonverbal reactions to advertising. As explained in a Research Department document:

Attempts to measure nonverbal, imagaic aspects of advertising communication have suffered from the dissimilarity of the stimulus to the reaction mode; i.e., the advertising is (partially) nonverbal, but the questioning technique is verbal.

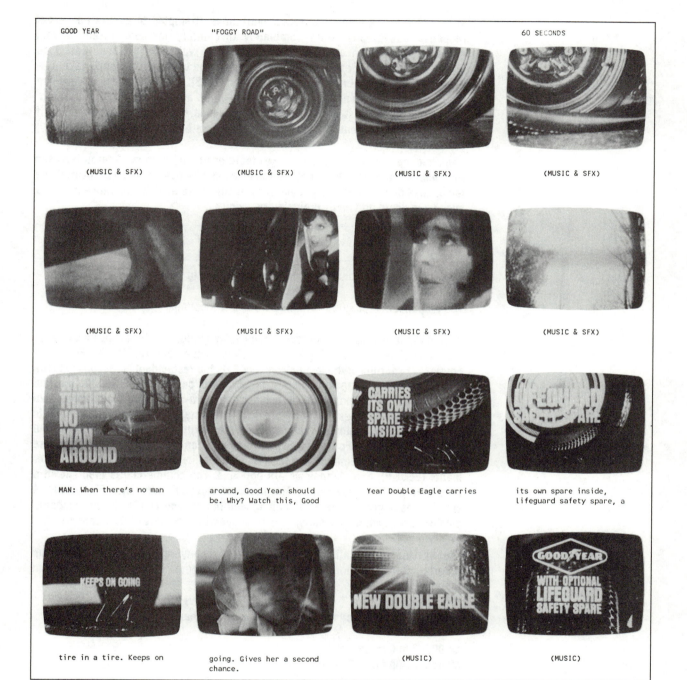

FIGURE 8-1

In recent years, a number of researchers have attempted to assess nonverbal response nonverbally, from completely involuntary methods (brain waves, galvanic skin response, voice pitch analysis) to voluntary methods based on high-tech electronics or distraction techniques. The voluntary methods have proliferated from three in 1984 to eight today (1988). Their value for advertising research varies, depending on the objective of the advertising and the research. They seem to be most useful where the key research objective is evaluation of interest and excitement levels, as in entertainment-based advertising.

The attached summary outlines the key features of each method. Appropriateness for specific issues should be considered on a case-by-case basis. Moreover, these techniques do not in any way replace traditionally productive qualitative methods such as in depth and focus group interviewing.

The following are two pages from the list of eight methods:

To assess viewers' conscious nonverbal reactions to advertising

100 respondents recruited in malls across 3–4 locations.

As part of the standard Prolog methodology, the respondent first views a clutter of 8 commercials (one test spot), and is asked commercial recall. The *Frame-To-Frame* (FTF) portion of the test follows. For FTF, the respondent is reexposed to the test commercial, along with the first three control commercials. He/she is asked reactions to the commercials by using a *keyboard* with buttons containing five different facial expressions (very positive—very negative). The start position is ☺ (neutral). Respondents must push a different button or last button pushed will continue to record. Following FTF, communication playback, scaled response (VRP type) to entertainment, emotionality, credibility and product attribute statements (EEC&P), and diagnostics are obtained. The commercial is then shown a third time for the FTF Refocus. Respondents view only their own FTF profile. A superimposed graph of reactions along with the commercial is shown. Respondents are asked what their feelings were at specific moments of the commercial.

Prolog: Unaided recall, main idea, interest in buying (post only), scalers on entertainment, emotional reaction, credibility, product attributes, and custom diagnostics.

Frame to Frame Reactions on pictorial scale and reasons for attitude shifts.

$6,000–6,500 for Prolog
$2,000–2,500 for FTF option

- Potential to elicit partial verbalization of initially spontaneous nonverbal reactions
- Anonymity of response which reduces biases associated with the influence of others in group
- Custom design possible
- Part of long interviewing procedure; fatigue possible.

Purpose   To assess viewers' conscious nonverbal reactions to advertising.

Sample   Custom designed.
              Up to 100 per session.

Procedure   Respondents record their reactions second-by-second on Ballot Box computers. These are hand-held touch sensitive *keypads*. Viewers are instructed to express constantly their attitudes while watching, using a five-point scale (A = very positive, B = somewhat positive, C = neutral, D = somewhat negative, and E = very negative). The Pulseline score which reflects reactions to advertising is the percentage of those whose reactions are very positive at a given moment less the percentage of those who are somewhat positive, plus 25% of those who are somewhat positive, less 25% of those who are somewhat negative. In addition, VRP type items can be administered. Respondents are asked to participate in focus group interviews for probing reasons for Pulseline ratings.

Criteria   *Custom Designed*

- Pulseline ratings (second-by-second reactions)
- VRP type items rated
- Content playback
- Refocus with reasons for pulseline ratings

Base Cost   Custom designed. Based on incidence and sample size.

Advantages
- Potential to elicit partial verbalization of initially spontaneous nonverbal reactions.
- Anonymity of initial response which reduces biases associated with the influence of others in a group.
- Custom design possible
- Diagnostics available

Disadvantages   Small organization (but more experienced than Speedback or Perception Analyzer).

To assess viewers' conscious, nonverbal reactions to advertising.

Custom designed—usually a total of 120–150 children per commercial across three locations.

Children watch TV in small groups (6–7). The TV plays a program along with commercials (the test commercial will appear twice in the program). While the TV is on, a mild distraction, in the form of a slide show, plays on a second screen. The slides are provided to give children's eyes something else to focus on, should their interest in the TV material wane. The children are free to look at the TV or the slides. By videotaping their faces, a record is kept, moment to moment, of where each child's attention is directed. Attention is sampled at 2-second intervals, with each child tracked individually. Following exposure, each child is probed on reactions and communication (can be custom designed).

- POINT SCORES—percent of sample looking at the TV at any one point in time.
- COMMERCIAL ATTENTION SCORES—percent who paid close attention to the whole commercial (at least 90% of the time) compared to norms.
- PRODUCT ATTENTION SCORES—reflect the attention children pay to those portions of commercial which focus on product.
- VIDEOCHARTS—based on point scores, show changing attention levels superimposed on the screen.
- COMMUNICATION & ATTITUDES

Per cell of 120—$9,000–$10,000
Per cell of 150—$16,000

- **Potential to elicit partial verbalization of initially spontaneous nonverbal reactions.**
- **Relatively large sample**
- **Custom design possible**
- **Follow-up one-on-one interview—for diagnostics**
- **Extensive experience with children's research**
- **No machinery to interfere with response**

Possible misinterpretation of whether or not child is looking at the slide show (inter-rater agreement).

The Ideal Answer: Creative/Research Partnership	In the copy research chapter of my book *The Compleat Copywriter*, (McGraw-Hill, 1966), I talked about the incredible multiplicity of factors affecting a consumer's desire to buy, and cited a former Y&R researcher, Bob Mayer:

Charting the measuring methods, both in his agency and from outside services, Mayer demonstrates all the variables which can affect the meaning of a given test result in any of the sequential steps. As you can see from [charts of various research methods], each research method has different variables. Calculating the number of relevant criteria which could affect a decision, given the many methods and variables, Mayer comes up with a conservative figure of 480,000, each of which purports to measure the performance of a single ad or commercial.

How can you possibly use *any* kind of research, or even combination of research methods, and account for all such variables? Here is how I resolved the subject at that time:

When you consider that staggering number of variables, you wonder how anyone can fairly make a decision based on copy research. One answer was that given by [Russell B.] Colley—that only specific, measurable objectives be stated and researched (e.g., that the awareness of a brand should be increased by such-and-such a percentage). Colley did not feel, however, that advertisers could go beyond the measurement of attention, comprehension, and believability, into the areas of intent to buy, purchase, and repurchase. It was when advertisers insisted that they must measure those areas that a research method like the Schwerin audience jury (which claimed to predict sales intent) became popular.

One creative answer which more copywriters and researchers, in collaboration, are trying to use is the assumption that copy research should parallel the thought process involved in copywriting. "Research must be *integrated* into the process of creating advertising," said (Stuart H.) Britt, in an address before the Advertising Research Foundation, and he called for empirical research methods, never relying on any one pat answer. This is precisely how our creative minds operate.

A year after my book was published, I attempted to follow Britt's advice, when I worked for several months in our London office, on the Daz account, P & G's British equivalent of Cheer detergent. I collaborated *daily*, not just with an art director, but with a full-time assigned researcher. And we tried a process I called "CDR" (copy development research). Every day, as we worked on strategies and executions, we immediately involved consumers in the process.

In this way, we enjoyed constant feedback, simultaneous with every step of the creative process. We kept a record of all our activities, and we also involved the rest of the agency product group and the client representatives. Thus, the research and creative process became one.

One of the problems with normal research methods is that they are so slow, cumbersome, and costly that it's next to impossible to match the speed of the creative efforts. In our case, our researcher, Jenny Bowen, had the skill and the contacts to be able to arrange daily consumer feedback which dovetailed with our creative output. Concepts might evince one response, while people might respond very differently to the same concepts, given executions. Furthermore, we wanted to get reactions to varied executions.

What we were constantly searching for were gross areas of "coincidence" and "contradiction." Our creative judgment was the main criterion. But we also used the method of the very honest scientist ("Whenever you get an idea, try to disprove it"). Research was an integral part of the real-time loop, so when decisions *were* made, everyone could feel that objective research and subjective intuition had been sincere partners.

When I returned to America, I gave a speech, before a meeting of the 4A's, on my new hobby horse—"Must Science Be a Dirty Word in the Creative Department?" I pleaded for a renaissance in the attitudes of the "creatives" and the "researchers." My speech was reprinted in the trade magazine *Madison Avenue* and achieved some currency. But the concept never fully took hold, not even in my own enlightened agency. (Perhaps *you*, dear reader, can help me to carry the banner for such an empirical attitude and system.)

There has been one influential voice at Y&R for empirical research, in the person of Joe Plummer, our research director from 1980 to 1987. Internally, and in public talks, Joe always maintained that such enlightened research should become the wave of the future:

Advertising will diminish in its value and effectiveness if we continue to rely on overly simplistic single number tests and do not expand our models, theories, and methods. Our track record in the past of greater and greater reliance on a single model and a single system like day-after recall has not advanced the ball at all. "When the only tool I have is a hammer, pretty soon the whole world looks like nails."

We should use every ounce of consumer feedback we can muster to make the most informed and intelligent judgments possible. Ultimately, we must take some risks, think harder about the questions, and be innovative in our selection of the best tools from an expanding "kit bag."

If we do *all* these things, take this approach and think about the objectives of science and the goals of our professional growth, no longer will we hear "research is the enemy of the new and different," but "research is a driving force for the new and different."

. . . .

CHAPTER CHECKLIST

. . . .

1. Research should always be the hand-maiden of creativity. It cannot measure the effectiveness of advertising. It can help us create the message.

2. We need a "knowledge base" in order to create the most effective advertising.

3. This knowledge is needed to help achieve four short-term goals and five long-term goals (review the goals).

4. Among the common subjects calling for research would be

    a. The demographic and psychographic market for a new product.

    b. How best to preempt a position (i.e., strategy) for a new parity product.

    c. What advertising should say and how to say it.

    d. How well specific ads and commercials communicate their message.

    e. How well an entire campaign is doing over time.

5. There is a vast number of sources for such needs as

    a. Product research.

    b. Message research.

    c. Campaign tracking.

    d. Market research.

    e. Channels of distribution.

(Review Dr Pepper case history on how methods were selected and knowledge used.)

6. Among research methods are qualitative ones, used directly by the creative people, including in-depth focus groups. (Review the Geico and Kentucky Fried Chicken case histories.)

7. Quantitative, single-method measures, such as Day-after recall scoring, have their flaws, but if clients insist on using this testing, it can be used creatively. (Review Goodyear "No Man Around" case history.)

8. Day-after recall scores can often be improved by simple commercial production revisions.

9. The most difficult factor for advertising research is the emotional, nonverbal response to advertising. Eight relatively new methods, however, are available.

10. The best kind of research is a creative/research partnership, with many different kinds of research being used to discover gross areas of coincidence and contradiction, which in turn aid the purely intuitive creative process.

. . . .

CHAPTER

9 Creativity in Direct Marketing and Direct Response Advertising

Bob Stone, speaking of marrying Y&R general methods with the special needs of direct marketing

We expanded only one of the (Y&R) tools — the Strategic Selection Outline — to include THE OFFER, an essential in any direct marketing plan.

(AUTHOR'S NOTE: Bob Stone, direct marketing consultant, and former head of Stone & Adler, graciously agreed to contribute this chapter to my book. Bob is responsible, therefore, for the following words and exhibits, in their entirety, about this specialized and fast-growing discipline.)

By 1984 Y&R was the unquestioned leader in direct marketing among the top 20 advertising agencies in the United States with billing reaching the $200 million level. This substantial volume came from three direct marketing agencies: Wunderman, Ricotta & Kline, the largest (now Wunderman Worldwide), along with their sister agencies, Chapman Direct and Stone & Adler.

Consistent with Y&R's goal to take a leadership role in all advertising and marketing disciplines, Ed Ney acquired Wunderman in 1973. Stone & Adler (S & A) was acquired in December of 1978.

Within hours after joining the Y&R family I attended my first Y&R conference in Carefree, Arizona, attended by chief executives of Y&R offices from around the globe. The presentations boggled my mind. One presentation in particular, by Lester Wunderman, gave me an insight to how Y&R, the world's largest general agency, was integrating specialized disciplines, such as direct marketing, into its total arsenal of client services.

It was at this same Carefree, Arizona, conference that I learned of the plethora of training programs and research available to Y&R units. The Traveling Creative Workshop, the Resource Center, the Advertising Skills Workshop. Likewise concepts, new to me, entered my consciousness for the first time: "mission statements," "company culture," "brand personality."

It wasn't that Y&R had to sell us on the importance of training: Aaron Adler and I had hosted an annual retreat each year for our creative and account people. What we now had to add to our training was a tremendous infusion of additional state-of-the-art training programs created by the best professionals in the business.

At subsequent Y&R workshops we learned about the "tools" of Y&R and how to use them: the Creative Work Plan (CWP), the Strategy Selection Outline (SSO), the Media Work Plan (MWP), Values and

Lifestyles (VALS). As impressive as these tools were, a burning question arose: Would these tools, sculptured for general advertising, be applicable to direct-response advertising? We found they were. Very much so. As a matter of fact, we expanded only one of the tools—Strategic Selection Outline—to include "The offer," an essential in any direct marketing plan.

ENTER "THE WHOLE EGG"

With the fruition of Ed Ney's master plan—acquiring leading firms in each communications category—everything was in place to fill any need of a client, or potential client. The concept, as described previously, came to be known as "The Whole Egg."

Direct marketing, the subject of this chapter, was thus sold as a part of the total package to world-class clients such as AT&T, General Foods, Time-Life, Lincoln-Mercury, and Merrill-Lynch. The concept was sound.

A Hole in the "Whole Egg"

By 1983 I was serving my fourth year on the Y&R U.S.A. Board. I asked that a proposal I had in mind be put on the agenda: a proposal to conduct a two-week intensive workshop on direct marketing, primarily for Y&R units around the world with little, or no knowledge of direct marketing.

When my turn on the agenda came I stated flatly that I saw a hole in the whole egg concept, at least as far as direct marketing was concerned. The hole, I continued, was that if a general advertising unit didn't have a basic knowledge of what direct marketing could contribute to the total marketing mix, how could we expect them to recommend its usage with their clients?

My thesis was generally accepted by the other members of the board. And that pleased me. But deep down I knew I hadn't made a total sale. Remembering the sage advice of Mark Stroock, I knew I had to get commitment from Alex Kroll, the chairman of the U.S.A. board. Alex said "Yes." It was a done deal.

Weeks went into preparation for the first Y&R direct marketing workshop. The venue selected was the Harrison Conference Center in Glen Cove, New York. The dates were April 1–13, 1984. Action groups were formed in both Chicago and New York. Frank Daniels, an experienced training director in our Chicago office, was appointed coordinator and assisted by my capable executive secretary Joan Reynolds. In New York we had Cindy Butchko, training director of Wunderman, and Nick Rudd, the astute Y&R training director. As a side bar, without a capable team like I had, there is no way an intensive workshop can succeed.

While I agreed to conduct many of the class sessions, I saw to it that I was strongly reinforced by heavyweights from both Wunderman and

S & A. An important member of the Chicago team was Craig Campbell, a Chicago vice president, charged with developing a client case, to be solved by the class over a two-week period. Craig built a case for IBM—an important client.

The in-house instructors were supported by noted industry leaders of this ilk: Bob DeLay, then president of Direct Marketing Association; Pete Hoke, publisher of *Direct Marketing* magazine; John Wyman, vice president, AT&T Telemarketing; Mike Manzari, executive vice president, The Kleid Company—a leading list broker; and Jo-Von Tucker, an eminent authority on catalog marketing. In short, the workshop was developed in the Y&R quality mode.

Registrants for the workshop were selected with extreme care. Only senior-level executives were eligible: we wanted those who had the ability and authority to take the word back to their respective offices. Representatives came from Y&R offices across the States and from as far away as England and Japan.

THE DIRECT MARKETING WORKSHOP

In constructing the workshop we identified three prime objectives:

1. To establish the basic differences between general advertising and marketing and direct marketing.

2. To explore the body of knowledge available for direct marketing.

3. To show general agencies how direct marketing can be integrated into the total marketing mix.

All attendees were furnished a workbook filled with a comprehensive outline of the two-week program, pertinent reprints supporting subjects to be discussed and the IBM case to be solved by teams formed from the attendees. In addition, each person was given a copy of *Successful Direct Marketing Methods,*[1] a 500-page book, to serve as a permanent reference in their respective offices.

What follows is a delineation of the 1984 workshop updated.

Direct Marketing Defined

The starting point was the official Direct Marketing Association definition of direct marketing:

Direct Marketing is an interactive system of marketing which uses one or more advertising media to effect a measurable response and/or transaction at any location.

[1]Bob Stone, *Successful Direct Marketing Methods* (Lincolnwood, IL.: NTC Business Books.

Important point: The two most important words in the definition are: "measurable response," for if response can't be measured, if costs and income can't be calculated precisely, it's not direct marketing.

While measurable response is the touchstone of direct marketing, it doesn't define the differences in objectives between general advertising and direct marketing, particularly when it comes to the sale of goods and services. Here are the basic differences:

Direct Marketing	General Advertising
• Selling to individuals. Customers are identifiable by name, address, and purchase behavior.	• Mass selling. Buyers identified as broad groups sharing common demographic and psychographic characteristics.
• Products have added value or service. Distribution is important product benefit.	• Product benefits do not always include convenient distribution channels.
• The medium is the marketplace.	• Retail outlet is marketplace.
• Marketer controls product until delivery.	• Marketer may lose control as product enters distribution channel.
• Advertising used to motivate an immediate order or inquiry.	• Advertising used for cumulative effect over time to build image, awareness, loyalty, benefit recall. Purchase action deferred.
• Repetition used within ad.	• Repetition used over time.
• Consumers feel high perceived risk—product bought unseen. Recourse is distant.	• Consumers feel less risk—have direct contact with the product and direct recourse.

Total Scope of Functions and Media

Ask a neophyte for a definition of direct marketing and you are likely to hear, "Oh, that's another term for direct mail." Or "That's really a new term for mail order." Both are incorrect. Figure 9–1 shows all the major functions and media available in the totality of direct marketing.

The flowchart dramatizes the fact that direct marketing is a subset of the total marketing concept and that there is a wide array of media available to accomplish stated objectives.

The Wide Body of Knowledge

Testing is a basic precept of direct marketing. Thus all efforts are measurable. Best lists. Best offers. Best publications, radio stations, TV and cable stations. Best formats. Testing possibilities are without limit.

But of the thousands and thousands of tests conducted over the decades, certain tests have come out the same, time after time—regardless of the marketer. Knowledge of these consistent results constitutes an invaluable body of knowledge.

Direct Marketing Flow Chart

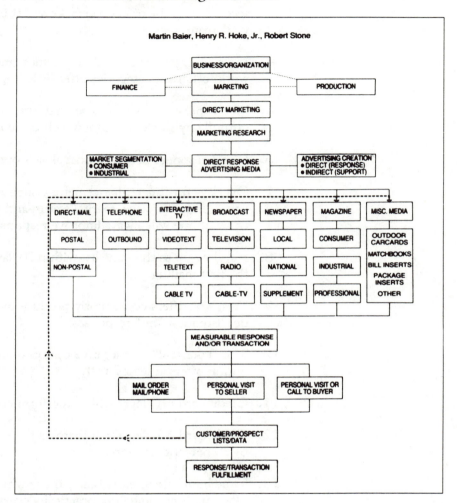

FIGURE 9-1

Over the decades I have identified 30 timeless direct marketing principles and have confirmed them with colleagues around the world. I'm so confident of the outcome of tests involving these principles that I'd feel free to guarantee the outcome 95 percent of the time with a 10 percent limit of error.

Here is the priceless list of 30 principles:

Thirty Timeless Direct Marketing Principles

1. All customers are not created equal. Give or take a few percentage points, 80 percent of repeat business for goods and services will come from 20 percent of your customer base.

2. The most important order you ever get from a customer is the second order. Why? Because a two-time buyer is at least twice as likely to buy again as a one-time buyer.

3. Maximizing direct mail success depends first upon the lists you use, second upon the offers you make and third upon the copy and graphics you create.

4. If, on a given list, "hotline" names (most recent responders) don't work, other list categories offer little opportunity for success.

5. Merge/purge names—those that appear on two or more lists—will outpull any single list from which these names have been extracted.

6. Direct response lists will most always outpull compiled lists.

7. Overlays on lists (enhancements), such as life-style characteristics, income, education, age, marital status, and propensity to respond by mail or by phone will always improve response.

8. A follow-up to the same list within 30 days will pull 40 to 50 percent of the first mailing.

9. "Yes/No" offers consistently produce more orders than do offers that don't request "no" responses.

10. The "take rate" for negative option offers will always outpull positive option offers at least 2 to 1.

11. Credit card privileges will outperform cash with order at least 2 to 1.

12. Credit card privileges will increase the size of the average catalog order by 20 percent, or more.

13. Time limit offers, particularly those which give a specific date, outpull offers with no time limit practically every time.

14. Free gift offers, particularly where the gift appeals to self-interest, outpull discount offers consistently.

15. Sweepstakes, particularly in conjunction with impulse purchases, will increase order volume 35 percent or more.

16. You will collect far more money in a fund-raising effort if you ask for a specific amount from a purchaser. Likewise, you will collect more money if the appeal is tied to a specific project.

17. People buy benefits, not features.

18. The longer you can keep someone reading your copy, the better your chances of success.

19. The timing and frequency of renewal letters is vital. But I can report nothing but failure over a period of 40 years in attempts to hype renewals with "improved copy." I've concluded that the "product"— the magazine, for example—is *the factor* in making a renewal decision.

20. Self-mailers are cheaper to produce, but they practically never outpull envelope-enclosed letter mailings.

21. A preprint of a forthcoming ad, accompanied by a letter and response form, will outpull a postprint mailing package by 50 percent, or more.

22. It is easier to increase the average dollar amount of an order than it is to increase percentage of response.

23. You will get far more new catalog customers if you put your proved winners in the front pages of your catalog.

24. Assuming items of similar appeal, you will always get a higher response rate from a 32-page catalog than from a 24-page catalog.

25. A new catalog to a customer base will outpull cold lists by 400 to 800 percent.

26. A print ad with a bind-in card will outpull the same ad without a bind-in up to 600 percent.

27. A direct response, direct sale TV commercial of 120 seconds will outpull a 60 second direct response commercial better than 2 to 1.

28. A TV support commercial will increase response from a newspaper insert up to 50 percent.

29. The closure rate from qualified leads can be from two to four times as effective as cold calls.

30. Telephone-generated leads are likely to close four to six times greater than mail-generated leads.

Data Bases: The Backbone of a Successful Operation	As we have seen thus far, there are many differences between general advertising and marketing and direct marketing. But the most distinguishing difference, without doubt, is the availability of data bases for direct marketers.

Successful direct marketers know who their customers are—by name and address. What they buy. How often they buy. What they spend. Marketers selling through traditional channels, with the rarest of exceptions, can't identify customers by name, address, or buying behavior. In short, direct marketers can identify that golden 20 percent of their customer base that accounts for 80 percent of their sales. Traditional marketers can't.

The data base requirement varies greatly by category of business, to be sure. But regardless of category of business, there is a guideline to follow that should lead to a meaningful data base. Ask this question: "What data will I need in order to carry on a meaningful dialogue with my customers either by phone, or mail, or both?" Depending upon the nature of a business, here is basic data which should go into the data base:

☐ Name of individual

☐ Mailing and shipping address

☐ Telephone number

☐ Time zone

☐ Standard industrial classification (SIC) number (if a business firm)

☐ Source of inquiry card/or order

☐ Date of inquiry/or order

☐ Cost of inquiry/or order

☐ History of purchases
  ☐ By dates
  ☐ By what items purchased
  ☐ By dollar amounts of purchases
  ☐ By cumulative sales dollars

By putting basic data into your customer base, the opportunity to maximize profit by manipulating the data increases a hundredfold.

The concept of manipulating customer data came about almost out of sheer desperation during the Great Depression. Catalog giants like Sears and Wards were feeling the impact of bread lines, as were all businesses. Working against the maxim that "All customers are not created equal," they developed a formula that changed the way mail-order customers were promoted. And this formula, with refinements, is being used to this day.

This magic formula was tagged as R-F-M (recency, frequency, monetary). Best customers, and therefore those most likely to buy again, were identified as those who had bought most recently, those who bought most frequently within a specified period, and those who had spent specified amounts.

In its simplest form, the R-F-M formula calls for a point system to be established with purchases broken down by quarter of the year. A typical formula might be as follows:

Recency points:

24 points = current quarter

12 points = last 6 months

6 points = last 9 months

3 points = last 12 months

Frequency points: Number of purchases × 4 points.

Monetary points: 10 percent of dollar purchase with a ceiling of 9 points. (The ceiling avoids distortion by an unusually large purchase.)

Number of points allotted varies among those using R-F-M formulas, but the principle is the same. Once the system is established and point values are assigned, the opportunities for maximizing profits are almost phenomenal. Under the system, each account is isolated from all other accounts. Buying habits dictate how frequently an account is solicited.

Our concern thus far has been with capturing data about those who inquire and those who buy. National Demographics & Lifestyles (NDL) of Denver, Colorado, for example, is in the forefront of compiling and providing massive compiled lists of consumers with precise selections of demographics and life-styles.

Figure 9-2 shows sketches of two men: David Day and Nick Night. Same household incomes, but different life-styles and therefore different interests in products and services.

It is through the selection of life-style criteria that direct marketers can match prospects to customer profiles.

The Importance of Offers	Earlier in this chapter I mentioned that the Y&R training tools adapted easily to our direct response needs. The only embellishment we made was in the Strategic Selection Outline, to which we added *the offer*, an absolute essential in direct marketing. Indeed, more often than not, we put the offer in the headline of a letter or print ad ("*Time Magazine* at 50% Off Cover Price," for example).

The number one objective of any offer: to overcome *human inertia*. It's so easy to toss a mailing piece, to turn the page of a magazine, to turn a deaf ear to a radio commercial, to get a beer during a TV commercial.

Tip: **The offer has to "turn the prospect on," often within 90 to 120 seconds!**

There are ten factors to consider when creating an offer:

1. *Price.* Pricing. There's nothing more important. Testing to determine the best price is vital to maximizing long-term payoff.

David Day—Bloomington, Minnesota		Nick Night—Bloomington, Minnesota	
Demographics		*Demographics*	
Sex	Male	Sex	Male
Household income	$40,000	Income	$40,000
Age	34	Age	34
Marital status	Married	Marital status	Married
Occupation	Sales/marketing	Occupation	Professional/technical
Spouse occupation	Clerical	Spouse occupation	Homemaker
Home ownership	Single-family home	Home ownership	Single-family home
Length of residence	Eight years	Length of residence	Four years
Children at home	Two, ages four and one	Children at home	One, age five
Life-style Activities		*Life-style Activities*	
Golfing		Fishing	
Foreign travel		Working on automobiles	
Physical fitness exercise		Camping	
Investing in stocks and bonds		Watching sports on TV	
Home workshop		Personal computing	

FIGURE 9–2

2. *Shipping and handling.* Many merchandisers follow a rule of thumb that shipping and handling charges should not exceed 10 percent of the basic selling price. But, again, testing is advisable.

3. *Unit of sale.* Will your product or service be offered "each"? "Two for"? "Set of X"? Once more, test.

4. *Optional features.* Optional features often increase the average order. For example, when the publisher of a dictionary offered thumb indexing at $2 extra, 25 percent of total purchasers opted for this added feature.

5. *Future obligation.* Most common are book and record offers that commit the purchaser to future obligation. ("Take ten records for $1 and agree to buy six more in the coming 12 months.") A continuity program offer might state: "Get volume one free—others will be sent at regular intervals."

6. *Credit options.* The average credit card order is usually 20 percent or more larger than a cash order.

7. *Incentives.* Incentives include free gifts, discounts, and sweepstakes. Toll-free ordering privilege is likewise an incentive—ease of ordering. Not unlike credit options, toll-free ordering privileges tend to increase the average order 20 percent and more.

8. *Time limits*. Time limits add urgency to an offer. It helps to overcome human inertia.

9. *Quantity limits*. There is something in the human psyche that says, "If it's in short supply, I want it!" Even "Limit—two to a customer" often outperforms no limit.

10. *Guarantees*. Of the ten factors to be considered in structuring an offer, there is one that should never be passed up—the guarantee.

From the ten factors to consider when creating an offer, a wide array of single and multioffers can emerge. Jim Kobs, later to form Kobs & Brady, was Stone & Adler's first account executive. Over the years Jim became a master at developing offers. The culmination was the accompanying "Checklist of 99 Proven Direct Response Offers." (See Figure 9–3.)

THE MEDIA OF DIRECT RESPONSE

Over the two-week duration of The Direct Marketing Workshop the participants were exposed to the complete array of direct response media. The emphasis was always on the selection of media within categories and the execution from a direct response standpoint. For our purposes here, we will detail only the major media: print, direct mail, and telemarketing, and television.

Print

Our first point about print media was that circulation alone is not the criterion for success. The number one criterion is *direct response atmosphere*. Does the publication carry direct response ads, issue after issue? (*Reader's Digest* has the circulation, to be sure, but *Better Homes & Gardens* has the direct response atmosphere.)

When it came to testing national magazines, we emphasized the economies of using regional editions to test response viability. *TV Guide*, for example, has over 100 regional editions.

Another advantage cited for regional editions was the opportunity to run controlled tests of a variety of ads in one weekly or monthly edition of a publication, using regional editions. One example given was a simultaneous test of eight different ads in one issue of *Time*, using A/B splits in eight different regions. The best pulling ad pulled two and a half times better than the poorest pulling ad. This technique of simultaneously testing a multiplicity of ads is known as "telescopic testing" in direct response jargon.

The body of knowledge about direct response print advertising was explored thoroughly. What follows is a capsule summary.

1. Test magazines by category—news, special interest, shelter, and so on—using a region of a publication in each category. The *pilot publications* that are successful serve as reliable guides to the use of other publications in the category.

Checklist of 99 Proven Direct Response Offers

Basic offers
1. Right price
2. Free trial
3. Money-back guarantee
4. Cash with order
5. Bill me later
6. Installment terms
7. Charge card privileges
8. C.O.D.

Free gift offers
9. Free gift for an inquiry
10. Free gift for a trial order
11. Free gift for buying
12. Multiple free gifts with a single order
13. Your choice of free gifts
14. Free gifts based on size of order
15. Two-step gift offer
16. Continuing incentive gifts
17. Mystery gift offer

Other free offers
18. Free information
19. Free catalog
20. Free booklet
21. Free fact kit
22. Send me a salesman
23. Free demonstration
24. Free "survey of your needs"
25. Free cost estimate
26. Free dinner
27. Free film offer
28. Free house organ subscription
29. Free talent test
30. Gift shipment service

Discount offers
31. Cash discount
32. Short-term introductory offer
33. Refund certificate
34. Introductory order discount
35. Trade discount
36. Early-bird discount
37. Quantity discount
38. Sliding-scale discount
39. Selected discounts

Sale offers
40. Seasonal sales
41. Reason-why sales
42. Price increase notice
43. Auction-by-mail

Sample offers
44. Free sample
45. Nominal charge samples
46. Sample offer with tentative commitment
47. Quantity sample offer
48. Free sample lesson

Time limit offer
49. Limited-time offers
50. Enrollment periods
51. Pre-publication offer
52. Charter membership (or subscription) offer
53. Limited edition offer

Guarantee offers
54. Extended guarantee
55. Double-your-money-back guarantee
56. Guaranteed buy-back agreement
57. Guaranteed acceptance offer

Build-up-the-sale offers
58. Multi-product offers
59. Piggyback offers
60. The deluxe offer
61. Good-better-best offer
62. Add-on offer
63. Write-your-own-ticket offer
64. Bounce-back offer
65. Increase and extension offer

Sweepstakes offers
66. Drawing-type sweepstakes
67. Lucky number sweepstakes
68. "Everybody wins" sweepstakes
69. Involvement sweepstakes
70. Talent contests

Club and continuity offers
71. Positive option
72. Negative option
73. Automatic shipments
74. Continuity load-up offer
75. Front-end load-ups
76. Open-ended commitment
77. "No strings attached" commitment
78. Lifetime membership fee
79. Annual membership fee

Specialized offers
80. The philanthropic privilege
81. Blank check offer
82. Executive preview charge
83. Yes/No offers
84. Self-qualification offer
85. Exclusive rights for your trading area
86. The super-dramatic offer
87. Trade-in offer
88. Third-party referral offer
89. Member-get-a-member offer
90. Name-getter offers
91. Purchase-with-purchase
92. Delayed billing offer
93. Reduced down payment
94. Rush shipping service
95. Secret bonus gift
96. Stripped-down products
97. The competitive offer
98. The nominal reimbursement offer
99. Establish-the-value offer

FIGURE 9–3

2. Bind-in cards—they flag down the reader—will increase response up to 600 percent.

3. If you are running an ad calling for direct response from a monthly magazine, here is a general guide to the likely response flow:

After the first week	3–7%	After two months	75–85%
After the second week	20–25%	After three months	85–92%
After the third week	40–45%	After four months	92–95%
After one month	50–55%		

From a weekly publication, such as *Time* or *TV Guide*, the curve is entirely different: 50 percent of total response usually comes in the first two weeks.

4. With the exception of seasonal propositions, there are two major direct response seasons: January through March and August through November.

5. The rule of thumb for frequency of insertion in a publication is (a) if the first insertion pulls well over 20 percent better than planned response rate, repeat within a three or four month period; (b) if the cost per response is in an acceptable range or up to 20 percent better than expected, wait six months and follow with a second insertion; (c) if response to the first insertion is marginal, it usually makes sense to wait a full year for another try in that publication.

6. Determining proper ad size usually requires testing. Generally speaking, advertising for inquiries requires less advertising space than does copy seeking orders. As a matter of fact, the nature of a proposition might require two-page spreads, and more. Experience has shown, for example, that book and tape clubs require a two-page spread to be cost efficient.

7. Four-color advertising usually increases response 30 to 60 percent at an increased cost of 20 percent. On the other hand, adding a second color to a black and white page usually doesn't pay out.

8. For direct response advertisers, position in a book has a telling effect on response. Right-hand pages are always preferred regardless of position, because the normal position for the coupon is the lower right-hand corner of the ad. But when it comes to position of an ad within the book, here is about what you can expect the relative response to be from various page positions as measured against the first right-hand page arbitrarily rated at a pull of 100.

First right-hand page	100	Back of book (following main	
Second right-hand page	95	body of editorial matter)	50
Third right-hand page	90	Back cover	100
Fourth right-hand page	85	Inside third cover	90
Back of front of the book		Page facing third cover	85
(preceding editorial matter)	70		

9. Generally speaking, run-of-paper (ROP) advertising has not proved effective for direct response advertisers. Preprints, however, with the advantages of full-color, quality paper and response forms, have proved very effective.

10. Another favored medium for direct response advertisers is Sunday newspaper supplements, notably Sunday Magazine Network, *Parade* and *USA Weekend*. Likewise newspaper-owned Sunday magazines, such as *The New York Times* and *Chicago Tribune* Sunday magazines.

The Y&R "Stopping Power" Program From the body of accumulated knowledge about direct response print, we proceeded to explore the creative side of producing direct response advertising. Here again we were able to benefit from a Y&R training program—the "Stopping Power" Program (Chapter 4). The basis of our presentation was the principles and techniques of stopping power, a process for stopping the reader.

The Seven Principles of Stopping Power

1. Attracts the defined target audience, plus an audience beyond.

2. Demands participation.

3. Forces an emotional response by touching on a basic human want or need.

4. Creates a desire to know more.

5. Surprises the reader.

6. Exposes expected information in an unexpected way.

7. Breaks with the personality and rules of the product category.

The Eight Techniques of Stopping Power

1. Open-minded narrative (picture or thought) in which the resolution is not presented.

2. Ironic twists on ordinary behavior.

3. Play on words in the headline.

4. Incongruity of visual elements and/or words by unusual juxtaposition of elements.

5. Exaggeration.

6. Simplification.

7. Shocking visual and/or headline.

8. Participation visuals (e.g., tests, games, multiple visuals).

Scores of ads were shown imparting these principles and techniques. See Figure 9–4 for a direct response application of a stopping power principle.

FIGURE 9–4

Direct Mail and Lists

The differences in print—general versus direct response—were grasped easily by our workshop group. Direct mail, house lists, and prospect lists were new territory.

To gain attention to and respect for direct mail, we "dazzled" our attendees with some classic direct mail case histories. Here are five.

☐ The multimedia program for Hewlett-Packard, promoting the first scientific pocket calculator. Inquiry ads ran in publications like *Business Week*, answered by deluxe mailing packages. Sales were incredible: just under $40,000 in sales per thousand mailing packages.

☐ The AT&T lead generation program for its Telemarketing Center. A total of 11,600,000 mailing pieces to small business produced 174,000 leads over a 12-month period. All leads were screened by the Telemarketing Center. Qualified leads, depending upon categories, closed consistently at rates of 25 to 50 percent, either by phone or sales visit.

☐ The famous Wunderman "curriculum" program for Lincoln, which identified what the consumer wanted in a luxury car. Then proceeded through a series of mailings to show how Lincoln fulfilled these wants better than any luxury car. What the program did for Lincoln dealers is secret, of course, but the consensus is that "it drove Cadillac nuts."

☐ The five-page letter to 2,800 members of the Direct Marketing Association which brought pledges for support of direct marketing education in colleges to the tune of $227,000 for each 1,000 letters mailed. (I still can't believe it, but it's true.)

☐ The famous subscription letter from Kiplinger which, with minor changes, outpulled all other letters for almost 40 years. (The magic can be found in the lead: "More Growth and Inflation Ahead . . . And What YOU Can Do About It.")

These case histories—always an effective teaching tool—had the desired effect. For sure.

While we emphasized the fact that direct mail is the most testable of all media, we pointed out that there is a body of knowledge about direct mail that proves reliable most of the time. The following relates to the components of most mailing packages.

Mailing Format

☐ The letter ranks first in importance.

☐ The most effective mailing package consists of outside envelope, letter, circular, response form, and business reply envelope.

Letters

☐ Form letters using indented paragraphs will usually outpull those in which paragraphs are not indented.

☐ Underlining important phrases and sentences usually increases results slightly.

☐ A separate letter with a separate circular will generally do better than a combination letter and circular.

☐ A form letter with an effective running headline will ordinarily do as well as a filled-in letter.

☐ Authentic testimonials in a sales letter ordinarily increase the pull.

☐ A two-page letter ordinarily outpulls a one-page letter.

Circulars

☐ A circular that deals specifically with the proposition presented in the letter will be more effective than a circular of an institutional character.

☐ A combination of art and photography will usually produce a better circular than will one employing either art or photography alone.

☐ A circular usually proves to be ineffective in selling news magazines and news services.

☐ In selling big-ticket products, deluxe large-size, color circulars virtually always warrant the extra cost over circulars 11 inches by 17 inches or smaller.

Outside Envelopes

☐ Illustrated envelopes increase response if their message is tied into the offer.

☐ Variety in types and sizes of envelopes pays, especially in a series of mailings.

Reply Forms

☐ Reply cards with receipt stubs will usually increase response over cards with no stub.

☐ "Busy" order or request forms that look important will usually produce a larger response than neat, clean-looking forms.

☐ Postage-free business reply cards will generally bring more responses than those to which the respondent must affix postage.

Reply Envelopes

☐ A reply envelope increases cash-with-order response.

☐ A reply envelope increases responses to collection letters.

Color

☐ Two-color letters usually outpull one-color letters.

☐ An order or reply form printed in colored ink or on colored stock usually outpulls one printed in black ink on white stock.

☐ A two-color circular generally proves to be more effective than a one-color circular.

☐ Full color is warranted in the promotion of such items as food items, apparel, furniture, and other merchandise if the fidelity of color reproduction is good.

Postage

☐ Third-class mail ordinarily pulls as well as first-class mail.

☐ Postage-metered envelopes usually pull better than affixing postage stamps (and you can meter third-class postage).

☐ A "designed" printed permit on the envelope usually does as well as postage metered mail.

Before we were through with our session on direct mail we had our participants actually writing a sales letter—many for the very first time. I accomplished this by providing a seven-step sales letter formula which has stood the test of time:

1. Promise a benefit in your headline or first paragraph—your most important benefit to the reader.

2. Immediately enlarge upon your most important benefit.

3. Tell the reader specifically what he or she is going to get.

4. Back up your statements with proofs and endorsements.

5. Tell the reader what might be lost if no action is taken.

6. Rephrase your prominent benefits in your closing offer.

7. Incite action. Now.

JAMAICA

More than you bargained for.

Jamaica is a land of serendipity. Drop in to buy a straw hat or a bunch
of bananas, and find yourself dancing to Mr. Kelly's accordion.
Walk along a beach, and discover a waterfall foaming into the sea.
Drive into the mountains, and find a cool green world a mile above the sea.
Follow a farm fence, and happen upon an 18th century manor house,
complete with Palladian windows and shady verandas.
Go to Jamaica with someone you love,
and discover that you're both more wonderful than you realized.

Make it Jamaica. Again.

Jamaica Tourist Board

FIGURE 4–3

FIGURE 5–1

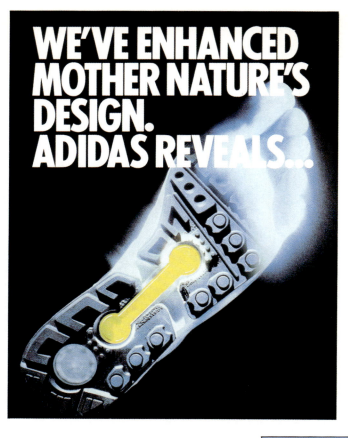

FIGURE 5–2

FIGURE 5–4

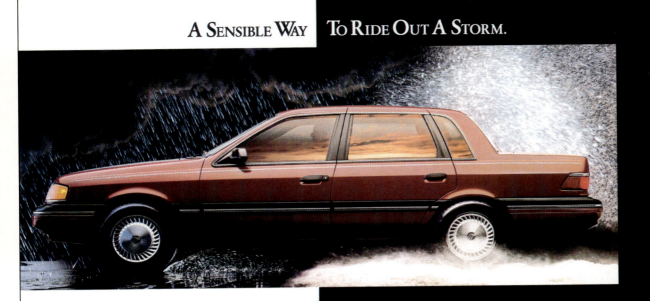

A SENSIBLE WAY TO RIDE OUT A STORM.

MERCURY TOPAZ. There's a reassuring feeling of security in the way Mercury Topaz combines comfort and control to help you deal with the elements. Topaz couples the precision of rack-and-pinion steering with the traction of front-wheel drive. An arrangement that's especially comforting when you're on a curve and roads are slick. And if you encounter those kinds of roads frequently, Mercury Topaz makes available a superb answer to bad weather driving–optional all-wheel drive. Comfort and control are one in Mercury Topaz. To make you feel better about driving when the weather's trying to ruin your day. Experience the comfort and control of a Mercury Topaz at your Lincoln-Mercury dealer today. For more Topaz information, call 1-800-822-9292.

LINCOLN-MERCURY DIVISION Ford Buckle up–together we can save lives.

MERCURY

WHERE COMFORT AND CONTROL ARE ONE.

FIGURE 5–5

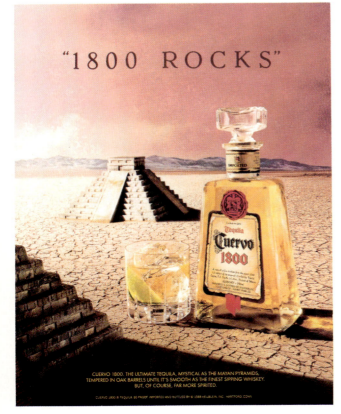

"1800 ROCKS"

CUERVO 1800. THE ULTIMATE TEQUILA, MYSTICAL AS THE MAYAN PYRAMIDS, TEMPERED IN OAK BARRELS UNTIL IT'S SMOOTH AS THE FINEST SIPPING WHISKEY, BUT, OF COURSE, FAR MORE SPIRITED.

CUERVO 1800 IS TEQUILA. 80 PROOF. IMPORTED AND BOTTLED BY © 1988 HEUBLEIN, INC., HARTFORD, CONN.

FIGURE 5–6

INGLENOOK NAVALLE THE **IN** WORD FOR WINE.

FIGURE 5–7

FIGURE 5-8

FIGURE 5-9

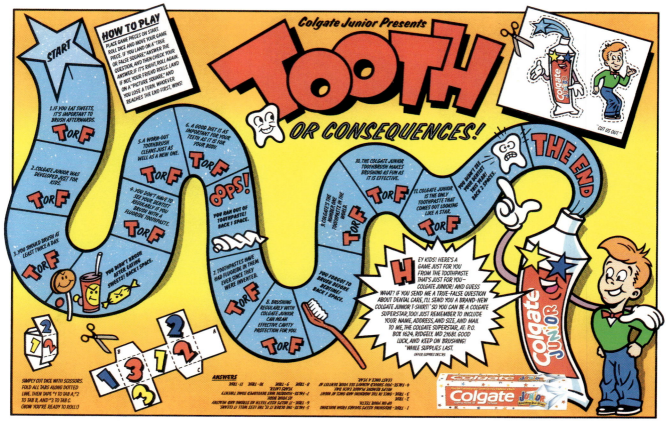

FIGURE 5-10

FIGURE 6-3

FIGURE 6-6

BAND-AID® Brand Adhesive Bandages

PRODUCT: BABAB
TITLE: "Boy/J&J"
COMMERCIAL NO.: JJYB-3668

LENGTH: 30 SECONDS
DATE: 3/10/86

BOY: Wanna see the cut under my BAND-AID bandage?

Mommy said keep it covered and it'll be all better faster. Wanna see it?

Hey,

where'd

my cut go?

ANNCR V/O: Only Johnson & Johnson has proven

that BAND-AID Brand heals cuts faster.

AFTER 4 DAYS

Up to twice as fast as uncovered cuts.

BOY: It was here. Honest, I mean it.

ANNCR V/O: Cuts covered with BAND-AID Brand

Heal up to twice as fast.

are proven to heal up to twice as fast.

Only from Johnson & Johnson.

YOUNG & RUBICAM NEW YORK

Johnson & Johnson

R-757 (rev.)

FIGURE 7–3

CLIENT: JOHNSON & JOHNSON
PRODUCT: JOHNSON'S BABY POWDER
TITLE: "WEDDING DAY"

LENGTH: 30 SECONDS
COMM. NO.: JJYP 3635
DATE: 5/30/86

DAUGHTER: Mama,

I thought you were dressed!
MOTHER: Oh, I forgot to put on my powder, honey.

DAUGHTER: I'm getting married in one hour.

MOTHER: And I'm going to be cool and collected even if it is the hottest day of the year.

DAUGHTER: Oh, I should have eloped.
MOTHER: Well, you told me not to be too emotional.

DAUGHTER: Oh, mama.
MOTHER: You know the first time I ever used this?

DAUGHTER: No, Mama. When?
MOTHER: When you were just a baby.

ANNCR VO: Johnson's Baby Powder. A feeling you never outgrow.

From Johnson & Johnson.

FIGURE 7–4

CLIENT: THE GILLETTE COMPANY
PRODUCT: RIGHT GUARD
TITLE: "BILLIARD PARLOR"

LENGTH: 30 SECONDS
COMM. NO.: GSGC 6043
DATE: 5/10/86

<u>WOMAN SINGS</u>: Men you'd better not

come on too strong . . .

. . . if you want to take me out tonight . . .

I've had enough

of Mr. Wrong.

I want to be with Mr. Right.

<u>MAN</u>: There are enough Mr. Wrongs.

Get the Right spray.

I've had enough

of Mr. Wrong.

I want to be with Mr. Right.

<u>SINGER</u>: Mr. Right

Mr. Right

FIGURE 7–8

WIZARD Air Freshener

TITLE: "EXPLOSION"
COMM. NO.: AHWF 3603
AGENCY: YOUNG & RUBICAM NEW YORK

LENGTH: 30 SECONDS
DATE PRODUCED: 8/25/86

(MUSIC: THEME MUSIC THROUGHOUT)
ANNCR: (V/O): The power

of nature's most beautiful fragrances

is recreated in WIZARD® Air Freshener.

Power to get rid of those really tough odors.

(SFX: EXPLOSION)

Power

against ugly odors.

(SFX: EXPLOSION)

Power against lingering odors.

(SFX: EXPLOSION)

Power against really

big odors.

(SFX: EXPLOSION)

The power of WIZARD. It begins with nature.

FIGURE 7-9

CLIENT: COLGATE
PRODUCT: COLGATE PLUS TOOTHBRUSH
TITLE: "ODD LOOKING"

LENGTH: 30 SECONDS
COMM. NO.: CLTB-7013
DATE: JULY 1987

ANNCR: The Colgate Plus toothbrush

meets old square head.

HERO: At first it was hard being the odd looking

toothbrush . . . (LAUGHTER)

But it's my dual bristle design and diamond shaped head . . .

(LAUGHTER)

that helps me clean teeth and massage gums so well.

(LAUGHTER STOPS)

And so comfortably.

No square head could beat that.

So . . .

My neighbor moved out . . .

and . . .

Peggy moved in!

ANNCR: Colgate Plus. The Odd-Looking, Super-Cleaning, Comfy-Feeling toothbrush.

FIGURE 7-10

CLIENT: CADBURY
PRODUCT: CREME EGGS
TITLE: "CLUCKING BUNNY"

LENGTH: 30 SECONDS
COMM. NO.: XSOC 5863
DATE: 9/6/85

ANNCR (VO): You're looking at a very unusual kind of egg, from Cadbury.

That's only around till Easter.

The shell is . . .

pure thick Cadbury's Dairy Milk Chocolate.

But inside sits a sweet, creamy yellow yolk . . .

surrounded by delicious white filling.

Creme Eggs from Cadbury.

Why, they're the best thing to come along since the Easter Bunny.

And when he's gone — they're gone.

FIGURE 7-11

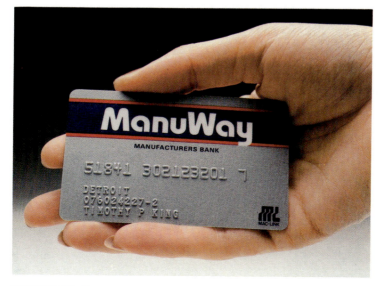

FIGURE 10-5

FIGURE 10-6

FIGURE 10-7

FIGURE 10-8

FIGURE 10–9

FIGURE 10–10

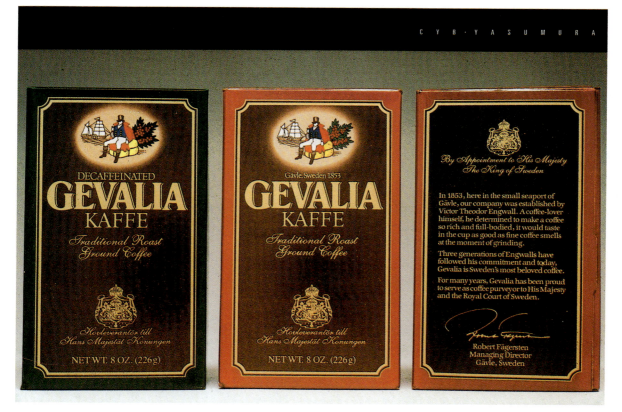

FIGURE 11-2

Telemarketing

By the time of our workshop telemarketing was becoming a major medium for direct marketers. But, not unlike direct mail, it was a medium that our participants knew little about. So we devoted a full day to telemarketing. It started with a field trip to the AT&T state-of-the-art Telemarketing Center in White Plains, New York. Our gracious hosts at AT&T were top sales, marketing, and operations people, including John Wyman, the head man.

They too got the attention of our workshop group with mini case histories.

☐ The story about American Express and its telemarketing program. How sales increased from $29 million to over $200 million within eight years.

☐ The use of an 800 number on Clairol hair-coloring packages, which creates over a half-million calls a year.

☐ How Beech-Nut Nutrition Corporation features a hotline with an 800 number that parents can call to get information on child development, resulting in over 80,000 calls a year.

☐ How White Castle, the hamburger chain, expanded beyond its trading area with an 800 number, selling 50 hamburgers at a crack for $57.00.

☐ The GE Answer Center in Louisville, Kentucky, operating 24 hours a day, 7 days a week, which handles over 2 million prospect and customer phone calls a year.

John Wyman, with whom I later had the privilege of co-authoring a book titled *Successful Telemarketing*,[2] clearly defined the spectrum of Telemarketing applications as a sales continuum. (See Figure 9–5.)

Full Account Management

Consultative Selling

Marginal Account Management

Sales Lead Qualification

Customer Service

Renewals

Seasonal Selling

FIGURE 9–5   Order Taking

[2] *Successful Telemarketing*, by Bob Stone and John Wyman. Copyright 1986 by Young & Rubicam, Inc. Published by NTC Business Books, Lincolnwood, IL 60646.

AT&T

2301 Main Street • P.O. Box 549 • Kansas City, Missouri 64141 • 1 800 821-2121, ext. 626

Dear Executive,

We are pleased to be able to present our special AT&T long distance services in one comprehensive "Business Services Guide."

This gives you the opportunity to review just what the new AT&T is offering. From AT&T Long Distance Service to AT&T Data Services, we bring you the best telecommunications network anywhere.

Our services are designed to help your business grow, and grow with your business, no matter how small or large your company is.

And along with the thorough outline of our services in your enclosed Business Services Guide, we're also offering a free consultation with a professional Consultant, to help you choose the AT&T long distance services that are right for you.

Simply call us toll-free at 1 800 821-2121, ext. 626 to speak to an AT&T Network Consultant.

Our Consultants have worked with businesses of all sizes across the country, so we can help you decide which services make sense for your company. And your Consultant will offer personalized service and advice to help your business use them to cut costs, increase your sales, and help your business grow faster. He or she can even coordinate implementation of the services for you.

So take some time to read through your Business Services Guide. And be sure to contact your Network Consultant at our toll-free number, or mail the enclosed postpaid card, to put these services to work for your business.

Sincerely,

Judy DeVooght

Judy DeVooght
Manager, Network Consultants

FIND OUT HOW YOUR BUSINESS CAN CUT COSTS AND IMPROVE PROFITABILITY WITH AT&T LONG DISTANCE SERVICES

CALL TOLL-FREE

1 800 821-2121, ext. 626

OR MAIL THIS POSTPAID CARD

YES! Please tell me more about AT&T long distance services

Please fill in Phone Number ______

If address is incorrect, fill out information below

Name/Title ______

Company ______

Address ______

City ______ State ______ Zip ______

33U-073

FIGURE 9–6

Wyman put special emphasis upon the application of telemarketing in qualifying sales leads (see Figure 9–6). He also emphasized the possibility of full account management from a telemarketing center for accounts not warranting the expense of personal calls. Not surprisingly, John Wyman pointed out that through telephone screening AT&T consistently identified 20 percent of total leads as high potential. This precious 20 percent was referred to the outside sales force immediately. The chart that follows shows how leads were handled by degrees of potential.

Code	Lead Disposition	Analysis	Follow-up Action	Result
A	High Potential	Refer to outside sales force		
B	Medium Potential	Sell by telephone		
C	Low Potential	Resurface at later date		
D	No Potential	No potential-information seekers		

On the charter bus back to the Harrison Conference Center all the new found knowledge about telemarketing was discussed with enthusiasm. But the day wasn't over. For Rudy Oetting—an international authority on TM—was waiting for us, ready to add to our body of knowledge. He really gave us the nuts and bolts of an efficient, well-mannered telemarketing center. Here are a few of the basics.

□ The average number of *incoming* sales/inquiry calls handled per hour by a telephone sales rep is 12; the average number of phone decision-maker contacts *outbound* is 5 per hour. (Explanation: *incoming* calls are at the buyers' initiative; *outbound* are at the sellers' initiative.)

□ On average, a field salesperson can make 5 to 6 calls a day, 25 to 30 a week; on average a telemarketing salesperson can make 25 to 30 decision-maker calls a day, 125 to 150 a week.

□ Every well-managed telemarketing center has at least 1 supervisor for every 10 telephone sales people. Monitoring and training must be constant.

□ Approximate cost per inbound call for business-to-business is within a range of $2.50 to $5.00; for consumer it drops to $1.50 to $3.00.

□ Approximate cost per outbound call for business-to-business is in a range of $7.00 to $14.00; for consumer the range is $2.50 to $4.00.

□ Telemarketing is often most cost-efficient when used in conjunction with print media, TV, or direct mail. (Example: inquiry by phone or mail, with fulfillment by mail, followed up by phone after receipt of literature.)

A mind-boggling day. Total exhaustion. But—to use an irresistible pun—it rang a lot of bells!

Television

A sure hit for our hardy group was the session on direct response TV, presented by star attraction Les Wunderman. TV was a medium that all attendees felt comfortable with.

For two-and-one-half hours Lester rolled one direct response commercial after the other: *Sports Illustrated*, *Time*, P & G, Time-Life Books, and scores more. The differences between regular TV and direct response TV gradually emerged. Before the session was over, Lester had the "students" actually writing direct response commercials.

The body of knowledge they took with them included the following:

☐ Direct sell commercials usually require 90 to 120 seconds as contrasted to 10 to 30 seconds for regular TV commercials.

☐ Support commercials—supporting another direct response medium— can hype response up to 50 percent with 10's and 30's.

☐ Frequent mention and display of the telephone number—as many as 9 to 12 times—is essential in direct sell commercials.

☐ Products that lend themselves to dramatic demonstration sell best on TV.

☐ Cable direct response commercials often bring responses at lower cost than regular TV, especially when the proposition matches the cable format: a sports offer on an all-sports channel, for example.

☐ Direct response commercials usually pull better during passive viewing time—old movies, for example—than during prime time.

☐ The first quarter of the year, in contrast to general TV, is the strongest for direct response.

☐ TV time is practically never bought at card rates. Experienced direct response media buyers negotiate constantly. They negotiate for late night or fringe time rates, weekend rates, seasonal rates. They also negotiate (ROS) deals, allowing stations to run commercials during unsold time periods and PI deals, agreeing to pay the station a set amount for each inquiry or sale. Their objective at all times is to get inquiries or sales at the lowest possible cost.

The Last Day in Glen Cove

During the two-week intensive workshop in Glen Cove amazing things happened. Camaraderie. Spontaneous laughter. Discussions. Debates. Friendly, but real Y&R competition among problem-solving teams. New friendships among Y&R personnel, both in this country and abroad. And, most important, new knowledge about direct marketing where there was little or none two weeks before.

Excitement ran high the final day in Glen Cove. The entire day was devoted to the five team presentations—each to present direct marketing solutions to the IBM marketing problem. While all teams were allotted free time to work on the problem between formal sessions, they opted to take that time plus endless after-hours "free time" to complete their projects. The desire to "win" was inherent in each.

After watching all five presentations, I felt they were all winners: I was astounded by the direct marketing know-how that surfaced. It was an incredible outcome.

That night we had an awards cocktail party and dinner befitting a superior gathering. (Nobody had more fun than yours truly.)

The Final Curtain

But we had one more event up our sleeves. It was decided, in advance, that instead of everyone dispersing on their own from Glen Cove, New York, we'd make an event out of the departure by busing everyone to Y&R headquarters on Madison Avenue in Manhattan.

We were treated royally by the top executives of Y&R—for some of the people, it was their first visit ever to headquarters. And the highlight for all was an informal address from Alex Kroll—the head man. He invited and fielded any and all questions. His parting message was: "Y&R is committed to direct marketing around the world." Mission accomplished!

THE RESULTS

From a direct marketing standpoint this question must be asked: "Did the Direct Marketing Workshop work?" Another question might rightly be: "Was it worth all the time and money?"

Events that followed indicated the workshop was worth every hour expended and every dollar spent. Questionnaires, requiring no signatures, asked participants to rate every session and to give an overall rating of "poor," "fair," "good," or "excellent." There were no poor or fair ratings. Close to 90 percent rated the workshop as excellent.

Our enrollees from Tokyo proceeded to start a direct marketing division at Dentsu. John Eighmey, whom you met in the very first chapter, moved from research to creative. He was later heard to say, "That workshop changed my life."

Most concrete evidence of success came from knowledge of direct marketing presentations which were made following the workshop by general advertising units of Y&R to such prestigious clients as Kodak and Massey Ferguson. And CMF&Z, a Y&R unit in Cedar Rapids, Iowa, later earned national recognition, winning many awards for its agri-direct marketing.

My own conclusions as to why the workshop worked involved four important points:

1. To warrant a workshop and the time and money involved, objectives must be clearly defined and long-term results must be reasonably expected.

2. Professionally structured workshops developed for one discipline can be successfully adopted to related disciplines.

3. Commitment for a training program must come from the top.

4. Successful training programs go "first class" all the way. Meticulous attention is given to the curriculum, the presenters, the facilities, and the students selected.

CHAPTER CHECKLIST

1. Direct marketers recognize that 80 percent of their repeat business comes from 20 percent of their customer base. They therefore develop data bases that enable them to identify and specifically promote the most profitable segments.

2. The offer is key to direct marketing success. The number one objective of any offer is to overcome human inertia. The objective is best achieved by developing incentives for prompt response.

3. The number one criterion in placing print advertising is to identify publications with a *direct response atmosphere* which indicates a strong propensity among the readers to respond by mail or phone.

4. The fastest way to identify "best ads" is to use "telescopic testing"— testing six, eight, or more different ads in regional editions of one issue of a national publication.

5. There are two major direct response seasons: January through March and August through November.

6. Direct mail is a primary advertising medium for direct marketers. Maximizing direct mail success depends first upon the lists you use, second upon the offers you make, and third upon the copy and graphics you create.

7. Direct response lists will most always outpull compiled lists.

8. Overlays on lists (enhancements), such as life-style characteristics, income, age, marital status, and propensity to respond by mail or by phone, will always improve response.

9. Telemarketing has become a major medium for direct marketers, both inbound and outbound.

10. It isn't unusual at all for 60 percent or more of catalog orders to come in by phone. And the average telephone order is usually 20 percent larger than the average mail order.

11. One of the most successful applications of telemarketing is to use the medium to qualify leads for salespeople, dealers, and distributors. This medium is effective in identifying the most qualified 20 percent of prospects who will account for approximately 80 percent of new customers.

12. Direct sell TV commercials usually require 90 to 120 seconds as contrasted to 10 to 30 seconds for regular TV commercials.

13. The first quarter of the year, in contrast to general TV, is the strongest for direct response.

14. Support commercials—supporting another direct response medium—can hype response up to 50 percent with 10 and 30 second commercials.

15. Direct response TV time is rarely bought at card rates. Experienced buyers consistently negotiate rates, thus effectively decreasing cost per order and cost per inquiry.

. . . .

CHAPTER **10** # Creativity in Design and Sales Promotion

From a CYB
capabilities presentation.

IN TODAY'S CLUTTER, WHAT ARE YOU? . . . Correct identification can roughly be defined as how you want the public to perceive you and your products. Not only through advertising, but through all image elements. Through graphics. Through packages. Through design. It is a delicate measurement. But an immensely important one. It looms increasingly more critical as technology accelerates, brands proliferate, corporations conglomerate. Too often the public is left with a fragmented image of who you are, what you stand for, what you do or sell.

The logotypes shown later in this chapter were designed by Y&R's design subsidiary, CYB, headed by Muts Yasumura. Each one fulfilled a stated purpose and followed a five-step creative process.

The process consists of basic principles similar to those reviewed in previous chapters about creativity in print, TV, and direct response advertising.

Gene Ptachinski, CYB production director, outlined the procedure as follows:

This is the design process **CYB-YASUMURA** uses to resolve design problems in order to help clients to position their product or image within the marketplace. In most cases, the design solution will help to give clients a distinctive edge over competition . . .

    Phase I. Orientation/Audit

    Phase II. Development of Objectives, Strategies, and Criteria

    Phase III. Design Exploration

    Phase IV. Refinements and Extensions

    Phase V. Final Art and Mechanical

Basically, this process means that

    —Initially, we get a detailed briefing and orientation from the client— outlining their interpretation of needs, goals, problems and marketing situation. A discussion of key issues that need to be resolved will be aired, i.e., perceived image characteristics, target audience, etc.

    —A field audit helps to give us a first-hand reaction to the projects/items environment and competition. In this process, we will talk to store managers and other personnel. We will also collect samples of important competitor items (packages, brochures, stationery, etc.).

    —Research (optional) . . . Often, research is used to help guide the design process. It is used to: establish a means by which we can assess the effectiveness of the existing design (if it is a redesign project) and its performance in the marketplace; aid in the formulation of a design strategy; assessing the effectiveness of alternate candidates.

—Before the actual design process (pen to paper) begins, it is critical to establish project criteria and marketing objectives. This will include the input from our orientation, audit and research. These image criteria will guide the creative process and will be used to evaluate the final design solution.

—Then we begin the creative search. We assign a team of designers to explore a choice of concepts based on the marketing and design criteria. Within this process, we will give particular attention to the following: desired image criteria; graphic options; color and typography; nomenclature; miscellaneous elements, i.e., endorsement considerations, existing equities, product descriptors, maintaining a family look, etc.

—We normally develop a wide range of approaches to a specific problem. *It is evaluation of many creative ideas, rather than a few, which assures the most satisfactory results.* The funneling process and cross pollination of ideas is part of our design discipline which leads us to the best single resolution.

—Following approval of the overall concept, the creative process continues with preparation of comprehensives or mock-up, line extensions, adaptation of the design to other elements and/or package sides, creating final artwork and mechanicals, etc. All dependent on the type of design project we are dealing with.

Naturally, each project is individual and requires different needs or steps for its unique specifications. Our usual design projects involve: packaging; corporate identity; environmental concepts; brand identities; marketing literature; miscellaneous, such as posters, special symbols (anniversary celebrations, Olympic), clothing (graphics for application on), etc.

CASE HISTORIES OF THE PROCESS IN ACTION

In design, perhaps more than in any other of the specialties we are discussing, there is no better workshop than to study the objectives and strategies of specific problems and to see the solutions. The following are a few of the CYB case histories, with the explanations presented by CYB in a handsome portfolio for prospective clients.

The expansion and diversification of Gannett in 1979 called for a new corporate signature (Figure 10–1) that would increase public awareness and reflect a broader spectrum of corporate involvement. The comprehensive identification program that was undertaken included analysis of the existing signature and its usage, an in-depth design study, development of a complete graphics standards and applications manual, and assistance in the implementation of key communications elements.

Gannett's new signature became the letter "G" partially superimposed over a strong black and white stylized globe, positioned above the distinctive all-cap Gannett logotype. The signature is intended to convey the dynamic growth of the company and suggest its broad range of communications activities. The symbol became the consistent identifier for

FIGURE 10–1

stationery, advertising, publications, promotional materials, vehicles, outdoor billboards, and even airplanes.

The Insurance Company of America was founded over 200 years ago, and for many years life insurance was the only product the company offered. In the 1970s, growth plans and diversification into a broad range of financial services created the need for a new corporate image and identity.

In designing the new company signature (Figure 10–2), CYB used the corporate initials as a symbol, rendering them in a bold contemporary, stylized fashion, and positioning the corporate name beneath. The strength of the type style reinforces the company's financial soundness and reputation. INA's original blue color was maintained, to provide another link with the company's long and illustrious past.

FIGURE 10–2

A project completed for Sperry Corporation in the early 1970s illustrates how an existing corporate signature can be revised, and its usage redefined, to create a more viable company identifier. (See Figure 10–3.)

FIGURE 10–3

PUERTO RICO

FIGURE 10-4

The revised Sperry signature features an enlarged blue Sperry star and the distinctive Sperry logotype. A horizontal format utilizes the star identifier as a linking device between the parent company and its major divisions, each of which maintains its own stylized logo.

The new corporate identification system increases recognition and awareness by utilizing the Sperry star more effectively, and by emphasizing the relationship between Sperry Corporation and its division.

A comprehensive corporate identification manual provides graphic and color standards and describes the application of the new identity to a variety of communications vehicles.

The Economic Development Administration of Puerto Rico felt that a common identifying symbol was needed to promote Puerto Rico's principal areas of commerce—tourism, industrial development, and rum production. Of primary importance was the selection of an identifier that would be unique to the island. (See Figure 10-4.)

An audit of island landmarks and a review of historical data clearly indicated that La Garita, or Moro Castle, was the symbol most people quickly associated with Puerto Rico.

CYB refined and stylized one of the Moro Castle guard towers, creating a distinctive and contemporary symbol. Two shades of blue—a translation of the blue water and sky—were used to project positive island attributes. The La Garita symbol is used extensively in rum advertising and other promotional efforts for the commonwealth.

The graphics system developed for Manufacturers National Bank of Detroit's new ATM (automatic teller machine) involved the selection of an appropriate name, the design of a new signature, and extension of the ATM identity to signage, brochures, ATM vestibules, and free-standing kiosks in nonbank locations. (See Figure 10-5, color insert.)

Although the ATM product was to be viewed as a separate service within the bank's spectrum of retail services, the name and graphics approach had to be compatible with the bank's corporate identification system, and be applicable to all subsidiary banks.

The distinctive, easy-to-read logotype is presented in white reverse against a banded background which is rendered in the bank's corporate blue. Red stripes on either side of the blue band provide bright, eye-catching color accents.

Package design for Peter Paul Cadbury's new Starbar entry was the result of a dedicated team effort between the company, the design group, and the advertising agency for the brand. The entire project was completed in less than 60 days from start to actual production. (See Figure 10-6, color insert.)

Starbar is a crunchy, chewy, chocolatey candy bar containing peanut butter, peanuts, crisped rice, and caramel, surrounded by a rich milk chocolate coating. CYB's design features a dominant layered logotype that relates to the product's composition. Warm yellows, golds, oranges, and browns reinforce special taste and texture attributes. Graphics are contemporary, lively, and memorable.

The unique Starbar logotype was extended to chipboard shippers, shelf talkers, posters, decals, sales kits, and so on. The design was also adapted to a multipak containing several regular-size bars and a poly bag of miniature Starbar Big Bites.

An evolutionary design program to modernize and upgrade package graphics for Don Q Rum (of the Serrales family distillery) assures that product packaging keeps up with changes in marketing strategy without sacrificing elements that have contributed to brand equity over an extended period of time. (See Figure 10–7, color insert.)

Changes made for Don Q packaging included

- Strengthening the primary identification elements—the Don Q shield and brand name—by rendering these important equities in a more impactful and contemporary form.

- Providing a strong manufacturer's endorsement that incorporates the family crest to reinforce a quality image.

- Adapting a single Don Quixote identifier to give the brand a distinct and promotable personality.

- Simplifying the package to appeal to a younger audience and to capitalize on the trend toward lightness.

- Creating an optimum, future graphic look and providing the evolutionary steps necessary to gradually move from present packaging to the new graphics.

La Yogurt, of Johanna Farms, is a French-style, stirred yogurt made with all natural ingredients and real fruit. The single-serving plastic cup is unique and distinctive, and it relates well in shape and color to the product's milk base. Full-color fruit and berry photographs dominate the package, providing strong appetite appeal. The French tricolor identifies the plain flavor. (See Figure 10–8, color insert.)

Packaging for La Yogurt is a good example of the importance of high-quality design in promoting and selling a new product in today's competitive marketplace.

A "First of Its Kind"; the Masthead for *USA Today*

After two years of planning and research, CYB's directive was to design a dramatic masthead and newspaper layout for the introduction of a nationwide newspaper called *USA Today*. The criteria demanded that the design be distinctive, but be compatible and work with the other sections of the newspaper; reflect *USA Today*'s image as a successful, informative, forward-looking newspaper; be visually attractive and interesting; be easily identified at point of sale; and project a contemporary, friendly, lively, and appealing image to the consumer. (See Figure 10–9, color insert.)

The *USA Today* design solution helped to create a distinct personality for the paper, portraying it as one of the most dynamic, fastest-growing information media in America . . . and now overseas.

Gevalia Coffee

In 1983, General Foods, using direct marketing, introduced Gevalia, a high-priced, specialty Swedish coffee into the United States. Its repackaging was a CYB assignment. (See Figure 10–10, color insert.)

CYB's briefing included the facts about the coffee's origin in Sweden; that country's high appreciation for quality coffee and Gevalia's leadership there; the coffee's fine taste and master blending; the need for packaging that would express an "Old World," imported, quality feeling; the need also for a premium decanter design; and the characteristics of the upscale target audience. Criteria included the use of visuals, color, and graphics to create a strong line identity and to communicate Gevalia's endorsement by the king of Sweden.

For the design exploration, CYB created over 50 design approaches. The preferred design fulfilled the objectives and measured well against a brand personality statement which reflected "Old World money, geared to someone who would probably drive a Rolls-Royce, Mercedes, or Jaguar." The preferred decanter design was classically beautiful, yet served a number of specific functional needs (to accept an expanding vacuum pack insert, facilitate ease in getting the coffee out of the container, etc.).

Through direct marketing, and also distribution in prestigious specialty retail stores, this premium coffee has been successful in America and has expanded for the past five years in terms of line extensions, types of coffee, size offerings, specialty packaging, and promotional offers. And the ultimate appreciation, in CYB's case, was the honor of receiving the International Clio Award for the best single packaging design in the world!

Helping to Solve adidas' Marketing Image Problems

While both Nike and Reebok were gaining prominence, adidas was losing share. Through the designs developed by CYB for its "Art" shirts, a new image has evolved which again places adidas as a leader within the sports marketplace. The textile division business

FIGURE 10–11

tripled over the three years since the designs were created. (See Figure 10–11.)

The Most Exciting Assignment

This story appeared in the summer 1985 issue of the *Young & Rubicam World* magazine. Some of its highlights:

It was a most exciting day when Muts Yasumura . . . was invited to meet with Emery Westfall, vice president of New York Telephone, as well as chairman of the Olympic Fund-Raising Committee. Muts then learned that he and his CYB design team had been chosen to create the USA Olympic Symbol for the 1988 World Olympics in Seoul, Korea.

Over the next weeks this excitement inspired Muts and his team to come up with over 120 designs . . . narrowed down to 16 . . . down to three . . . and then to his recommendation. This new symbol was displayed on letterhead, envelope, business card, flag, uniforms, pins, product tie-ins, advertising tie-ins and television.

There were three major presentations for the recommended design. . . . The third and most important presentation was to the USOC executive director, Colonel F. Don Miller.

That presentation was so well-received and Col. Miller so enthusiastic that champagne was ordered to celebrate! Not only did he agree with Muts' recommendations, but he said, "I want this commercial announcement on the air January 1!"

The article went on to describe how the team scrambled to make the New Year's deadline two and a half weeks away, working through the Christmas holidays and embarking during the first big New York snowstorm for Colorado Springs and the final screening and approval by Col. Miller. They made the air date.

The Olympics still were not over for CYB. After two tough assignments, we were given another three weeks to produce a 12-minute show for over 400 USOC delegates at their Colorado Springs Conference. The concept was to take the "symbol" presentation and create an inspiring multi-media event.

The production was able, dramatically, to show the 120 preliminary designs, the 16 finalists, and the 3 culled from those. It described one as following up on previous USOC symbols, which had been deliberately very traditional. A second was a bold symbol, more applicable to the present. But the third, with its stylized "A," italicized, better predicted movement and energy. It projected the sound of the *"U-S-A! U-S-A! U-S-A!"* at the 1984 Olympics in Los Angeles, when the crowd spontaneously started to chant in unison—and it introduced the new theme, "U.S.A. . . . '88!"

The presentation combined nine slide projectors and synchronized sound and video. The *World* story concluded with this description:

Imagine full theatre sound and a 27-foot screen! The magic of Ray Charles singing "America, the Beautiful"! The tears of the 1984 Olympic Gold Medalists! A new symbol for 1988, Seoul, Korea! A finale with dozens of young Olympic hopefuls wearing the new USA '88 symbol T-Shirt running down three aisles shouting, "USA . . . USA . . . USA!!!" Balloons dropping from the ceiling! Spotlights dancing on an excited crowd suddenly jumping to their feet cheering USA . . . USA! Frank Heffron calling Muts up onto the stage, and Muts presenting the new USA '88 symbol on "special edition" Olympic jackets to the leaders of the USOC . . .

As the lights went up, you could see the tears in the crowd's eyes.

THE ULTIMATE MEANING OF CREATIVITY IN DESIGN

That enthusiastic description, the emotional scene described, and the way *I* was moved when I saw a videotape, on a small screen, of their presentation—something that could only do *scant* justice to what it must have felt like to be there, in the live hall, with the full sound and the giant screens—illustrates how powerful the effect of a design symbol can be.

What *is* symbolism? It is what human communication is all about. Every word you speak, every word in this book, is a *symbol*. A symbol is something that *stands for* "an object, quality, process, quantity, etc., as in music, chemistry, mathematics, etc." (dictionary). We create symbols, and manipulate symbols, all in the hope of being understood and achieving some desired effect about the reality we symbolize.

So the ultimate achievement in design is when a symbol is so right, so expressive, and so compelling that it is instantly recognizable as what it stands for. Just think of the advertising symbols, in your experience, that have made a dominant impression on you, and that are both familiar and clearly defining. When they evoke an emotional response, as with that strong Olympic symbol by CYB, they achieve their highest creative objective.

PROMOTION MARKETING

From *The Whole Egg Catalog*

Promotion marketing is composed of those marketing elements which go beyond the communication of a product's basic function and benefit to the consumer. Included are the traditional disciplines referred to as promotion, merchandising, sales promotion, distributor/trade advertising and allowance programs, incentive marketing, collateral, etc.

Cato Johnson Promotion Marketing firm and Rogers Merchandising, which Y&R acquired, respectively, in 1979 and 1984, helped to round out the agency's move toward "The Whole Egg"—total commercial persuasion capabilities. The specialties of such firms are calculated to make sales through every kind of inducement one can imagine—cents-off couponing, sweepstakes, premiums, point-of-sale displays, design of product packages, and retail outlets.

The Growth of Sales Promotion

While sales promotion had at one time the aspect of complete "borrowed interest" (i.e., any kind of sales inducement, regardless of whether or not it had any relevance to the product or the product context), the attitude of strategic thinking has moved these specialties closer to the methods taught by Y&R at large.

Recognizing the increasing clout of these previously alien disciplines, Y&R at large formed a new unit in 1988, headed by Bill Power, former head of Y&R, Detroit. The training for creativity in these disciplines, for the *advertising* people, would be similar to going to school for direct marketing, a new frontier.

This was especially appropriate since by 1988 the money invested by marketers in sales promotion far exceeded their investment in traditional advertising. According to *Advertising Age* (June 13, 1988),

Marketers spent an estimated $106.7 billion on all aspects of promotional marketing in 1986. Measured media advertising that year was $31.1 billion. . . . In 1987, average gross revenues for full-service promotion agencies rose 28%, while gross income for the top 500 U.S. ad agencies fell 4.6%.

Marketing promotion is a below-the-line collateral service, and most marketers consider it essential to retail sales. In 1981, year of worldwide economic recession, Jim Castling (then chairman and managing director of Cato Johnson in London) explained how this attitude prevails:

One movement that marks the maturity of sales promotion is the fact that it has proven to be one of the last budgets to be cut when the going starts getting tough. Reduce the sales force, by all means; the ones that are left will just have to work a bit longer in the afternoons. You might be able to wing it for another season

without increasing the advertising appropriation. . . . But to pull back funds from in-store off-take incentive is far too great a risk.

Y&R has increasingly cross-ruffed the people in their various specialties, and creative leaders from the parent company have increasingly brought their skills and training to the specialized affiliates. They, in turn, in learning the new disciplines, change their way of doing their jobs:

There are two quite disparate abilities which, somehow, need to be combined in any person likely to succeed in sales promotion: the imaginative capacity to conceive new solutions to problems hitherto thought to be fully plumbed; and the knack of making things happen, exactly according to plan, at the appointed moment.

The Major Difference Between Sales Promotion and Traditional Advertising

Alan Zweibel, executive creative director of Cato Johnson, was one of the Y&R generalists who moved into a specialized affiliate job. He explains the basic difference:

I always worked, for twenty years at Y&R, on essentially long-term image enhancement of products or services. Over the course of a period of time, the commercials or ads would give the consumer a warm feeling with, hopefully, the motivation to buy the product when they were in the market for something of that nature.

The business I'm in now is much more short-term oriented—we're looking for a relatively immediate behavioral change as opposed to a long-term perceptual change.

In a perfect world, they work together. The stuff that Y&R does makes a person feel good about something, hopefully what we do here at Cato is to make them go out and buy it *now*.

Creatively, Try to Marry the Two Disciplines   How do you make the sale *now* and still uphold the image? Says Alan Zweibel:

The ideal combination is that what we do should not in any way detract from the overall positive perception of the product. Too much sales promotion is so driven that they will do anything to get action from the consumer, frequently at the terrible cost of ruining the long-term perception of the brand. Like, if you have a Johnson & Johnson, who for fifty years have been doing the most wonderful kind of advertising, which has gotten them a place in the consumer's mind as being high quality, pure products for your baby's needs, it would be destructive if you had to move a lot of Johnson baby powder in a particular week to do a slashing price with no attention paid to the fact that people are glad to pay a higher price because of the J & J quality.

What you hopefully do is to offer an added value—get Johnson Baby Powder this week and also get a new baby scale or a free special non-allergenic bathing cloth or something. It gives the consumer an added value, but it doesn't detract from the worth of the product.

A lot of promotion suffers from the fact that it's destructive to the brand even though it may be temporarily helpful to the bottom line.

Two Contrasting Examples   Alan cited antipodal examples of automobile promotion:

General Motors last year gave 1.9 financing. They sold a lot of cars, but what it said to the public was that a GM car must have some inferiority—it's not worth what you're asked to pay at real cost. The image of a General Motors product had to suffer in a firesale atmosphere.

Another car manufacturer, Peugeot, instead of cutting *price,* gave *their* customers a free cellular phone, which ran about a thousand dollars. So the buyer is getting a thousand dollars worth of extra value, and it did not cheapen the car. It said, this is a good car, we know what kind of person you are, and we are going to give you something extra to complement the kind of business you do, the kind of driving you do.

That's smart promotion, that's integrated intelligently, it supports the brand without destroying the image.

Promotion at Point of Sale

Sales promotion is most on its mettle in what I called, in my previous book, *The Last Chance Medium.* Says Alan:

It's very, very competitive, because you're not in the context of a magazine or a TV show—you're in the final decision-making arena, you're at the supermarket, you're in the store, you're approaching the shelf. So the tools that are available are constantly being invented. Now they have advertising on shopping carts, they have video on top of the aisles, they even have it at the checkout counter. . . . There are talking shelves and electronic coupon redemptions, which change the nature of cents-off promotion. Technology will probably have a bigger role to play in our business than it will in advertising.

How the Sales Promotion and Merchandising Firms Work

Cato Johnson describes the scope of its activities as follows:

Proprietary Products . . . We offer promotional concepts or services to the industry at large. Although tailored to a specific level or segment of commerce, the service is offered to all companies. For example, The Money Page (TM) is a run-of-press, best-food-day, cooperative-newspaper-couponing medium offered to all packaged goods manufacturers and distributors . . .

Promotion Marketing Plans. On a contractual basis, we develop, implement and evaluate promotion marketing plans for clients . . . In providing this service, Cato, Johnson recognizes that effective promotion marketing plans require strategic and creative development and judicious blending of various elements in order to motivate target audiences.

Rogers Merchandising calls itself "The Agency for Retail Action." In merchandising itself, the company stresses its specialties as follows:

Because consumers are now making 80% of purchase decisions and 65% of brand decisions in-store, marketing at the store level is essential. Rogers fills this critical need with our expertise in store level merchandising.

The focal point of our work is to extend product positionings through the planning, tactics and media we employ. At Rogers, we advocate merchandising as a means to enhance your advertising and brand positioning. This is in distinct contrast with traditional promotional thinking where the focus is placed on "buy this, get this."

The new wave in sales promotion is called *micromarketing*, to describe the narrowly targeted possibilities of today's sales promotion:

To profile store level trading areas, Rogers has created the FUSION (TM) micromarketing system for database planning, production and fulfillment.

For planning, the FUSION system uses U.S. Census data, psychographic data and product usage to zero in on what factors affect purchase decisions, and what message appeals most to customers of a particular store location.

For production, the FUSION system can personalize store materials economically. For fulfillment, the FUSION database driven distribution system ships the right materials to the right locations.

Learning by Example

The Y&R training method, of teaching by inspiration and example, provides promotional people with an ever-growing resource of successful case histories. The following are a few such examples from Cato Johnson:

The Fine Art of Great Desserts This promotion was designed to encourage food service personnel to use General Foods products to make "ambitious-looking" desserts. Ingredients: a dessert trade ad and a richly illustrated recipe booklet.

Aspiring food service personnel called an 800 number for the recipe book, and the ad won "highest response ever" in the *Restaurants and Institutions* magazine.

A Joint Lipton-Disney Promo Says Zweibel, "This Lipton/Disney promotional idea got seven brand managers at Lipton to agree on something, and the lucky kid got a customized birthday card (thanks to computer laser printing) on his or her birthday. Tickets to Snow White and Disneyland were also part of the promotion. Most successful and both Y&R clients happy."

A Promotional Sales Film Sales promotion takes many forms. Cato Johnson produced a short sales film for General Foods food service division promoting a $5,000 coffee maker. The low-budget film cost only $18,000 complete. But it had such a powerful product demonstration that it was highly successful as a sales tool and also won a 1988 Gold ADDY award.

3 DWAZE DAGEN   Sales promotion doesn't have to be only the purview of the sales promotion specialists. The Amsterdam office of Y&R staged a tumultuously successful promo for a retail client using a series of newspaper teaser ads. As reported in *Young and Rubicam World 19*:

De Bijenkorf Department Store in Amsterdam wanted to change its image from an exclusive, expensive, and luxury-class store into a lifestyle department store where everybody can buy beautiful fashion and trendy items for reasonable prices.

Y&R Amsterdam was called in to introduce and support an event called "Three Crazy Days." At a totally unexpected moment, for three days only, there would be remarkable sales.

Our challenge was to create an event that would become an institution for the store, generate an additional 50 percent turnover, and attract new customers. The timing of Three Crazy Days was unexpected for both customers and competition.

Through a teaser campaign (four ads on Monday, four ads on Tuesday), we attracted customers' attention by wrapping the promoted items in yellow plastic. The same was done in-store until the day of revelation. The suspense was mounting. On Wednesday we ran an ad with five different Bijenkorf buildings wrapped up in yellow plastic. Headline: "Tomorrow, Holland's craziest department store will be revealed." Thursday, the revelation ad. Friday and Saturday, reminders.

The campaign was a huge success. There were 600,000 customers in three days (a normal weekly average is 400,000). There was an additional turnover of 5 million florins. Spontaneous free publicity in national newspapers. Traffic jams. And a very happy client!

International Sales Promotion Coordination

Until the 1980s, sales promotion activities were largely contained by national borders. But as the European Common Market became more of a reality, more and more manufacturers wanted to promote their products in countries other than their own—as often as possible on a transnational basis.

Cato Johnson, at the time, was perhaps the only sales promotion company in Europe able to handle such an assignment. As reported in "The Whole Egg Catalog":

True international sales promotion has to take account of the detailed and complex laws and regulations that apply in each country. So, although coordination of such activities has to be handled centrally from a single office, it can be effectively carried out only with tangible and reliable facilities on the spot in each market.

One manufacturer who recently entered Europe with its products is Clorox International. It wanted to promote sales of its product, Twice As Fresh, in several

European countries at the same time; but it wanted, also, as far as possible, to avoid unnecessary marketing costs and duplication of effort market-by-market.

Cato Johnson, in concert with Young & Rubicam in London, mounted sales promotion activity for Twice As Fresh in the United Kingdom, Italy, and France:

Although sales promotion laws vary enormously country-by-country in the European Economic Community, Clorox wanted to find a single promotion technique which could be used in several countries. It selected money-off couponing but found that, even on such a simple sales promotion mechanism, each country requires widely differing inclusions and administrative provisions.

Reporting to the Coordinating Director, Kerry O'Connor in the London office, each Cato Johnson office provided the necessary detailed information to make the international action legal country-by-country. In addition to the consumer off-take promotion, Cato Johnson also handled trade communications activity, sales force briefings, collateral material and an impressive audiovisual program to introduce the new product to the wholesale and retail trade in each country. Cato Johnson was also responsible for adapting established American material, such as the package design and sleeve, for use in Europe. English material was translated into appropriate languages, and a strict reporting and evaluation system was set up between the headquarters of Clorox International in London, and Cato Johnson, the London coordinating office. . . .

This work could be of great interest to other potential entrants to the European market for packaged goods. A complete case history presentation exists in London.

Some Rogers Examples of Creativity

All of the following Rogers' case histories, like those of Cato Johnson, show how sales promotion can go beyond the mere expedient of offering cents-off to make a sale. In other words, the promotions are firmly based not just on coupons and discounts but on creative *ideas*.

A Multibrand Promotion   General Foods was interested in testing whether local-market, multibrand promotion was effective for gaining higher levels of retail display support and increased product movement in Denver. Rogers arranged a tie-in with the Denver Broncos football team and the Denver Broncos Youth Foundation. They then developed a strategically integrated promotional program involving a consumer sweepstakes, community events with Bronco players in attendance, Broncos coloring book self-liquidator, and a citywide Halloween party fundraiser.

Denver residents were exposed to promotional messages an average of 14 times during the six week event.

As a result, sales movement for all 15 brands combined showed a double-digit increase versus the national average.

A Continuity Promotional Program over a Long Period   After divestiture of its operating companies, AT&T sought a continuity program to increase brand awareness, differentiate the brand, and minimize switching to other long-distance carriers.

Rogers executed "AT&T Opportunity Calling," a value-added promotion that gave customers discounts on merchandise based on the dollar amount of their long-distance calls.

A big plus to the national promotion was the development of "local guides" packed with discount offers from local merchants for shopping, dining, and recreation. Rogers' Field Marketing Organization sold in the promotion to over 5,000 participating retailers and restaurants in 63 markets.

During the four years of the program, the number of local supplements grew each year, a tribute to the popularity, effectiveness, and success of localization.

AT&T Opportunity Calling was targeted to more than 22 million consumer households. And most important, AT&T judged the program successful in meeting their objectives by retaining over 70 percent of their base.

"Relationship Marketing"   Miller Lite beer, as the light beer category matured, wanted to communicate with their key consumers in a more "light adult" manner. Rogers created a relationship marketing vehicle enabling Miller to speak directly to its customers: the Lite Beer Athletic Club (LBAC). The club merchandised the equity in Miller Lite's phenomenally successful television commercials.

Each club member received a welcome letter from Lite all-star and self-appointed club president Bob Uecker, a membership card, certificate, decal, and a subscription to LBAC magazine.

The magazine supported local market activities such as Pro Beach Volleyball and the NFL Lineman of the Year program.

National Advertising in Merchandising Display   "It takes much more than another coupon drop or price promotion to 'make it' at retail," says a Rogers house promotion piece. "Retailers are taking the lead in creating promotions; manufacturers are 'buying' participation rights. Slotting allowances have become a way of life, especially for new products. Now, store 'rate cards' for in-store merchandising space are beginning to appear." An example of a "goofproof" merchandising display was for Greensweep liquid ready-to-use lawn and garden products.

Having obtained the rights as the official lawn and garden products for Disneyland, the company needed a way to leverage the Disney relationship to meet retail distribution and display goals.

Psychographic research revealed that target consumers were family oriented, not particularly interested in lawn work and gardening as hobbies, and wanted to minimize risk in selecting new products.

The magic of Disney came alive with an effective in-store 5-foot display. And that creative approach, just as it might have been for a general advertising campaign, was driven by a *strategic* positioning; that is, Greensweep was portrayed as so reliable, simple, and effective, even Goofy couldn't goof.

Customizing a Program in Incentive Marketing   "What do you need?" asked the Rogers promotion brochure. "Increased sales? Improved safety records? New accounts? Cost reductions? Achieving quotas? Increased productivity? You name it, we customize a program for the need."

Midas Mufflers and Rogers launched an aggressive multitiered incentive program aimed at promoting teamwork among shop employees. Prizes were awarded to all installers if the entire shop met its installation target.

For a different customized need, Rogers developed a safety incentive program aimed at Illinois Central Railroad employees. Customization included an award catalog with prizes appealing to specific interests of those employees.

Rogers also handled the database maintenance of the program, and the projected savings provided Illinois Central with a 10-to-1 return on investment.

The Right Display for the Right Store   Today, with consumers making most purchase decisions in store, and with the sophisticated micromarketing systems, displays can be customized just as magazine ads are, with specific messages for the specific interests of a store's customers.

adidas had won the bidding war for rights to basketball star Patrick Ewing, and the display featured the Ewing locker, constructed from a chrome steel frame with a silk-screened plexiglass locker door. The apparel/shoe rack displayed the Ewing line in a minimum of floor space. Working in tandem with the locker was the molded plastic ceiling dangler simulating a rim and net and a life-size free-standing display of Ewing in action.

Data Base Distribution: A High-Tech Edge   One of the key components of Rogers' FUSION micromarketing system is proprietary software and systems for directing all forms of fulfillment. These include the distribution of point-of-sale displays, administration of sweepstakes and contests, handling huge volumes of rebates, continuity and gift certificate programs, and localizing chapters for increasing membership interest in clubs.

An example was the strategy, idea, and followthrough of a premium program for Burger King's young customers.

Kids were a tremendous market for Burger King, with an average purchase frequency of nearly once a week. The competitive problem, however, was that they preferred McDonald's by a 3-to-1 ratio.

Rogers' strategy focused on the use of premiums to build purchase continuity. The complete program featured a different free premium every other week, supported by advertising on Saturday morning TV.

After the planning and creative execution, Rogers was responsible for sourcing, purchasing, warehousing, and distributing the premiums for the thousands of BK restaurants. Average store sales increased by 15 percent. And children's preference for Burger King equaled McDonald's in just six months.

The New and Improved Accountability of Sales Promotion

In 1987, Douglas F. Haley, director of Market Information for the Nestlé Food Corporation, described the advances in sales promotion sophistication, at a promotion conference in New York:

I believe we're at a special and exciting moment in marketing measurement: a time when the opportunity presents itself for theory to become translated into practice. This is occurring through a fortunate juxtaposition:

- of marketplace pressure, through increases in promotion spending

- of improvements in sales measurement, through weekly scanner data linked with weekly in-market measurement of causal data

- of improved consumer behavior measurement, through consumer purchase panels, some of which are linked directly to specific store activities

- of truly exciting advances in data processing technology, in the form of increased computer processing powers and database technology to make this information accessible to marketing decision-makers

- of modeling capabilities, and the capacity to actually validate models with empirical data

Haley went on to describe the management problem in the past of constantly having to balance the short-term *tactical* promotion spending with long-term *strategic* advertising spending. Now, with the measurements available, marketers are discovering that promotions and advertising are not mutually exclusive, that "there are such things as franchise-building promotions."

Haley reviewed ten major trends in the promotion industry:

1. Promotion proliferation

2. Scanner data

3. Increased retailer power and sophistication

4. Scanner data services

5. Decreasing response time

6. Data processing technology, decision support systems

7. Market response modeling

8. Increased consumer sophistication

9. Shifts in marketing structures

10. Event marketing

Sales Promotion's Position Today

Like direct marketing, sales promotion was, until recently, neglected by the large advertising agencies and considered a necessary evil by marketers. It was generally considered a form of purchasing customers rather than *creatively persuading* them. Now, as more and more agencies rush to acquire sales promotion companies and retail outlets more closely resemble advertising media, it is obvious that sales promotion has come of age and should inspire more imaginative ideas and *training for creativity.*

· ·

CHAPTER CHECKLIST
· ·

DESIGN
· · · · · · · · · · · · · · · · · · ·

1. "What are you?" . . . an increasingly important question for a company to ask and for design to interpret to the consumer.

2. The five phases of a design project: orientation, development of objectives and strategy, exploring many designs, refining choices, final production.

3. To learn by example, study how design solved a variety of problems: for expansion and diversification at Gannett and INA; for a common corporate ID system at Sperry and for Puerto Rican commerce; for a bank's ATM; and for products as diverse as candy, rum, yogurt, coffee, a national newspaper, and the Olympic symbol.

4. The highest goal of design is for a symbol to evoke instant recognition and positive emotional response.

PROMOTION MARKETING
· · · · · · · · · · · · · · · · · · ·

1. Clients invest more in promotion marketing than in advertising.

2. Major difference between advertising and promotion marketing: the former to achieve a long-term favorable image, the latter immediate short-range sales.

3. Ideally, the two would work in tandem. The sales promotion will combine favorably with the image building, never detract from it.

4. Sales promotion at the point of sale is increasingly competitive, needs constant innovation—the latest being technological.

5. Successful case histories include a recipe book promo for General Foods, customized birthday cards in a Lipton/ Disney promo, a low-budget, high-result sales film for General Foods, an amusing teaser promotion for a major Dutch retailer, the complex overseeing of an international sales promotion for Clorox—from Cato Johnson—and from Rogers Merchandising: a multi-brand promotion for General Foods, an AT&T continuity program, relationship marketing for Miller Lite beer, merchandising displays for a garden product and sports apparel, employee incentive marketing, the data base distribution of young people's premiums (Burger King).

6. With improved accountability through scanner data and other high-tech data processing, sales promotion in retail outlets can come closer to creativity in advertising media.

· ·

CHAPTER **11** Creativity in Public Relations

Harold Burson,
Founder and Chairman of
Burson-Marsteller

In my view, the definition of public relations is simple—even if the implementation is not. Public relations is any effort to influence opinion—to influence the attitudes of people. . . . You can do three things to public opinion. You can try to change it, if it suits your purpose to do so; you can try to create new opinion, where none exists; or you can reinforce an existing opinion.

Public relations has the same basic purpose as advertising—to *communicate*: to communicate about a company, about its employees, about its finances, and about its products or services.

The major difference, however, between advertising and the oldest and most familiar tool of public relations—publicity—is that you *buy* space or time for the advertising, while for publicity *you don't pay the media* for the stories you hope they will run.

Creating effective advertising is a great skill. It teaches you a lot about communication because it's the only form of communication where you have an involuntary, sometimes antagonistic, audience. You're most often in a borrowed medium, and you have to compete with the editorial content for attention, as well as with the competitive advertising.

But publicity, in some respects, is an even greater skill, because you're asking the media to give you space or time in their precious commodity, to run your releases and tell positive stories about you without payment. To do that, you must constantly convince experienced editors and broadcasters that what you have to say about your client is news*worthy*. If you can do that successfully . . . well, you're a man, my son.

Burson-Marsteller has done that successfully for more than 35 years. In addition, it's expanded its communications tools beyond publicity. In doing so, it has become the world's largest public relations firm. If you are interested in this special form of communication, therefore, you can't find better guidance than to see the way Burson-Marsteller goes about its business.

HOW TO BE A SUCCESSFUL PUBLIC RELATIONS COMPANY

The first requisite is to organize for success. Remember the five guides, in Chapter One, for achieving the ideal environment for creativity

☐ Have a high goal.

☐ Cultivate a company culture.

☐ Provide constant incentives.

Our Vision...

Burson-Marsteller has embarked on an adventure in communications...A journey without end; but one with a distinct destination.

We seek to build the most exciting counseling and communications organization in the world, adding new dimensions to the meaning of public relations and public affairs. The process is never ending; as the world changes, we will change with it. The only constant is our dedication to excellence in thought and deed.

The premises that drive us are simple but challenging. The consulting and communications organization that will rise above all others will be the one most relevant to the broadest range of client needs. It will be knowledgeable, strategically sound, but never timid...Efficient, executionally thorough, but never dull...Always reaching out to cross new frontiers.

We exist solely to serve our clients. Our client focus demands that we remain flexible, organic and dynamic so that we can apply our best resources to each client problem, program and project.

Ultimately, to be successful, we must be valued by our clients as true business partners, providing superior counsel and services that not only meet but anticipate their needs. We will not, however, allow client satisfaction to lead to complacency.

We recognize that there are no absolutes in our world... That we have no monopoly on people or product. We remain restless with what is, searching always for what could be. We will constantly seek out the best talent, the freshest ideas, the broadest concepts, the newest perspectives in our efforts to enhance our value to our clients.

Ours is a global business. It demands that we work to a single standard of excellence worldwide. We will build the systems and harness the technology that will give all our people, anywhere in the world, equal access to our knowledge, experience and skills.

Quality, innovation and value...Sensitivity to our clients and to each other...High energy, high reward...Impatience with the status quo...A willingness to take risks... Compulsive curiosity...These are our guideposts. And, while our destination will always be before us, it is absolutely essential we make the journey.

Burson·Marsteller
Imagination With Substance. Execution With Style.

Our Values...

We believe the most significant factor contributing to our company's progress has been an instinctive adherence to a unique set of values—rarely articulated, but always understood by our most successful people. Ours is a demanding business. High energy, hard work, even a high threshold of pain are constants at Burson-Marsteller. Given the pressures of our extraordinary growth, there is little room for any other kind of behavior. Beyond this, though, we admire certain qualities:

ACHIEVEMENT
The common thread that propels our most successful people is the constant need to excel, to achieve personal and professional goals beyond the expected norm. Our people are known for their results orientation. They are tireless in striving for real impact on their clients' businesses, for demonstrable value. They seek to define the real problem, develop the real solution, no matter what the obstacles or the personal sacrifices required.

TEAMWORK
Ours is a multi-disciplinary business. Sound strategy and creative execution require diverse talents to work in unison. B-M people realize that individual success depends on cooperation and support. We prize the individual, but celebrate the team.

COMMITMENT
We are profoundly committed to the goal. Our people let no obstacles interfere with the fulfillment of their responsibilities. We hold true to our word. Clients and colleagues alike can count on us.

CURIOSITY
B-M people are inherently uncomfortable with the traditional. They recognize there is no such thing as a single, correct perspective on any issue or problem...That today's absolute truth is often tomorrow's folkstory. They welcome new knowledge, new insights, new ideas, no matter the source. At Burson-Marsteller, ideas have no rank, no country of origin. While the company endeavors to train and grow its people, we firmly believe the ultimate responsibility for personal growth is up to the individual.

SHARING
B-M people are quick to share information, knowledge and experience. All of us, at any given moment, are students, teachers or mentors. Our instinct is to accept all who wish to contribute; to reject those who would try to use knowledge as power. We hold mutual respect for our clients, peers, subordinates and superiors. We accept blame individually. We share credit collectively.

RISK
We encourage prudent risk. We reject the notion that if it hasn't been done, it won't work. If we think it's right, we want to do it. And we will fight for the opportunity.

FIGURE 11-1

☐ Engage in perpetual self-renewal.

☐ Provide the best possible tools and training.

Burson-Marsteller is an excellent case history of how well those guides work.[1]

Burson-Marsteller expresses its goal and culture with its "Vision and Values" statement in Figure 11-1. The footline of its logo summarizes the overall goal: "Imagination with Substance. Execution with Style."

[1]Information, quotations, and case histories in this chapter are courtesy of Burson-Marsteller.

Quoting from the vision part of the statement:

Burson-Marsteller has embarked on an adventure in communications. . . . A journey without end; but one with a distinct destination.

We seek to build the most exciting counseling and communications organization in the world, adding new dimensions to the meaning of public relations and public affairs. The process is never ending; as the world changes, we will change with it. The only constant is our dedication to excellence in thought and deed. . . .

We exist solely to serve our clients. Our client focus demands that we remain flexible, organic and dynamic so that we can apply our best resources to each client problem, program and project.

The statement expresses six values which make up the company's culture:

□ Achievement ("The common thread that propels our most successful people is the constant need to excel.")

□ Teamwork ("Ours is a multi-disciplinary business. . . . We prize the individual, but celebrate the team.")

□ Commitment ("We are profoundly committed to the goal. Our people let no obstacles interfere with the fulfillment of their responsibilities.")

□ Curiosity ("B-M people are inherently uncomfortable with the traditional. They recognize there is no such thing as a single, correct perspective on any issue or problem.")

□ Sharing ("B-M people are quick to share information, knowledge and experience. All of us, at any given moment, are students, teachers or mentors.")

□ Risk ("We encourage prudent risk. We reject the notion that if it hasn't been done, it won't work. If we think it's right, we want to do it. And we will fight for the opportunity.")

Like Y&R, Burson-Marsteller offers employees a wide range of incentives to do good work and to enjoy doing it. They have the same restless spirit for positive change, and their tools and training, as I shall describe, are extensive.

The two companies couldn't have been a better fit when, in 1979, having been approached for acquisition by nine of the ten largest advertising agencies, Harold Burson and the late Bill Marsteller chose to join the Y&R family.

WHAT A SUCCESSFUL PUBLIC RELATIONS FIRM DOES

The organization has three broad categories of client services: corporate/institutional communications, consumer marketing communications, and to aid those two functions, communication services.

The company's guide to client services, the Resource Guide, describes these three functions:

CORPORATE/INSTITUTIONAL COMMUNICATIONS

A corporation has many broad constituencies beyond its customers. Each of these groups has special interests that can be crucial to the company's well-being.

The issues are based on ideas and values, and range from environmental concerns to business ethics or safety in the workplace, corporate culture, foreign trade, product safety, financial stability or trade with South Africa.

The list is endless and constantly changing, providing Burson-Marsteller with new missions.

MARKETING SUPPORT: CONSUMER MARKETING

Public relations support for the marketer used to mean strictly product publicity, but today our efforts go far beyond the press release.

We combine sound strategic planning, a broad range of specialists in marketing, merchandising and communications and the world's largest network of resources to offer clients a unique capability. We work at all levels of the sales and distribution system, stimulate interest in product or service, build traffic and generate excitement at the point of sale.

COMMUNICATIONS SERVICES

Research. The aim of the research department is to apply knowledge to client programs, to create more effective new business presentations, to develop basic strategy for communications programs, to provide answers to tactical questions, to refine messages, and to diagnose effectiveness.

International Liaison. The international liaison office acts as the bridge between B-M offices worldwide and international client activities. Any project that goes beyond the borders of a single country, even a routine assignment, is coordinated through the New York-based department.

New Communications Technologies. Cable, home video, computer-based systems like videotex and interactive discs—this group keeps up with all the new communications technologies. Re-established at B-M in 1985 after its launch at Y&R in 1983, NCT counsels clients and account teams on opportunities and new electronic media techniques.

Media. Media services provide counsel and direct media contact for clients around the world, in print and broadcast media.

Design. The Burson-Marsteller approach to design is referred to as Design by Objectives™ and applies to all communications—visual and verbal, packaging and positioning, corporate names and trademarks. Its focus is on developing design solutions that meet clear-cut objectives—a far less subjective process than is usually associated with design.

Burson-Sant'Andrea Productions. Sophisticated and creative audio-visual communications for clients' employees and customers. Services range from production of a single slide to orchestration of complex, week-long meetings, seminars, and expositions.

Communications Training. Helps clients become more effective communicators—in group presentations, one-on-one meetings, trade or consumer print interviews, broadcast media interviews, speeches, internal and external presentations.

THE PUBLIC RELATIONS TRAVELING CREATIVE WORKSHOPS

Burson-Marsteller has extensive, ongoing training for its 2,000 employees in 40 offices and 20 countries, with the objective to maintain a single standard of excellence worldwide.

Training begins with the orientation seminar, covering the company's "people needs," its resources, and how those resources are shared for client service and the development of B-M people. Like Y&R, the company holds regular worldwide and regional seminars, and videotapes and scripts from the central department train the trainers in local offices. The core activities are the "World Class Series," which cover such subjects as

☐ Creative Democracy. How to run a creative brainstorming session.

☐ Presenting to Win. Discusses and demonstrates presentation skills.

☐ Prospecting for Growth. A participative exercise in "prospecting" or "mining."

☐ Information Building. Emphasizing the need for public relations programs to be information driven and how best to go about it.

☐ Client Relations. How to achieve the best possible agency-client collaboration.

In addition to these "World Class" seminars, and periodic comprehensive seminars, there is an important writing workshop, which I shall discuss shortly.

The World Class workshops have a unique format, which is highly participatory. They show verbatim enactments of simulated situations in which key B-M executives play the roles of clients and public relations counselors. They deliberately show negative as well as positive situations and use periodic pauses in the role-playing situations when the workshop participants discuss and critique the actions.

To give you the flavor of these dramas, here are verbatims from one of eight scenes in the World Class "Client Relations" seminar:

DESCRIPTION OF SCENE 5 FOR SESSION LEADER

An account executive (AE) discovers that a story placed on behalf of a client mistakenly identifies the president of the company as the manager of marketing services.

Discussion leaders please note the following:

- Focus discussion on the AE's general attitude toward the client as well as on solving this problem situation.

SCRIPT OF SCENE 5: "A MISTAKE IN THE MEDIA"

SUZANNE: Good morning! That's a pretty scarf!

JUDY: Thank you! You're bright and early today.

SUZ: Yes, I want to write the call report on yesterday's meeting before the phones start to ring. I think it's going to be a busy day.

JUDY: Did you see the *Business Times* this morning?

SUZ: Not yet. Do we have a placement?

JUDY: Well, which do you want first, the good news or the bad news?

SUZ: Oh, no. Give me the good news first. It's much too early for bad news.

JUDY: Well, the good news is that your client Treadwell is one of the companies interviewed for that roundup article on import-export duties. Remember when the publication called last week? Well, they wrote a major story, all right. And they quoted Mr. Barksdale, Mr. Rudy, and Debbie Cooper extensively.

SUZ: That *is* good news. I think I'll phone Mr. Barksdale on the stroke of nine.

JUDY: Yeah. Congratulations.

SUZ: Uh-oh. What's the bad news?

JUDY: (unfolding newspaper) Take a look at the photo.

SUZ: Great! They used our portrait shot of Jim Barksdale.

JUDY: But look at the caption. They didn't identify him as J. Barksdale, chairman. They identified him as D. Cooper, manager of marketing services.

(There is a moment of stunned silence.)

SUZ: I don't know who's going to feel worse about this—me, Mr. Barksdale, or Debbie Cooper. What do you think we ought to do?

(STOP TAPE)

SESSION LEADER'S GUIDE FOR SCENE 5

Q: How serious is this problem?

A: It's more of an embarrassment than a crisis situation; nevertheless, it requires immediate attention.

Q: What can the AE do at this point?

A: • Call the client immediately and explain the problem. He will appreciate hearing about it from the agency rather than discovering it for himself.

• Offer to find out if corrections can be made in time for other editions.

Q: What can be done to prevent this type of situation from occurring?

A: • Closer contact with the media. The AE wasn't even aware that the story was running that morning.

• Stricter supervision of photo releases, making sure they are properly captioned and the captions are securely attached to the photos.

Such an enactment is part of the training process in all the World Class workshops. Here are some of the lessons taught in the sessions.

Information Building

This workshop emphasizes the need for public relations programs to be information driven. It shows two account handlers presenting an annual program, their third year with this client. The presentation is a failure because the program is not knowledge based. The executives return to the office, where they discuss the presentation with the director of research, who guides them on how to do their homework in the future. The support papers include the following two checklists for thorough information gathering.

MARKETING COMMUNICATIONS AUDIT FORM

I. *MARKETING SITUATION*

   A. *Sales Analysis*

• What have sales been the past two years?

• What is your sales forecast for the next two years?

• What accounts for the increase? Decrease?

• What is being done about that?

• How many of your customers (both in numbers and by percentage) account for 80 percent of your business?

• If 80 percent of your business is from 20 percent of your audience, are monies and efforts being proportionally allocated?

- What about geographic trends?

    Is business concentrated in a limited number of markets?

    Are your efforts taking this into account?

    Are there market trends? i.e., Should we begin to "plant seeds" in growing markets?

- What about seasonally?

    Is your product seasonal?

    Does that create problems?

    How are you solving those problems?

    Can you help flatten the demand curve?

B. *Your Reputation in the Market*

- What is your product's reputation?

- What is your reputation in terms of service?

- What is your corporate reputation?

- Does your reputation need refining? Building?

- How do you communicate the reputation you want?

- Do you know its effectiveness?

C. *Current Promotional Mix*

- Items in this mix:

    Personal selling

    Advertising

    Public relations

    Trade shows

- Is the current mix right? How do you know?

- Has the mix changed over the years as market conditions have changed?

- How do you see the mix changing in the near future?

- What is the goal of each promotional item?

- Does everyone agree on those goals?

D. *Increasing Sales*

- Increased sales will come from

    Expanding markets

    New markets

    Broader line, new products

    Greater use of product

    Competition

- What is being done to secure these increased sales?
- What are you doing to support that effort?

E. *Your Competition*

- Who are your primary competitors?
  national? regional?
- Have you identified your own "unique selling proposition(s)?"
- What is your competition's "USP"?
- Compare your own strengths, weaknesses across the board to those of your competitors.
- How are you communicating those strengths?

II. *MARKET*

A. Audiences—Who are they?

- Primary
- Secondary
- Tertiary

B. *Audience Segmentation*

- Who are the influences in each audience category?
- How is each being addressed?
- How are you reaching the key decision makers?

C. *Audience Needs*

- What are the needs of each audience?
- What do they look to you for?
- How do you know their needs?
- What are their current problems, if any, in terms of product, service, and so on?
- What's each audience's hot button in terms of accepting your product? Your service?
- How does each of your audience's needs match up with your own marketing objectives?

D. *Purchasing Factors*

- How does the purchase develop?
- Is the purchase considered or impulse?
- How do your communications take this into account?

- Are you addressing the influence of a middleman (e.g., retailer, dealer, distributor)?

E. Brand Loyalty

- Why is your brand purchased versus others?
- Why are competitors' brands purchased?
- Which competitor or market segment is vulnerable? Why?

III. DISTRIBUTION

A. Product Distribution

- What is the role of your distributors?
- What is their relationship to your company?
- What percentage of your business is through distribution?
- Is proper time and attention being put against this audience?

B. Problems

- Are your distributors competitive in nature?
- Are you offering solid sales support? Training?
- What is the audience's primary complaint (if there is one)? How are you dealing with that?

C. Communications

- How do you routinely communicate with distributors?
- Are they satisfied? If not, why?

IV. SALES FORCE

A. Communications with Sales Force

- How is it done?
- Does it take into account other demands placed on the sales force?
- How do you measure its effectiveness?
- What is the sales force's biggest problem with communications from headquarters?
- Are you addressing that concern? How?

B. Sales Force Support

- How do you help the sales force communicate to their audiences?
- How effective is what you provide them?
- How do you know?

V. *INTERNAL MANAGEMENT*

A. *Does Management Know What You're Doing?*

- Does it know the results?
- How does it know?
- Is that vehicle effective? How do you know?

B. *What Are Your Problems/Challenges with Marketing?*

- Do they understand your needs?
- Do you understand theirs?
- If they need to be better informed about your efforts (and the value of those efforts), how do you propose to do that? When?

  Access to debt/equity

  Portfolio analysis (relative importance/direction of all business units)

VI. *THE CLIENT/PROSPECT*

- Corporate personality/profile/"bio"
- Aggressive, progressive, slow, cheap, short-versus-long-term perspective
- Engineering/manufacturing/marketing/service driven, etcetera
- Business mission
- Communications (awareness/capability)
- Distinctive competencies/weaknesses (what is it they really do best/worst?)
- Direct opportunities
- Direct threats
- Sales force analysis

INTERNAL COMMUNICATIONS ANALYSIS

What it is

A comprehensive process designed to evaluate the internal communication system within an organization.

What it does

A. Deals with all of the variables in the system

- Informal and formal
- Corporate, divisional and human resource
- Top down, lateral and upward

- Inner-departmental, supervisory

- Audiences

- Messages

- Vehicles

- Distribution

- Resources—staff and budgets

B. Combined with feedback, it provides all of the data needed to create a strategic internal communication plan

How it works

PHASE I: Internal Communication Matrix

A. Preliminary evaluation of existing communication system

- Audiences

  - Corporate directors

  - Senior management

  - Divisional management

  - Middle managers/supervisors

  - Other professionals

  - All other employees

- Messages

  - Mission/strategies/goals/values

  - Products/services

  - Customers/competition

  - Business environment/trends

  - Public affairs/legislative news

  - Management information

  - Policies/procedures

  - Training/orientation

  - Benefits/personnel announcements

  - Human interest/employee recognition

  - Community involvement

- Vehicles

  - Corporate publications: magazines, newsletters

  - Electronic: video, wire services, hotlines, dex, telex, electronic mail/bulletin boards, teleconferencing

  - Direct: face-to-face dialogue, meetings, telephone, grapevine, special events

- • Other: paycheck stuffers, letters from management, news bulletins, memos, reports, posters, bulletin boards

- Distribution

  - • Internal: hand delivery, inter-office mail, telex, dex, video, wire service, bulletin board, word-of-mouth (meetings, telephone, grapevine)

  - • External: regular mail, overnight delivery, messenger, business and trade media, personal visit

- Resources, Staff, and Budgets

  - • Communications management

  - • Editors, writers

  - • Creative

  - • Support staff

PHASE II: Qualitative and/or quantitative research—internal communications audit

- We conduct an audit of management and employee attitudes toward internal communication to determine

  - • Information they need to perform better

  - • Information they would like to receive

  - • Feedback on current forms of communication

  - • Ideas for ideal communication.

- We also probe attitudes toward internal communication, its credibility and effectiveness in meeting corporate objectives

  - • Top down

  - • Bottom up

  - • Lateral

  - • Supervisory, inner-departmental

- The audit is generally conducted in four stages:

  - • Senior management; one-on-one interviews

  - • Focus groups of a cross-section of employees, including development of custom questionnaire

  - • Administration of questionnaire to sample of employees (see attached examples of questions)

  - • Report on audit findings.

- We begin preliminary research and budgeting for alternate vehicles or communications systems of interest, that is, electronic mail, video news releases. We may also begin to work on existing corporate publications, that is, new design, better writing.

"Presenting to Win"   This tape shows two communications training specialists making a commentary on a new business presentation to a national computer company. The supporting papers include the verbatim script, the key teaching points, and the biographical notes.

The last-mentioned support, biographical notes, is a good policy because it not only gives the tutors' credentials, to add credibility to what they teach, but also helps to acquaint the personnel of a large organization with their peers and to build pride in the caliber of their company. Here are the key points in this session:

1. Preparation and anticipation are absolutely vital to an effective client presentation.

2. The B-M executive who takes the brief from the client must share all the information he or she's received from the client with the rest of the team.

3. We need to know how many people will attend from client organization and their positions.

4. Need to know when and where meeting will be held and how long we have available to present.

5. Rehearsals are a must. It's virtually impossible to make a good presentation if you are not familiar with your material before you go on.

6. Do everything you can to ensure that the *whole* team rehearses. A presenter who was absent from the rehearsal can inadvertently do a lot of damage to the professionalism of the presentation.

7. Make as much effort in preparation for your stand-up presentation as you did for the original proposal. All those hours working on the program can be thrown away by a hastily staged presentation.

8. Ideally, only involve those people in the presentation who will be directly concerned with the account.

9. If you can, hold the presentation on B-M premises where the client can see our facilities.

10. Find out all you can about your audience. How old are they? What are their titles?

11. If the presentation is being held first thing in the morning, be sure the room is set up on the night before. If the meeting starts before office-opening time, make sure there's someone to meet the client.

12. Make sure the receptionist is alerted and knows the names of the visitors. Make sure she knows where to find you when the client team arrives.

13. If you are presenting on the client's premises, make sure you know everything about it. Best of all, go and see it. Can it be blacked out? Are there power points? What audio-visual equipment exists, and so on?

14. Make client feel important from the start. Don't keep him or her waiting in reception.

15. Make sure your presentation content is entirely relevant. This point is shown in the video by group manager discussing our overseas capabilities when client is only interested in his or her domestic market.

16. When presenting, stand your ground. Be calm and authoritative.

17. Distribute handout material at the end of the presentation. Handing it out earlier distracts the audience.

18. Copy on boards, flip charts, and slides should be concise and clear and in *outline* format. The copy should only be a reference point for the speaker, not something to be read aloud.

19. Wordy copy also causes speakers to lose eye contact with the audience.

20. Video outlines some pointers for developing effective slides or other visuals:

    ☐ One idea per board or slide

    ☐ Be telegraphic

    ☐ Every board or slide has a title

    ☐ Every title is underlined

    ☐ Titles in different colors from text

    ☐ Every subpoint set off from the next by an asterisk or a dash

    ☐ Keep to four or five items per sheet or slide

    ☐ Color is better than black and white

    ☐ Make light pencil notes on the charts to prompt yourself

    ☐ Number the pages and write next page number on previous one

    ☐ Put words you want to stress in blank spaces for better emphasis

    ☐ Circle figures or underline them while you are talking

    ☐ Presenter "Susan" won points from commentators for using the client's name during the presentation. Personalizing the presentation gets clients more involved

21. We're all nervous. The secret of nervous energy is to make it work for you, not against you.

22. Your audience normally want the presentation to go well and are silently supporting you. Breathing exercises or tension-reducing exercises can help reduce initial tension during presentations.

23. If you have a tendency to use "filler words" when you are nervous—"um," "ah," "you know"—speak slowly and clearly, and this will often eliminate them.

24. Use pauses. A short silence at the right moment can be effective in making a point more dramatic.

25. Watch your volume. When rehearsing, check that your voice reaches the whole room.

26. Always check beforehand that your boards or slides are in the right order.

27. Decide how you're going to handle questions. You can allow the audience to ask questions in midpresentation or to keep their questions afterward unless something isn't clear while you're speaking. Asking the client to keep questions until the end creates better continuity.

28. Unlike "Fred," make sure that your appearance is as professional and polished as possible.

29. Again, unlike "Fred," make it clear to the audience that you are enthusiastic about the program you're presenting.

30. With a well-prepared presentation and adequate visuals, no speaker should need handheld notes. These prevent eye contact but can also show that the presenter is unfamiliar with the material he or she's presenting.

31. Avoid overuse of public relations jargon. It's tempting to blind the client with our communications language such as "vertical" and "horizontal publications," but it could well confuse the client and lose points. Use clear and concise language. Talk about the client's business, not yours.

32. Avoid unpositive phrases such as "we would try," "we will attempt to." They have no place in presentations. Be enthusiastic and positive.

33. Never close a presentation without seeking the audience's reaction by asking if there are questions. If the decision maker likes it and says so, you can save a lot of time.

34. Anticipate as many questions as possible before the presentation and have the correct answers ready.

35. If you intend to build results evaluation into your program, present the measurement plan when you present the program. It's much more difficult to get approval for results research when the program's up and running.

36. Remember the purpose of the presentation—to get a new account or the next part of a program. The ultimate aim is to get the order—so ask for it!

THE BURSON-MARSTELLER WRITING WORKSHOP

This is one of the most important workshops, for it concerns the first and original purpose of public relations and publicity: to create releases about a corporation or its products or services that will effectively garner space.

The agenda includes

> Leads and headlines
>
> Tightening copy
>
> Organizing your story
>
> Photo captions
>
> Backgrounders
>
> Applying workshop skills to actual client project
>
> Review and an open discussion

Here are some of the important guides:

The "Grabber" Lead

Get the lead out of your leads!

A real "grabber" first paragraph on a release should be your goal, especially on wire service and consumer press copy.

Remember you're competing for the editor's, and ultimately the reader's, attention. And your competition includes important hard news and some fine writers. Competition can be pretty stiff, too, on the good trade journals.

How do you write a lead that grabs? You don't write it; you create it. You use your imagination. You think in terms of concept, not words.

Following are some products of this process.

□ Heating an uninsulated home is like cooking with the oven door open. It's not very efficient.

—a release on home insulation

□ A Florida resident can save as much as $143 a year on air conditioning costs by spending eight hours in his attic.

—another insulation release

□ Someone wants to sell you old tires to spread around your garden.

—a release on plastic packaging

□ Question: What frightens many hospital patients more than injections, blood tests, and medications?

Answer: The bedpan.

—a general news release on a trade magazine story

□ Newspapers are making news, not just reporting it.

—another release on a trade magazine story

□ "Money talks," says the old adage. Penny, nickel, dime, quarter, dollar are the words every youngster grows up with. Now with the new "cashless society" a partial reality, everyone will have to learn a new "money language."

—a release on terms used in electronic banking

□ Some towns take time to grow. Boone is one of them.

—a release on a banker's involvement in building a town

□ If a letter is a vehicle of communication, then the postmark slogan is its bumper sticker.

—a release on zany one-liners on envelopes

□ Bathrooms as bathrooms are dead. Long live the "revitalization" room! A retreat. A place to indulge yourself, lazily.

—a release on bathroom fixtures

□ When vacationers were looking for a beach, India used to be considered the last resort. Somehow her image never conjured up sunbathing, surf, and sand—even though she has more than 2,500 miles of coastline.

—a release on, what else, India tourism

Getting Attention   Each lead invites you to read on.

Your curiosity is piqued by something funny or familiar—the oven door, money, the bedpan, newspapers, postmark slogans—put in a new context.

You get an offer you can't refuse—saving $143.

You're attracted by a statement bordering on the outrageous—old tires, bathrooms.

Or an old fact is presented in a fresh way—Boone, India's beaches.

Fun and Games   How do you get leads like these? Have some fun with your facts. Let them run around in your head for awhile. Play games with them. According to psychologist Carl Jung:

The dynamic principle of fantasy is play, which belongs also to the child, and as such it appears to be inconsistent with the principle of serious work. But without the playing with fantasy no creative work has ever yet come to birth. The debt we owe to the play of the imagination is incalculable.

No Restrictions   You can play the idea game anywhere, anytime—at your desk, on a stroll, on the train. Keep paper and pencil handy, and you can catch the fleeting thought when it occurs. After all, playing is one thing, but it's important to score.

"Well," you say, "I've played the game, and my story doesn't lend itself to a really bright lead."

OK. Tell it straight—as concisely and clearly as possible. But only after you've tried the other way—only after you're sure your decision to go straight was arrived at intelligently and imaginatively.

Editing Tips

While looking over your freshly minted copy, you should be correcting a lot of things—typos, misspellings, grammatical errors (do subjects and verbs agree in number, for example), style violations, mistakes in arithmetic, and so on.

Most important, though, you should be tightening your copy, eliminating words and phrases that add no meaning or, worse yet, garble your meaning.

Of course, some sentences are obviously bloated, such as

The expansion program will enable the plant to manufacture welded tubular steel at nearly twice the size of its present capacity.

Without the bloat, it says

The expansion will nearly double welded tubular steel production.

Nine words did the job of 21—and did it better.

In addition, you should look for

☐ Passive voice. This is the worst offense. Almost never can a writer justify it. "The ball *was hit* over the fence by Jackson" is just not as good as "Jackson *homered.*" Even if you say "Jackson *hit* the ball over the fence," it's patently better than the first sentence. Passive voice is the classic instance of words getting in the way.

Consider:

Skidmore, Owings & Merrill was *challenged by* Northern States to optimize the building's energy savings.

Northern States *challenged* Skidmore, Owings & Merrill to optimize the building's energy savings.

The distinct signs of passive voice are the verb "to be" (have been installed, were built, are being sent, etc.), the preposition "by," and a more than vague feeling that you don't know who is doing anything.

☐ Adjectives and nouns that have hidden verbs.

The four-bar linkage has a nearly *hypnotic* effect on . . .

The four-bar linkage nearly *hypnotizes* . . .

Fat men have a *tendency* to get fatter.

Fat men *tend* to get fatter.

☐ The expletive "there is" or "there are."

ature *There are* many instances where the quantities needed will not support standard charges.

Often, needed quantities will not support standard charges.

There is an increase in health maintenance organizations in which testing is standard procedure.

Health maintenance organizations, in which testing is standard procedure, are increasing.

☐ The article "the."

This work involved *the* gathering of a great deal of data.

This work involved gathering a great deal of data.

☐ What doesn't mean anything to your reader.

This includes the undistinguished service record of a newly appointed sales representative and, for trade publications, his or her family status.

Remember, every word you cut makes the reading easier. Two words cut from a ten-word sentence may not seem like much, but it's a 20 percent saving. In a five-page case history, that's a whole page.

Organizing Your Story

The basic building block in journalistic (and, therefore, Burson-Marsteller) writing is the inverted pyramid. The newswriter, unlike the lawyer, states his or her conclusion or paints the broad picture first, then gives the details—in descending order of importance. The writer uses as many pyramids as needed to complete the story.

For example, your client, Automaker, is reducing prices because of lower materials and labor costs. Materials costs fell because of a depressed steel market; labor costs fell because of increased plant automation. Prices will go down about 8 percent, or an average of $1,000 per car.

Your story for the general public would read:

TORONTO, December 12, 1984—Automaker Ltd. today announced it is reducing prices on its 1985 models 8 percent, or an average of $1,000 per car. The new prices will take effect Jan. 1.

President F. S. "Stick" Shift said the company was passing on to the motoring public reductions in its materials and labor costs.

Automaker's top-of-the-line model, the Palm Beach convertible, will be priced at $23,450, down from $26,800. Its least-expensive model, the Dawg, will be $5,675, down from $6,485.

Mr. Shift said the chief factor in the lower materials costs was a depressed steel market. Steel prices, he noted, have fallen $7–8 a ton in recent months.

Automaker's labor costs went down, Mr. Shift said, because of increased automation in all three of the company's plants.

The last time Automaker reduced prices was 18 months ago. That move increased the company's unit sales about 15 percent, auto industry analysts reported.

Besides lower steel prices, the company is also beginning to benefit from a switch to reinforced plastic in many body parts.

"That change has been going on for nearly two years," Mr. Shift said, "but it is only starting to show up on our balance sheet now."

The automation, also begun two years ago, should be completed by July 1985, Mr. Shift added. It has not resulted in any worker layoffs, he said; all reductions in Automaker's staff have been through attrition.

As you can see, the story is built in modules, or pyramids. Each pyramid contains information on price (A) and influencing factors (B). You can end the story at the point of any pyramid and not destroy the impact.

This is the basic skeleton of the routine news story. It is the preferred structure for the everyday news release—the product announcement, the personnel release, for example.

In other stories—the case history, the feature, the backgrounder—you embellish the skeleton but still keep the rudiments. The lead may be softer; each pyramid may be deeper; the ending may be less abrupt. But the backbone must still be just as strong. It must hold your ideas together—in good order.

Photo Captions

The caption tells the reader why he or she is looking at a given picture. Alone, the picture is an example of the photographer's skill. The caption completes the message.

Keep the following things in mind when writing captions:

- Always use present tense (Willie Stargell *powers* a Tom Seaver pitch into the stands). It gets the reader involved in the action.

- Use a kicker, also called a "cap lead-in," to attract the reader's attention. This is three or four short words, all in capital letters, that characterize the picture in such a way as to jog the memory or tease the imagination.

- Explain what is going on in the photo so the reader is not left in doubt. Do not, however, labor the obvious.

- Keep it short. Outside limits: 40 words, or four normal lines, if picture accompanies a story; 70 words, or seven lines, if it goes alone.

- Also when a picture goes with a story, do not summarize the story in the caption. This gives the editor the option of throwing away the story.

□ Remember the client. Get the client or product name into the caption in such a way that it is almost impossible to delete.

The Backgrounder

Any event, to paraphrase an old saw, occurs in an environment. When an event involves your client, an important part of your job is to supply the details of the environment to the editor who must print or broadcast the story of the event.

In many cases, you can supply the environment, or background, in a few sentences in your story of the event. Often, however, the environment is large or complicated, and you must write a separate story, a backgrounder.

Case Histories

The best kind of training is through inspiration and example. Burson-Marsteller maintains a case book file that is dog-eared with use. The case histories are designed (1) to serve as guidelines for program development and implementation, (2) to ensure that each B-M account and new business team will be aware of the company's reservoir of experience in creative public relations, and (3) to enable account teams to adapt and present this knowledge with more confidence and less duplication of effort. Some case examples follow:

Examples in Corporate/Institutional Communications

Met Life (Internal/External Image Building)   A joint Y&R/Burson-Marsteller integrated communications program addressed a serious corporate problem at Met Life. Internal surveys showed a sense of drift. A *Fortune* magazine survey rated the company last of ten in its industry. John Creedon, Met Life's CEO, knew that an internal and external communications program had to be part of the solution.

First, B-M involved management in developing a mission statement on the company's role and its vision and values. The group defined the company and its future, articulating needs and goals. The resulting program integrated virtually all techniques—from advertising to public affairs leadership to corporate philanthropy. The theme was "Met on the Move."

The next step was to lift employees' perception with involvement programs, such as a family day in New York City with 15,000 attendees.

A consumer broadcast and print campaign spoke through "Peanuts" cartoon characters—a dramatic departure for a conservative company. (See Figure 11–2, color insert.)

A second print campaign was aimed at internal and opinion leader audiences, highlighting Met's leadership and record-breaking

FIGURE 11-3

performance. (See Figure 11–3.) The "On the Move" theme became the foundation for a series of innovative product launches.

B-M also publicized management's involvement in industry issues to demonstrate leadership. B-M counseled on corporate philanthropy to maximize visibility and created communications programs for a comprehensive, long-term quality program across all operations.

Finally, a major media publicity program was launched to reveal Met Life CEO John Creedon as an industry leader and architect of his company's repositioning to external audiences.

Result: Media awareness increased substantially, employees embraced the company's new style and vitality, and Met Life moved from tenth to fourth place in the *Fortune* survey.

BellSouth (After Deregulation)   With the breakup of AT&T, BellSouth was one of the seven new communications companies scrambling for investor attention. Research showed that analysts lacked know-how in assessing these new companies and were interested in short-term prospects. BellSouth decided to stress its geographic location backed by technological leadership and strong management: "Right Company, Right Place, Right Time." The messages were rolled out via "analyst schools," a source book, and analyst meetings. Result: BellSouth emerged from the breakup with one of the strongest perceptions among the seven.

Volvo (Entering New Markets)　The Swedish industrial firm wanted to enter U.S. capital markets, but B-M research showed that its "conglomerate" image, successful in Europe, would not be favorably received by U.S. analysts. Positioned as an advanced manufacturer with established niches in worldwide markets, Volvo's share price and volume increased.

Johnson & Johnson and Tylenol (Crisis Management)　This is a classic case of the most difficult form of public relations—how to turn the disaster of a crisis into renewed success. Working closely with J & J top management, Burson-Marsteller, and many others, helped to rebuild public confidence in the company and its over-the-counter analgesic after a series of product-tampering cyanide poisonings shocked the world.

Y&R (although Tylenol was not one of its brands) also helped during the crisis by doing overnight research every day the crisis lasted.

Jim Burke, the president and CEO, literally took over the job of brand manager on the product, delegating the running of the rest of the company to members of the executive committee. He set up a "war room" where a tightly-knit team worked round-the-clock to determine policy and actions.

Fifteen months after the crisis, Y&R's Alex Kroll (at a major agency seminar devoted to the subject of managing creativity) described what happened:

Burke doesn't even have a desk. A conference table is all he uses. He sits at the head, but there is no hierarchical desk, no throne. Burke is only the first among peers. He was also head ideator, chief thinker, throwing out ideas, bouncing them off people, trying them out, listening to everybody's ideas in turn. He became the quintessential open man, both with his own people and any of the reporters, all the press.

This quality of candor was the key to weathering the problem. And the first dimension was to define that problem:

Early in the first week, Burke correctly defined the problem in its largest context. It is not an attack on J & J, but an act of terrorism against the entire national health care delivery system, and by extension, the food delivery system. We are all being terrorized.

The second key to the solution was that Burke sought out the press, both broadcast and print, and eventually succeeded in making the press J & J's allies in the battle:

And they needed allies: Tylenol and death, Tylenol and murder appeared on the front pages of every paper in the U.S., for the better part of six weeks.

Burke and his team analyzed the nightly telephone research, with Jim Dowling, head of Burson-Marsteller, as well as Ney, Kroll, and others constantly advising. The heads of the FBI and the FDA were urging J & J not to surrender to the terrorist by pulling in all the capsules. But Burke and his team came to the opposite conclusion:

Shyly (because this is an enormous amount of money we are talking about) we say, "Sir," screwing up our courage, "pull them, pull the capsules. Until you do, nothing you say or do will be credible."

Burke looks around the room for possibly ²/₁₀ths of a second and says, "I think you are right." No emotion. He had come to that conclusion himself, but we all reinforced it. And then he ordered the recall of $100 million worth of product which we would proceed to incinerate.

But remember, Burke has assessed the potential damage in the billions. $100 million (or 50 cents per share in that quarter, as it turned out) was really small beer. However, I know other companies in this field who would have thought to cut their losses. Stop the hemorrhaging. Not Burke, who had correctly defined the problem and the stakes both in their social and economic terms.

The dramatic case history went on with a series of decisive actions, including the daring decision to rebuild the product's franchise—with the medical profession, with the public, and through the press:

Burke makes the astonishing announcement of the true mission—"The idea here is not just to save the franchise, or save part of the franchise, but to restore the franchise to a full blooming health."

The principle was "high expectations"—the highest. Given those expectations, his people were energized. They moved quickly to capture all the best packaging facilities in the U.S. under the useful rationalization that since Tylenol was most hurt, Tylenol deserved the first crack at the best packagers.

Over two million pieces of literature were shot out of New Brunswick in those first weeks to doctors, nurses, dentists, and hospital managers with the facts, and the key fact, THE PROBLEM HAD NOT ORIGINATED AT THE FACTORY. Advertising began, not to sell the brand, but to tell people who threw away their Tylenol capsules, that they could get replacement tablets free from their retailer, or by writing directly to J & J.

Through the daily research feedback, with thousands of feet of film of consumer opinion, the team learned what people needed to hear:

As to how to say it, Burke pulled the astonishing coup of getting the networks to allow J & J to use a doctor to talk about the situation. Dr. Thomas Gates of McNeil Laboratory. Probably the first, and possibly the last, doctor ever in an analgesic commercial . . .

As for the press coverage, I think that if Burke had not been so upfront and open all along, he would not have gotten the kind of cooperation he needed. The press was both the enemy, in one sense, and in another an ally. Jim Dowling estimated that the real competitive media expenditures were well in excess of $2 billion—$2 billion of free press given to the story linking Tylenol and death. How could J & J get that kind of media money behind the positive side of the story when it came? Jim Dowling correctly assessed that the only way was to turn editors and reporters into copywriters and to build on that franchise of interest—not to mislead them, but to give them the positive facts when there were positive facts. And the most appropriate messenger was Mr. Burke himself.

But it had to be a nationwide message, because the competition was nationwide—Peoria, San Diego. . . . To do that, Dowling and his people constructed a unique press conference by satellite. . . . Connecting 30 cities all at once, and hundreds of reporters, so each and every major city reporter would have open access to Burke and J & J—they were not subject to the interpretations of *Time* and *The New York Times* and the networks.

This is masterful psychology. Everybody gets the news at once. It turns reporters into copywriters. . . .

How well did it all work with the public? What happened eight days later, when Burke went on the Phil Donahue show and revealed the new tamperproof package? The people cheered. Ever heard anyone cheer for a package before?

"48 days deep into the crisis and J & J was on the way back. . . .

This classic case, in crisis management, conclusively proved the power of creativity in public relations:

What is so extraordinary is that almost all crisis breeds caution; this crisis bred creativity. By the time Burke appeared on the "60 Minutes" program, cynics had become believers, the evangelist was winning back his flock. . . . In the latest Nielsen, January–February, Tylenol has achieved a 29 share.

It is already the greatest miracle in marketing history!

Examples in Consumer Marketing

Coca-Cola, Inc. (New Coke/Classic Coke Launch)   It might appear that generating news coverage for a product like New Coke or the introduction of Classic Coke was easy. While the stories were certainly newsworthy and of interest, their strategic development and execution were the kind of work that only a comprehensive company like Burson-Marsteller could accomplish.

B-M worked at the highest levels of the Coca-Cola Company to help develop the New Coke strategy. They wrote speeches, set up and conducted satellite press conferences that electronically hooked up journalists in major markets around the United States, informed the bottler system, delivered product in person to editors, and unveiled new advertising.

When the public reacted so strongly to changing a hundred-year-old formula, B-M responded, helping create a new package and a new name for Classic and then monitoring the Great Coca-Cola Controversy day by day.

Out of the turmoil came the sweet taste of success. Coca-Cola soon enjoyed a larger share of the sugar cola market than it had at any time in a decade.

General Electric (Answer Center and "Quick Fix")   B-M research showed that consumers wanted manufacturers to provide them with more helpful advice in choosing and caring for their household products. B-M recommended that GE create the following consumer help services:

The Answer Center, a 24-hour hotline service set up to handle consumer questions about GE products and service. B-M's assignment was to publicize the service nationally. Through editorial events, spokesperson tours, press mailings/contacts, and a syndicated radio series, B-M's program resulted in a sevenfold increase in calls to the Answer Center over a three-month period, from 2,000 per week to 15,000 per week—during which time no advertising mentioned the Answer Center.

GE's "Quick Fix" System, a do-it-yourself repair program, was developed to enable consumers to handle repairs and replace parts on a variety of GE appliances. Burson-Marsteller was assigned to generate widespread consumer awareness of the Quick Fix System without advertising support. B-M trained eight spokespeople, including GE executives and women, "do-it-yourselfers," then launched a nationwide, 90-market print/broadcast media tour. The program generated more TV and print coverage for GE appliances than any program in the company's history.

Example in Business Marketing

Dow Chemical Co. Ltd. (Styrofoam)   This architectural product, available in the United Kingdom for 20 years, was faced with a declining growth rate and new competition. To increase awareness among architects, who specify the product, B-M recommended a national raft race for architects, in cooperation with the leading weekly trade publication, positioned as part of the Architecture Year celebration. The resulting fun event generated tremendous publicity, reaching 99 percent of all architects in the United Kingdom.

Example in Health Care Service

Fair Oaks Hospital   Fair Oaks started an 800 telephone number as a helpline for cocaine users and needed to publicize its availability. B-M created national attention for the helpline and used it to reposition the hospital as the nation's leading center in the diagnosis and treatment of cocaine abuse.

Example in Entertainment Marketing

AT&T (Spirit of America)   Twenty-one cities, 5-kilometer races, and a five-city concert tour helped AT&T celebrate the "Spirit of America." Top AT&T consumers were entertained by headline performers such as Frank Sinatra, while the campaign featured many celebrity spokespersons. In addition, the 5K fun runs tied AT&T to its biggest project that year, the Olympic Torch Relay, by giving runners the opportunity to win a free trip to the Olympic Games or run in the torch relay.

Sports Marketing

AT&T (Olympic Torch Relay)   The assignment from AT&T was straightforward: Make its sponsorship of the 1984 torch relay happen. Calling on all its sports executional resources, B-M organized, staged, and publicized the passage of the Olympic flame from New York to Los Angeles.

Over 82 days, the relay caravan escorted the torch through 1,600 cities, towns, and villages in 33 states. More than 90 B-M people, including specialists in graphic design, audiovisual, legal, accounting, videotaping, community relations, news bureau operations, and logistics, arranged for the caravan's support, security, and transport needs.

More than 30 million spectators witnessed the relay live, making it the largest-attended event in history. Billions more watched and read about the relay. A client survey showed 96 percent awareness of the event and 48 percent awareness of AT&T's sponsorship. The Los Angeles *Herald Examiner* called the relay, "the public relations coup of the century."

. . . .

CHAPTER CHECKLIST

. . . .

1. **Public relations influences opinion by changing or reinforcing it, or by creating a new opinion where none exists.**

2. **Major activities are corporate/institutional and consumer marketing communications.**

3. **Services required for thorough public relations today include research capabilities in depth, media, design, and audiovisual expertise.**

4. **Public relations program development includes situation analysis, communication objectives and**

strategies, and program tactics, such as a creative concept ("the big idea"), corporate and/or marketing activities, a media plan, and the measurement/evaluation of results.

5. Training curricula for successful public relations should include grounding in information building, idea generation, executional expertise, client relations, and presentation skills.

6. Information-driven programs begin with (a) a thorough audit of the marketing situation, the audience make-up, distribution, and sales force characteristics, and (b) a comprehensive preprogramming situation and competitive analysis.

7. Writing resultful releases requires skill in story organization, "grabber" leads, copy editing, photo captions, and backgrounders.

8. Successful case histories have in common originality, relevance, credibility, thorough media integration, and newsworthiness.

. . . .

CHAPTER 12

Creativity in Event Marketing

Al Schreiber, about the successful AT&T "Long Distance Baseball Series," the event in which youngsters from the recently open Republic of China toured the United States, competing with American Little Leaguers

I said "Think about it when you get older, think about it when you look back and say to yourself, here are the things I did that I'm proud of and here are the things I just did 'cause everybody else did 'em." And he came through. To his credit, AT&T funded it, and it worked out."

The great thing about our business is the fun you can have solving the seemingly unsolvable—inventing new ways to break through the clutter, to rise to the challenges of segmentation, zapping and communication overload.

Y&R is pioneering in the explosively growing field of event marketing, which is helping to solve a lot of marketing difficulties, as you shall see. Burson-Marsteller is the Y&R team leader, under the direction of Executive Vice President Al Schreiber.[1]

THE OPPORTUNITIES AND PROBLEMS OF EVENT MARKETING

In its latest brochure on the subject, Burson-Marsteller discusses the opportunities and the problems to be solved:

> *Event marketing . . .*
> *Relationship marketing . . .*
> *Cause-related events . . .*
> *Sponsorships . . .*
> *Ambush marketing . . .*

These are the buzz words of the burgeoning field of Event Marketing. A field on which some 3,400 U.S. companies now enthusiastically play. A field in which those companies invest over 3.5 billion dollars—proportionately just as high in Europe and Asia. A field growing at a 40 percent rate—typically at the expense of other marketing activities.

But the buzz words of Event Marketing can easily become buzz saws!

> *High sponsorship program costs . . .*
> *Poor event execution . . .*
> *Lack of event integration with other corporate or marketing efforts . . .*
> *Irrelevance with marketing or corporate communications strategies . . .*
> *Ultimately, poor or unknown results.*

---

[1]Information, quotations, and case histories in this chapter are courtesy of Al Schreiber, executive vice president, in charge of sports/events marketing, Burson-Marsteller, Inc.

Clearly, well-conceived events or programs can provide significant rewards. But these benefits accrue to those companies that rigorously apply a disciplined approach to their event programs, as with other marketing efforts.

Although event marketing is a new subject in Y&R's curriculum, the department can already draw on the experience of many sponsored events, including more than 50 sports events in four continents—events with such provocative ideas as the P&G-sponsored "BounceStyles" (gymnastics) in North America, the Union Bank of Switzerland/Whitbread "Round-the-World Sailboat Race" from Europe, the Nike "Fun Run" in Asia, and the Wang "Race Against Time" in Australia.

Marketers' Problems Which Event Marketing Can Help Alleviate

In 1987, Al gave an overview of the lessons he and his colleagues had learned, in a speech before the International Events Group. This summary became the matrix for seminars he is starting to conduct within Burson-Marsteller and the other Y&R companies.

In his introductory remarks, he said:

On the marketing scene, event sponsorship is booming. It's a phenomenon. The American II Spinnaker, the Breeder's Cup, the Manny Hanny finish line banner, none of these were even conceivable 10 years ago. But in the last few years people have been conceiving the inconceivable. Why is that? Because mass advertising is increasingly less able, by itself, to provide product differentiation. We believe that events can.

He then outlined the current concerns facing the agency's clients.

Four major concerns were expressed by marketing executives and product managers in response to a research survey by Burson-Marsteller:

One, marketers are concerned about the erosion of brand loyalty. People are simply less loyal to a favorite brand these days.

Two, marketers are concerned about the maturation of categories. TV dinners are simply no longer new.

Three, marketers are concerned about the shift in marketing domination. Once advertisers were king. Heavy advertising created consumer pull. Retailers in gratitude submitted to the requirements of the advertising. Now, consumers are not as effectively pulled. You simply can't count on their loyalty anymore. The advertisers are no longer the kings. The retailers are.

Four, marketers are concerned about segmentation. Marketing is often turning its back en masse to search out class. Let me suggest to you that events can be that class. Events can be a strong segmentation force.

How Event Marketing Helps Solve These Concerns

"Obviously," Schreiber continued, "event marketing is not a cure-all. But, interestingly, event marketing can help assuage *every one of the four major concerns* shared by marketing and product managers. Here's how:

Concern One: Erosion of brand loyalty. Today's heavy emphasis on couponings and premiums has weakened the value of individual brands. Price is everything and value is often forgotten. An event we feel can contribute value back to the brand in an area that's difficult for the competition to match. *It's a value that goes beyond price.* Indeed, association with an event can even help command a premium price for a product at times. When Tang associated itself with the Mothers' Against Drunk Driving march, it became more than a breakfast drink. It became a symbol of righteousness. And righteousness, I suggest, is worth a whole lot more than plain old Vitamin C any day of the week.

Concern Two: Maturation of categories. The battle for share within a mature category changes the marketing attack. One brand must now wage war directly against another. The marketing emphasis usually shifts to price promotion, which results in driving down the margin. When the margin hits zero or less, a brand can die. In this case, again, an events-oriented marketing plan can provide a product differentiation that transcends price.

Concern Three: Trade domination. There's no question, power is shifting to the retailer. The challenge to the marketer, then, is to enhance his retailer relationships. It behooves him to become a partner, or at least a friend, of the retailer. Events are naturals for relationship building. You invite him or her to meet Michael Jordan or Whoopi Goldberg. One vice-president of a major AT&T account, a lifelong Sinatra fan, shook hands with Frank after one of our concerts, smiled, turned to his AT&T host, and said, "I'm yours for life." Events are superb for building relationships.

Concern Four: Segmentation. Marketing managers see segmentation creating many problems. They mentioned fragmentation of budgets, higher selling costs, dilution of effort. But they recognized segmentation as a growing trend. Many of you have read the recent cover story in *Business Week* about the Campbell Soup Co., the original mass marketer, and its segmentation by regions, regionalization. The article describes the variations in production, in advertising and in promotion that Campbell is implementing regionally, in fact, tailoring to fit specific neighborhoods within a single city. These are the first rumblings, says *Business Week,* of a seismic change at Campbell that could eventually redefine mass marketing in America.

What brings us together at this conference is that literally we are the group creating that redefinition. Event marketing offers tremendous potential for segmentation, not only by geography but by psychographics also. Through events, you might want to reach your prime audience in Kansas City, Missouri, with a bike race, but a bake-off might work better in Kansas City, Kansas. If segmentation is the right route, events certainly support a strategy of segmentation.

Seven Steps for Successful Event Sponsorship	Through its experience in assisting event marketers, Burson-Marsteller has developed a seven-step process, with certain proprietary techniques to assure efficiency.

1. Establish Objectives. What do you want to accomplish? What do you want to be measured against? Obviously, this is a basic imperative before anyone can consider event sponsorship and promotion.

2. Develop the Strategy. This is precisely the same part of the process followed by Y&R in every discipline discussed in this book.

"Here," says Schreiber, "is where you can consider whether or not an event is suitable. In some cases, event sponsorship is simply not a reasonable approach to achieving your objectives. Maybe you really need a flood of 30-second commercials; maybe you need a media tour, or an employee incentive program. But, on the other hand, events are frequently called for. When you think of strategy, consider Gillette. They wanted to reach an international audience in a high-impact, high-profile way. Their solution: World Cup Soccer. A perfect strategy. It's also a perfect fit, and that's step number three."

3. Ensure a Strategic Fit. This fit should be among the three elements of audience, event, and product. Schreiber describes Burson-Marsteller proprietary methods of accomplishing this goal:

If it's a sports event, we conduct a *sports compatibility profile* which we call SCOPE. Through SCOPE we analyze users or prospective users of the product by their stated involvement with 45 amateur and professional sports which we have captured in an extensive data base. That way we determine which sport is most suitable for the product in question. It takes the hunch out of selecting sports for a program. SCOPE is quantitative and quite objective.

We also put an event through an RVA, a Relative Value Assessment. An RVA assesses any event, sport or cultural, against the whole fabric of a brand's objectives and strategies. The Relative Value Assessment subjects the proposed event to a matrix of 25 criteria in categories like tactical effectiveness and executional efficiency. The person doing the judging assigns a point value to each response. Ideally, a group of potential events is judged simultaneously and more than one person is asked to do the judging. So what you wind up with is a point score with some events pulling scores of 5.5 and others 9.9. The criteria of course are the key. Any good brand manager asks himself those same questions instinctively, but the RVA forces the brand manager to consider every question.

Among the perfect fits Schreiber cites: Coca-Cola's long-time alliance with the Olympics; Alpo dog food's sponsorship of sled-dog racing; Rolex's association with polo.

4. Negotiate the Package. Having determined your strategy, you will then negotiate the terms by which you sponsor and promote an event. Negotiate with the athlete or performer, with the lawyers, the agents—whoever is required to okay your participation.

"Sometimes," says Schreiber, "there may not be an event in the city in which you are promoting the product. Then you have to create it. Albuquerque may just be awaiting the first underwater demolition derby. Or Des Moines may not yet have a frog jumping contest. . . . When Equitable Life wanted to reach families, there wasn't any fitting sponsorship available. So Equitable created the Family Challenges in skiing and tennis. Today these events are among the most popular participatory events in the country."

5. Implement the Event. You can do this by yourself or in conjunction with an outside events organization. If you have a large staff or if the event is a simple one, confined to one or two locales, you may want to do it in-house.

"The key," says Schreiber, "is to execute with excellence. Poor execution can create nightmares. When we worked with AT&T and the Los Angeles Olympic Organizing Committee to do the Olympic Torch Relay, we spent over a year planning that event, and it took a year to get it all together. Hershey found the perfect group to implement its coast-to-coast track and field youth program, the National Recreation and Parks Association."

6. Extend the Event. "That means to use it throughout your marketing mix and throughout your marketing efforts. Sometimes you can use an event as the key element in your advertising. You can build retailer promotions around it. You can make it work in employee incentive programs and dealer promotions. You can make it a springboard for couponing or sweepstakes. Looking at the retail displays of the beer and tobacco companies gives us a clue as to how to do it right. They're experts at extending events. The point of extension: you paid good money for your event, so use it or lose it."

7. Measure the Results. "When you're setting your objectives, make sure you can say that every one is measurable. Show how you move the needle, how many cases were sold. What about audience attendance? Awareness changes? Intent to buy? Dealer interest? If you've expressed the objectives properly, you can read the effect the event has had on them and that can tell you a lot about choosing and selling in the next event. Use your figures to modify your execution, or to convince the vice president of marketing or the CEO that you're on to something good."

Al cites Jerry Welsh, a former colleague, now with E. F. Hutton, who never considers an event unless measurement criteria are built directly into that event. He knew, for instance, that the Statue of Liberty promotion increased his card usage 20 percent.

HOW TO GET CREATIVE IDEAS FOR EVENT MARKETING

While every creative professional can succeed in getting good ideas for events, you approach this medium with an attitude and aptitude somewhat different from your approach to traditional advertising.

Al Schreiber lists three basics for creating events, starting with the basic mind-set:

---

1. Study and Know the World of *Entertainment.* The difference between thinking of ideas for events vs. ads is that for events you need to cultivate a specialized knowledge of sports and music and the cultural world. You need to adopt the attitude of an expert, and consult experts, and be very aware and attuned to what's out there and what's available—what's the inventory that you can draw upon. To come up with the concept of a Torch Relay, you have to be familiar with the concept of relays, to come up with a special kind of baseball decathlon, you have to be familiar with different sports.

The event marketing creator has to be very specialized in terms of his currency with sports, music, and cultural events.

2. Thoroughly Know and Consult the *Experts.* For the baseball tour of the Chinese youngsters, Burson-Marsteller consulted the former U.S. Baseball Commissioner Bowie Kuhn, and Bowie has been a regular consultant for the agency since.

If you need an Arnold Palmer or a Jackie Stewart as spokesman for your event, you will be contacting organizations like Mark McCormack's IMG. And if it is feasible you will have acknowledged experts on your staff. Burson-Marsteller could never have staged such musical events as the American Express "Front of the Line" concert program with Frank Sinatra, Liza Minelli and Sammy Davis, Jr. without the enthusiastic expertise of Herb Karlitz, its resident musical expert. Herb is also an entertainment lawyer specializing in the music field. (Burson-Marsteller has recently undertaken a joint venture with Premier Artists Services, to be called CEP—Corporate Entertainment Productions—with Karlitz as president of the new organization. Premier Artists is one of the most highly-respected entertainment packagers, representing such stars as Frank Sinatra, Liza Minelli, Paul Anka, Steve Lawrence and Eydie Gorme.)

3. And, of Course, *Resist the Usual.* Burson-Marsteller prides itself on having religiously followed the Y&R credo in every event their ingenuity has dreamed up. If those events had not had the spark of originality, they could never have garnered the press, the positive company images, and the sales results you'll find in the case histories that follow.

Event marketing of a sort began a long time ago, when the beer and cigarette companies wanted to target their heavy consumers and logically turned to sponsoring events where their products were heavily consumed. However, today, to stand out in modern event marketing, you need those ideas that can penetrate the clutter of mere sports or music sponsorship—the "Hands Across America," the AT&T "Torch Relay," the Amex "Front of the Line" privilege of advance ticket sales—ideas which have that touch of magic which is the seed of success because nobody has ever done it before.

Originality can often consist of anticipating a trend—finding through your contacts and intuition a sport or music talent which is new, on the leading edge, and of course the perfect fit for the marketer's objectives.

Successful Case Histories

The following are nine successful event marketing examples using the Burson-Marsteller seven-step process.

Promoting to the Hispanic Market   Procter & Gamble felt that it was not getting its fair share of the Latin market. The company decided to test an event in New York City, the largest Hispanic market in the country. Burson-Marsteller helped to attract that audience for several P & G brands with a Latin concert in New York's Madison Square Garden. The concert featured the hottest Latin talent of the day. Admission fees were steep, at $20 a seat or $10 a seat with a proof of purchase of Cheer, Crest, Downy, Ivory, or Joy brands.

The promotion, though constrained by severe time limitations, involved all areas of advertising, publicity, and retail. Three thousand distributors and retailers attended the cocktail party and concert. Fifteen thousand product samples were distributed. Best of all for Procter & Gamble, despite the short notice, 13,500 attended the concert and, significantly, 60 percent of the paid attendees brought along a proof of purchase—measurable results.

Wooing the Affluent Customer   Merrill Lynch, on the other hand, was trying to reach a totally different audience, also in New York—the city's most affluent people. The company seized the opportunity to sponsor an event honoring the city's most cherished cultural institution, the 90th Anniversary Celebration of Carnegie Hall. Not content with a mere name association, Merrill Lynch pulled out all the stops to maximize its linkage with the landmark.

The centerpiece of the program was the re-creation of a concert played at the hall's opening in 1891, followed by an 1890s gala party. At the gala, Merrill Lynch's financial advisors mingled with the New York 400. ("That," said Schreiber, "is a euphemism for selling.")

For this event, Burson-Marsteller helped to form a committee of hundreds of the city's most important socialites and businesspeople, plus one out-of-town chairperson, Nancy Reagan. They created a glittering 1890s postevent supper, with a menu that re-created suppers of 90 years ago, and a full-scale stage show.

The guest list of affluent citizens was drawn from Carnegie Hall patrons, each of whom paid $500 to Carnegie Hall for the privilege of attending. Merrill Lynch reported that the event was a door opener for literally tens of millions of dollars in new business.

A Different Affluent Psychographic Segment   Iveco Trucks was also keen to meet businesspeople, but in this case the audience was truckers. A virtually unknown Italian company, Iveco wanted to increase awareness among fleet truck owners, operators, and dealers, both here and overseas. Recent surveys suggested that vast segments of this audience were heavily sports-oriented. Soccer, tennis, sailing, and track and field were among the sports indicated, and in the United States boxing offered excellent potential. So Burson-Marsteller helped Iveco to negotiate sponsorship rights to several major bouts, dominating the scene with signage. They also ran a spread in *Sports Illustrated*. Similar I.D. was on camera throughout TV coverage of all the fights.

The total campaign included sponsorship of 57 world championship events in 15 countries. The result: After three years, Iveco's name was recognized and identified with trucks by more than a third of its American market and by more than 70 percent of European audiences.

Burger King and New York's Finest　Just about the time that the song "New York, New York" was becoming popular, the city wanted to issue bulletproof vests to its policemen. At the same time, Burger King concluded that it did not have the community presence enjoyed by other New York City fast-food outlets like McDonald's. The event idea: Burger King should take a leadership role in raising funds to buy vests for the New York City cops.

The program was twofold: Sixty-three New York Burger King restaurants sold coupons for french fries. All the proceeds were donated to the vest fund. But to gain maximum exposure, and provide entertainment, Burson-Marsteller staged a VIP night on Broadway—a vast salute to New York's finest with dozens of celebrities, including the casts of three Broadway shows, Mayor Koch (the Burger King himself), and the biggest orchestra ever assembled on a Broadway stage. Tickets were priced at $24 for the show and $96 for the show and the cast party. All monies went to the vest fund.

Promotion was formidable. An advertising blitz, in-store announcements, bumper stickers, 200,000 playbills, and heavy print and broadcast publicity. The result was great for the New York City police. The VIP night and coupon programs raised enough money for 1,400 vests. The results were excellent for Burger King too: thanks given to the company at the mayor's home before the show and during the show, the Times Square message board continuously flashed the word "Thanks," and afterward the police department gave Burger King its highest humanitarian award. Finally, the 63 participating outlets saw a significant increase in traffic, selling some 2,000 coupon booklets.

Target: A Mass Audience　M&M/Mars came to Burson-Marsteller with a serious concern. Candy sales were declining and the public was getting multiple messages from many sources that suggested that eating candy was not in the interest of good health. Obviously, too much candy *is* harmful, but some candy is advantageous. Burson-Marsteller

novel suggestion at the time. They recommended that the company align itself with the greatest example of health and fitness on earth, the Olympic Games.

In a unique arrangement with the LAOOC, Mars signed on not as the official candy but as the official *snack* food of the Olympics. That official sponsorship became the core for a series of public, distribution chain, and employee programs on health and the Olympics. Many programs were implemented to position Mars products as foods, which have an appropriate place in a healthy diet, or even an athlete's regimen. For instance, nutritionists held clinics for athletes at Olympic training centers.

The company held sales promotion activities as well. One sales promotion had 6-foot M&M jars (replicas of smaller 20-ounce Olympic jars sold at retail) circulating around 20 major markets in a "Count the M&Ms" competition, with winners receiving tickets to the Olympics.

When the Olympics were over, research showed that there was a decided reversal in the public's negative attitude toward candy. Dealers were enthusiastic, plant managers reported that morale had never been higher, and for the first time in the company's history, it could not produce enough M&Ms and Snickers to keep up with demand.

Global Media Coverage Helps Avon Go the Distance   When Avon needed help in marketing its products to women in Japan, it turned to Burson-Marsteller, who, after extensive analysis of the marketplace, recommended a series of running events open only to women.

More than 60 journalists attended the program's kick-off announcement. Pre-race publicity included newspaper and wire service interviews and TV appearances for the program's spokesperson, a world-famous marathon runner. The coverage helped make the initial race the nation's largest running event ever.

Total coverage of the first year's activities—three races—reached more than 251 million people through 300 press reports and 13 radio, and 14 TV programs—all this in a country with a population of only 115 million. Constant media attention of Avon as sponsor helped create strong client identification with positive women's activities.

The runs were considered a key element in boosting consumer awareness of Avon's Japanese presence by more than 70 percent and in helping the company's Japanese sales exceed industry averages during the year.

The XXIV Olympic Games in Seoul   I've already discussed, in Chapter Ten, CYB's exciting assignment in 1985, designing the U.S. Olympic symbol for the games in Seoul.

That same year Roh Tae Woo, who became Korea's first democratic president two years later, was the president of the Seoul Olympic

Organizing Committee (SLOOC), and he hired Burson-Marsteller as worldwide public relations consultant. (See Figure 12–1.)

The assignment was not only a great challenge in event marketing, but also a huge responsibility in crisis management. Indeed, it was partly because of the positive reputation Burson-Marsteller had achieved through successfully helping Johnson & Johnson to weather its Tylenol crisis that Korea chose Burson-Marsteller. Another reason was the positive impression Harold Burson made on the Koreans during his early meetings with them. An article in *Sports inc.* magazine (9/26/88) explained why:

South Korea, a country where department stores hire young women to stand in the doorways and bow to customers, is tailored for Burson's style. "He has all the right qualifications that Koreans respect," Rylance said. [Bill Rylance was Burson-Marsteller's overall manager of the program.] "They're used to American businessmen coming in being brusque and aggressive. They find it refreshing to meet a company chairman who is a quiet, humble gentleman."

The Korean director general of SLOOC's international press and public relations, Shin Hyong Ung, had outlined the major objective. Reported the *Sports inc.* article,

"Through the world press, we have to show that Seoul is a most peaceful and secure city," Shin said. "Korea is very open in a democratic society. Every society has discord, but here it's very minor." . . . Except on foreign TV, of course. There, riots often seemed to be engulfing the city. Maybe it would have helped if someone had taken the strategy of explaining that this year's demonstrations were isolated gatherings of radical students lacking the support of the populace that last year's riots had. But Burson-Marsteller remained committed to a low-key approach.

However low key the approach, the strategy Burson-Marsteller did adopt, during the three years of this challenging event marketing, was to involve the world press to a greater and greater degree in the reality of the happenings before and during the games. Al Schreiber explained how this was done, in a September 1988 article in *PR WEEK* magazine:

Of primary importance was communicating SLOOC's philosophy: to hold an Olympics dedicated to harmony and progress, and to return the Olympics to the athletes. This message is consistent with Korea's desire to play a role in bringing about a world of peace and harmony, and to demonstrate the vitality of its economy and culture.

To do this, we formed a global team led by Bill Rylance, who moved from our Bahrain office by way of London to Seoul to manage the program, supported by Artie Solomon in New York.

Working closely with the Organizing Committee, these two, plus Brian Matthews, our number two man in Seoul, assisted by our world network of offices, have coordinated a multifaceted public relations/public affairs program that has included writing dozens of speeches; writing and placing over 17 Op-Ed pieces on behalf of SLOOC officials in major world media; arranging press conferences in

FIGURE 12–1

London, Frankfurt, Madrid, Barcelona, Paris, Calgary, and Tokyo; and obtaining television coverage in Spain, Germany, Switzerland, Canada, the U.K., and the U.S., through media tours and general media relations. Solomon has also been authorized to serve as spokesperson for SLOOC. . . .

TRADE SHOWS AND SALES MEETINGS

A unique feature of the Y&R family of services is virtually a one-man show that's gone on at Y&R for several decades, in the person of Dave Berman, in charge of Show & Meeting Services.

Dave is a Renaissance man, who can build a display, light a show, write a script. He's an Origami expert who transforms dollar bills into birds and gives them to you as you're shooting the breeze. A no-b.s. guy, the delight of CEOs, whose testimonial letters cram his files.

Here, you can catch the flavor of the man as be begins his training presentation to the Advertising Skills Workshop:

As you know, I am here to tell you about Show & Meeting Services.

I'd like to start by pointing out that we are living in a world of "specialists." There's a doctor who knows all about what's happening in your right ear, but doesn't know a damn thing about what's going on in the left. In fact, it reminds me of a friend . . . a salesman who called on National Biscuit Company and requested to see the Vice President in charge of Fig Newtons. He was taken aback when the receptionist asked: "Loose or packaged?"

Now . . . I am one of the number of specialists who make up the various collateral services that Y&R offers. Show & Meeting Services is basically in the business of producing presentations.

It is a unique service in that the presentations are produced and staged by the department rather than merely supervising the activities of outside vendors. That doesn't tell it all. Probably the best way to *tell* you what we do is to *show* you what we do. But before I do, I want to talk a moment about presentations.

The Three Basic Principles of Shows and Meetings

Dave then pulls an envelope out of his pocket and proceeds to hammer home to his audience the three essentials of a successful show or meeting. (Once again, we learn how closely related are the basics of all our specialties.)

From time to time, high school and college groups come through the agency to see "how it works," and I am asked to talk to them about what makes a good presentation. As they come in they are given an envelope like this. It says, "Don't open until requested." (See Figure 12–2.)

I start by saying: "Over the years, we have developed three basic rules for what makes a good presentation. The first of these rules is in the envelope." I ask them to open it, and as you can see, they discover this bit of nylon cord, on the end of which is a fish hook. I tell them this is the first thing that makes for a good presentation. I then proceed to go around the room and question them about what they think the fish hook represents. After half a dozen answers, I stop and explain that the first point is represented by the fish hook . . . the ATTENTION-GETTER . . . a "GRABBER." But most important, I have gotten them to think about what I *wanted* them to think about even before I started to speak!

The second point is PARTICIPATION. I got them to *participate* by asking them what the fish hook represents . . . and even if I didn't call on them, they were participating because they weren't sure I *wouldn't* call on them. . . . So I had my whole audience's attention . . . they were all participating.

My final point is RELEVANCY. Relevancy to the audience to whom you're speaking. Disregarding this point has caused more presentations to fall flat on

FIGURE 12–2

their face than anything I can think of. You can screw up the slides, blow a projector bulb, make do with a bad sound system—all of this can affect the impact of a presentation. But if it's relevant, you can survive. IRRELEVANCY leads only to DISASTER.

Each time we sit down and start to plan a project, we strive to get the strongest *fish hook* we can come up with . . . to get as much *participation* as we can . . . and certainly, and foremost, that the message is *relevant* to the audience that is going to see and hear the presentation.

Dave's case histories are ideal for presentation in a creative workshop because most of them are done on a low budget and in a short time. It's a fine example of ingenuity when you can take those three basic principles and make them work in jigtime, on a small budget, and galvanize an audience into enthusiastic action—as is the crucial goal of all sales meetings and trade exhibits.

The following case histories are told in Dave's own words as presented to the Advertising Skills Workshop.

Eastern Airlines (Motivating Travel Agents)   Eastern asked us how to tell travel agents in 15 cities about a new set of packaged tours. The problem: limited money, time, and a tough audience.

Travel agents are notorious for being a rude audience, anxious to drink your booze without giving a damn about your message. Plus, the principals of the major agencies tend to pass along the invitation to one of the underlings.

Solution to the time, money, and audience problems: We created a minimusical—about as mini a musical as you can get. A cast of two plus a stage manager and a prerecorded music track to which the cast lip-synched.

For the setting, we designed and had built an inexpensive expandable modular unit (at that time $125 per set). One was sent to each city. It was made of preformed corrugated cardboard, so that it could be modified, depending on the individual hotel room in which they were playing. (See Figure 12–3.)

We "fish-hooked" the program by sending a *series* of mailings as a buildup, and we were able to manage a 25 percent increase in travel agency principals' attendance.

The actors carried two trunks of costumes and made quick changes to personify the types of travelers who would be interested in various tours. Relevancy was hit all the way through, since we constantly pointed out how easy and profitable it was for the travel agents to book the tours.

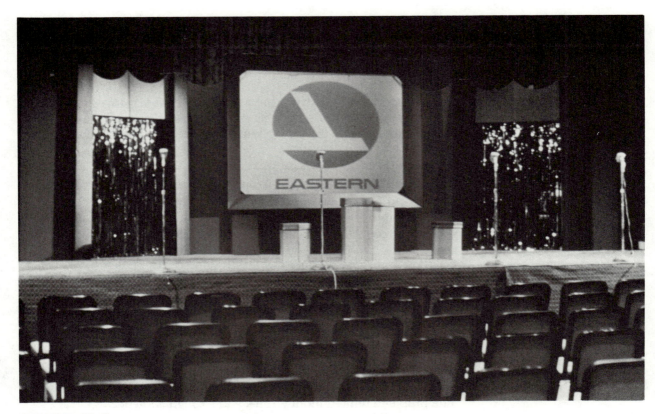

FIGURE 12–3

Bristol-Myers (Getting More Facings)   Bristol-Myers came to us with this problem. It was trying to impress on the sales force that although distribution was good, shelf facings could be better, and so the objective for the next push was "more space." The meeting coincided with the interest in the space program, so we built it around a "space" theme.

We got them all out on the beach, ostensibly for calisthenics, but dressed in NASA-white coveralls and crash helmets. In the midst of the exercises, a huge orange parachute appeared and dropped into the Atlantic Ocean. We could see the jumper being picked up and brought aboard a boat in the distance. In a few minutes, the rescue boat came up to the dock, and the national sales manager, dressed in a parachutist's outfit, emerged from the boat. (Of course, he hadn't jumped, we pulled a quick switch.)

Once inside, the meeting room was set up like a space control center. We even had miniature space ships. (The photo was taken with regular film. The space ships were actually covered with black light paint and appeared from nowhere and floated over the audience, then linked up in the dark overhead.) The space ships each represented part of the program, and with the linking up of the two parts, distribution and shelf space, the program would be successful. (See Figure 12–4.)

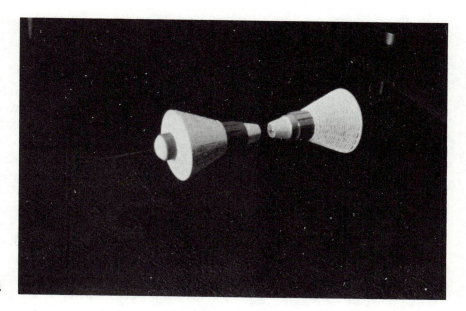

FIGURE 2–4

There can be no doubt that when the salesmen left the auditorium, they knew what the objective was for the next six-month period. Fish hook: Space theme. Participation was built into the presentation. And it certainly was *relevant.*

General Foods Sanka Brand (A Consumer Promotion)   Sanka put out a cookbook by Amy Vanderbilt that the consumer could get with a label and 50 cents. At the sales meeting, we presented this trade piece: a rolling pin on which we had attached a piece of dye-cut sponge rubber to look like a piece of dough, with a silk screen message, "We're rolling out the dough." (See Figure 12–5.)

The salesmen removed the end of the rolling pin and pulled out a card presentation of 3 × 5 cards that resembled recipe cards: "Take a pinch

FIGURE 12–5

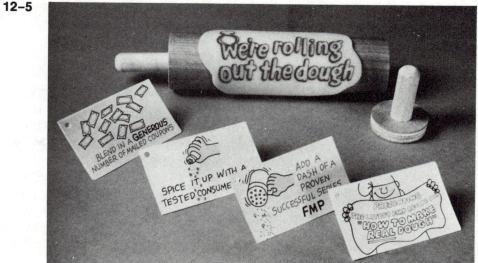

of a good thing . . . Sanka," "Add a dash of couponing," "Spice it up with a feature," and so on.

This technique was so successful that I've continued to use the principle. First, each point in the presentation is done on an individual card so that the salesman can adjust the presentation to meet his needs. Every salesman doesn't sell the same and the same salesman doesn't sell the same to every client. With this technique we give them flexibility. In addition, we give them blank cards and colored pens so that if they want to create their own additional cards, they can do so. We hardly ever do them in set type—just hand lettering, so the salesman can make his cards look like the rest of the presentation. In addition, we try to personalize the presentation. Figures are given on the basis of what is *relevant* to that particular buyer. The advertising card, for example, lists the media outlets in *that* buyer's city.

J & J Baby Lotion (Increasing Retail Displays) The problem: Trying to get druggists not only to display baby lotion in the baby department but also in the adult section. We built it around the fact that there are hidden profits on the druggist's shelf, and we invited him to peer through a magnifier.

Again the cards were separate and could be rearranged, and the little magnifier was attached to a leave-behind card that ticked off the key elements in the program. That little gimmick was much more effective than a simple $8\frac{1}{2} \times 11$ sheet of paper.

Dr Pepper (To Establish Distribution) This was a presentation to get distribution of Dr Pepper before the kick-off date for sale in New York City. The salesmen offered this tiny gavel to the buyer, with this trade piece—a legal brief:

Handing the buyer the gavel, they said, "You be the judge: if you have a question, bang the gavel!" The salesmen then presented a series of facts on why the buyer should carry Dr Pepper. I am proud to say this had an almost 85 percent usage. It was quick and dirty and an attention-getter which salesmen liked. (See Figure 12–6.)

Clairol (Strictly Entertainment) This is an example of the fun and games part of our Show & Meeting Services. Most of our clients are members of an industry association for the particular business they're in, and from time to time, one of the clients is given the honor of being either the chairman or "picking up the tab" for the evening's entertainment at one of the association affairs.

Clairol's turn was at a beauty operators' convention in Chicago. Hairdos being shown that year were the in the Twenties' style, the speakeasy days. So all the invitees were sent an invitation that looked like the exterior of a speakeasy door, and when you pulled back the flap, you saw the password. When you arrived at the hotel there was a

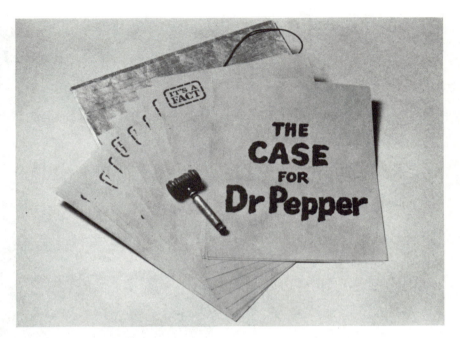

FIGURE 12-6

full-sized speakeasy door to match the one on the invitation. When you knocked at the door, the opening slid forward and the young lady asked for the password, which happened to be "Curly sent me." Once inside, set up on the platform was an old-fashioned claw-foot bathtub filled with ice and at least 50 bottles of champagne, surrounded by champagne glasses. The guests could then walk over to a "free lunch" counter, where they could enjoy hors d'oeuvres of the period. To continue the mood, we ran a contest. We blew up pictures of happenings in the Twenties—such generally known events that even though you may not have been there, you could answer the questions. We then had a drawing for prizes.

The object of these types of events is to impress a general idea on people who are coming. In this case, Clairol was trying to tell people that they had all the necessary equipment for the hairdresser to be able to do a good, efficient job in creating the Twenties' hairdos. To do that, we had a number of hairdressers around the room demonstrating the techniques, using Clairol products.

Bristol-Myers (Dramatizing a New Line) Bristol-Myers asked us to put together a party, at the National Wholesale Drug Association meeting, to dramatize some new products it was introducing that came from France. With a set similar to the expendable stage settings we used for the Eastern meeting, we put together a French street. In this case, the unit was set up to look like the exteriors of different shops. At the entrance was a real "fish hook": a gentleman tipping his hat to young ladies while at the *pissoir*. (See Figure 12-7.) Next, as we continue down the street we pass the cheese booth, where you could taste a number of French cheeses. Further along, a crepe shop where you could be

FIGURE 12-7

tempted to try some delicious crepes—my mouth still waters when I think about the chocolate ones. And on the right side an onion soup booth where we had a cauldron perking away serving delicious, thick onion soup. We also had a handwriting analyst, a cartoonist who did quick caricatures, and a magician and down the center of the street were sidewalk-type tables with umbrellas—everything very, very French. (See Figure 12-8.)

Dave went on to describe, for the workshop, many other such events—for Johnson & Johnson, an evening's entertainment using a variety of foreign games he obtained from members of the United Nations; for Bristol-Myers a sales award dinner in Hawaii, in a Japanese tea house (see Figure 12-9); horse races for a Chrysler dealer's meeting; for the first anniversary of selling Dr Pepper in New York, a mammoth birthday cake resembling a can of Dr Pepper.

Finally, having got the attention of the Advertising Skills Workshop members (who are recruited from offices all over the world), Dave, ever the creative entrepreneur, concluded with:

Have Show—Will Travel: If you need a problem solved, we may be able to help you . . . please call us and give us an opportunity to do so.

FIGURE 12-8

FIGURE 12-9

CHAPTER CHECKLIST

EVENT MARKETING

1. Event marketing is a fast-growing medium because it helps to solve all four major problems marketers face today:

    a. Erosion of brand loyalty.

    b. Maturation of product categories.

    c. Shift from the marketer's to the retailer's domination.

    d. Segmentation—the need for better targeting.

2. Event marketing solves these problems by providing products with extra *value*, by going a quality step beyond price promotions, by building positive relationships with retailers as well as consumers, and by tailoring sponsored events to specific market segments.

3. The seven steps to successful sponsorship are:

    a. Establish objectives.

    b. Develop a strategy.

    c. Ensure a strategic fit.

    d. Negotiate your package.

    e. Implement the event.

    f. Extend the event.

    g. Measure the results.

4. In order to get creative ideas, you should study and know the world of entertainment, as well as the experts you will consult.

5. As in all forms of commercial communication, seek to stand out with originality—resist the usual.

6. For inspiration, review the successful case histories cited in this chapter.

TRADE SHOWS AND SALES MEETINGS

1. These programs require show business capability.

2. The three basic principles are to have an attention-getter, a "grabber," a "hook"; to compel participation; and to be relevant to the audience.

3. Case histories illustrating successful use of these principles include Eastern's minimusical for travel agents, a "More Space" NASA theme for a Bristol-Myers sales meeting to encourage getting more shelf space, launching a Sanka brand cookbook to the sales force with 3×5 recipe cards for salesmen's success, promoting increased store displays for J & J baby lotion through a "magnifier" on the subject, Clairol's re-creation of the Roaring Twenties, and Bristol-Myers' re-creation of a street in France (both for the benefit of trade associations).

CHAPTER

13 Creativity in the Use of Media

Remember the opening of *The Music Man*, when the traveling salesmen kept repeating the refrain "You gotta know the territory"? Well, if you want to be creative in the use of media, that's the first requisite: *You've got to know the media.*

To know the media best, you should begin with an efficient organization of your media personnel and give them all the assistance and training they need to know and understand media backward and forward.

ORGANIZING TO UNDERSTAND MEDIA

Understanding media is a complex undertaking because there are so many media, they keep proliferating, and there's so much to know about them. Here is a table of organization for the Y&R Media Department (a.k.a. Communications Services). This is the kind of comprehensive organization a truly full-service agency might have:

1. Media planning

2. Research

3. Broadcast purchasing and programming; and

4. Specialists in the other categories of media, old and new

Of those four groups, the first—media planning—is the key contact with the product group and the clients and the final arbiter of media strategies. The other three are the "resource" groups, to provide the information the planners need to exercise sound and creative judgment.

The Training Program

In the past, while there have been single seminars, a number of which are described in this chapter, there was no formal, ongoing program. Recently, such a program, administered by one of the media supervisors, Barbara Delfyett-Hester, was designed to familiarize entry-level employees (minimum of three months' experience) with the various areas of the Communications Services Department.

The program provides an overview of each departmental discipline by having the trainees spend two to three days in each area with an instructor, thus supplying a telescoped hands-on overall experience.

Instructors are department personnel who have been selected because they are

☐ Senior in position

☐ Diversified in experience

☐ Capable of interpersonal communication skills

☐ Competent in coordination, able to involve participants in all group activities

"We will spread the training over several weeks," read the announcement of the program, "so that no one is away from his desk for more than two or three days during any week. For example, if a trainee is observing the local broadcast group for two days during the week of 2/25, he may not participate in the program again until the week of 3/11, thus leaving his daily responsibilities uninterrupted during the week of 3/4."

The trainees participating in the program are selected by the various area heads.

Why Communications (Media) Services?

This is the first question to be answered in any training about media. And the answer given:

To serve the client, to serve each product group, to communicate thoughtfully and effectively with media representatives, and to study and understand the clients' prospects.

The objective:

To deliver advertising messages to the right people, in the right place, at the right time, in the best environment and at the lowest possible price, a sufficient number of times to ensure effective communication.

To accomplish this objective, Y&R's comprehensive Media Department has these seven functions:

1. Assessment of marketing environment

2. Review of marketing objectives and strategies

3. Development of media strategies

4. Creative interaction

5. Evaluation and selection

6. Execution

7. Stewardship

How to Use Media Research   If you are to do your media planning effectively, you have to do your homework, and if you are fortunate enough to have a research resource group, those experts do a lot of it for you. They can provide all of the following: evaluation of syndicated research, consulting on research issues, point of view on media trends, models for test marketing, and models for plan evaluation.

Among the forms of information and systems a media research group deals with: syndicated data; audience measurements, such as Nielsen, Arbitron, Simmons, VALS; competitive measures, such as BAR, LNA/PIB, Multi-Client Cable Study; computer systems, which manage and analyze data, assist in vehicle selection and plan evaluation, and control budgets and scheduling.

Special study projects for media research include such subjects as

> *Marketing*: Working women, singles market, black consumer market, the South, leisure time, the prime of your life, teenagers in the 1980s, the New York market, the West.

> *Insights into Demographic Groups*: Population trends; purchase habits; media habits; life-styles; media considerations about radio, cable, daytime television; media in the 1980s, couponing, magazines, out-of-home.

A Y&R seminar about media research covers the categories of information, types of research needed, and the structure and functions of the department. It reviews the purposes of media research and the alphabet soup of resources (NTI, ARB, SMRB, PIB, NSI, AIS, ORC, G&R, BAR, MRI, etc.), otherwise known as "information overload," a characteristic of today's research scene.

Media research, says the seminar, must review and evaluate *all* the information out there. Before making recommendations, ask yourself these four questions:

1. *Is the research projectable?* Decide after you examine the technical research design and methods.

2. *Is the research valid?* Decide after you study the conceptual purpose and measurement concept.

3. *Is the research reliable?* Decide after you analyze the results of the data reported.

4. *Is the research useful?* Decide after you determine the practicality and utility of the data.

The effect of all this effort, concludes the seminar, is to:

---

reduce the overload and make available to planners the *best* possible source for their needs. Furthermore, in the case of Y&R, the decisions have tremendous impact on the industry, so the responsibility extends *beyond* the Media Department.

How the Planner Determines Media Strategy   Just as you need a creative work plan, you need a media work plan (Figure 13–1) to guide your media planner in the selection of the best possible media.

A seminar entitled "The Media Planning Process and You" trains the media planners. It explains that their plan is based on the best possible media research input and the marketing objective and strategy (as described in Chapter Two), which all result in the communication goals (effective reach and frequency). Those goals provide a quantitative basis for effective communication to target prospects and are based on the premise that repetition is necessary to ensure message comprehension and purchase motivation. The development of effective reach and frequency goals should be directly linked to a brand's marketing strategy and requires substantial product, marketing, and consumer knowledge, plus, of course, seasoned judgment. A summary of the seminar is as follows:

The media plan is the link in communicating the message to the consumer:

- Channel of communication.
- Strategic selection of appropriate environments can add value to the message.

The Marketing Group's role in media plan development is to:

- Provide complete marketing information and insight, updating as necessary.
- Evaluate media strategies based on their fit in the marketing program.
- Provide input and raise any concerns to direct the planners on the right path.
- Evaluate the media plan based on achievement of agreed upon strategies.

The goal in the media planning is to develop strong plans that:

- Are based on clear understanding and direction.
- Result in effective communication to the consumer.

The seminar reviews the overall characteristics of each medium.

The Y&R Media Work Plan

A. Background

B. Key Inputs for Media Work Plan

C. Section I—Marketing Background

D. Section II—Strategic Decision Summary

E. Section III—Execution

A. *BACKGROUND*

    1. What is a media work plan?

        a. Is comprised of three sections: Marketing Background, Strategic Decision Summary, and Execution.

        b. Serves to identify the business and marketing conditions which direct the formation of media strategy.

        c. Serves as a discipline that helps translate marketing and advertising objectives into functional media strategies.

    2. Why use a media work plan?

        a. Aids in developing strategically sound media plans that address agreed-upon marketing and advertising goals.

        b. Facilitates agency/client agreement on the objectives and issues which impact upon strategy.

        c. Identifies the execution of the recommended strategy.

B. *KEY INPUTS*

    1. Working media budget

    2. Target audience

    3. Seasonality

    4. Geographic definition

    5. Marketing objectives/strategies

    6. Promotional activity

    7. Competitive information

    8. Testing activities

    9. Creative requirements

    10. Other factors deemed relevant

C. *SECTION I—MARKETING BACKGROUND*

    1. Describes business situation that will impact upon media strategy development.

    2. Most important section of media work plan; forms framework for media strategies.

FIGURE 13–1

Components of Marketing Background

1. Advertising period

    a. Campaign period

    b. Fiscal year

    c. Calendar year

2. Media budget

3. Marketing background

    a. Brand history: Provides recap of brand in terms of past advertising, business overview.

    b. Competition: Analyzes competitive media pressures that will be faced by the brand.

        (1) Competitive marketing background

        (2) Expenditures

        (3) Media class

        (4) Activity

        (5) National versus local efforts

    c. Geography

        (1) Review of brand's distribution and business strength on a national/regional/local basis.

        (2) CDI, BDI used to determine geographic strength. BOI to identify markets of opportunity.

    d. Seasonality: Provides consumption patterns.

    e. Purchase cycle: Does the brand have a long or short purchase cycle?

    f. Pricing: Brand's pricing relative to category.

    g. Other factors that may impact on media planning.

4. Key marketing objective/strategies

    a. Marketing objective and strategies as it relates to media planning.

    b. Provides a statement of purpose for media.

        (1) Introduce new product

        (2) Gain trial and conversion

        (3) Maintain/increase share

D. *SECTION II—STRATEGIC DECISION SUMMARY*

1. Describes how media strategies will accomplish the marketing objective from a media perspective.

Components of Strategic Decision Summary

1. Prospect audience

FIGURE 13-1 *(continued)*

a. Basic designation: General description of consumers media will reach (i.e., current users, nonusers, heavy users).

b. Demographic

(1) Provides detailed information regarding prospect audience (i.e., sex, age, percentage of population, percentage of media effort).

(2) Market research provides information to identify demographics.

c. Psychographics

(1) Provides insight into the attitudes and life-styles of target audience.

(2) Provided by market research.

2. Media strategy: Defines how media will be used based on marketing information provided in Section I:

a. Competition

b. Geography

c. Seasonality

d. Weight allocation by quarter, continuity versus flighting.

e. Effective reach/frequency goals

3. Media selection/rationale

a. Based upon media strategies

(1) TV dayparts

(2) Radio

(3) Print

(4) And so on

b. Reasons for media selection

(1) Daytime network for its efficient frequency against women, and so on

E. *SECTION III—EXECUTION*

1. Description of media plan.

2. Completed after plans have been developed according to agreed-upon marketing/media objectives and strategies.

Components of Execution

1. Media mandatories: Describes situations which have impacted upon planning process.

a. Client directives (i.e., daytime weight levels)

b. Creative directives (i.e., plan must make exclusive use of :30s)

FIGURE 13–1 *(continued)*

     c. Spending considerations (i.e., 60 percent of media funds must be spent in first half of campaign period)

  2. Key executional factors: Identifies and provides rationale for

     a. Flighting patterns

     b. Continuous advertising

     c. Commercial length usage (i.e., 60/30)

  3. Media purchasing guidelines

     a. Types of programming

     b. Type of editorial

     c. Daypart usage

     d. Creative units

  4. Performance Data: Provides information that compares media execution to established goals.

     a. Reach/frequency

     b. Impression delivery by percentage of media effort

     c. Quarterly weight allocation

     d. Budget reports: quarterly, monthly

  5. Media Testing Activity: Provides brief review of all testing activity that will be considered during the advertising campaign.

EFFECTIVE REACH/FREQUENCY

Discipline that attempts to examine what frequency levels mean to effective communication; recognizes that repetition (frequency) is a key factor in the learning (message comprehension) process.

Effective frequency   The frequency of message exposure against a target prospect within a specified time frame which is judged necessary to ensure message comprehension and to motivate to consider purchase.

Effective reach   The percentage of the target audience exposed to the advertising message at the effective frequency level.

INPUTS TO THE DETERMINATION OF EFFECTIVE FREQUENCY LEVELS

1. Primarily a judgmental decision.

2. Based on the examination of a variety of marketing/media/creative factors.

3. Each factor must be evaluated relative to the needs/strategies/ position of each individual brand.

FIGURE 13-1 *(continued)*

Some of the factors examined are

Marketing

- ☐ Established versus new brand
- ☐ Brand dominance
- ☐ Purchase cycle
- ☐ Usage cycle
- ☐ Brand loyalty
- ☐ Brand awareness
- ☐ Category dynamics
- ☐ Competition
- ☐ Pricing
- ☐ Prospect definition
- ☐ Marketing objective

Creative

- ☐ Message uniqueness
- ☐ Message complexity
- ☐ New versus continued campaign
- ☐ Message variations

Media

- ☐ Competition
- ☐ Share of voice
- ☐ Scheduling
- ☐ Media selected
- ☐ Editorial environment

FIGURE 13–1 *(continued)*

THE CREATIVE TV MEDIA BUYER

There is no training seminar per se that can adequately arm a TV media buyer to be creative about his or her work. In this immensely powerful, changing, and expanding medium, experiential knowledge—even seat-of-the-pants agility—is the most realistic training.

Essentially, to understand the medium, you must keep constantly current and in contact with the following areas of expertise:

1. National TV buying
   a. The networks
   b. Cable stations
   c. Syndicated programming

2. Local spot buying

Frank Zingale, a veteran group supervisor of the Broadcast Purchasing and Programming Department, explains how the national TV buying works:

We traditionally buy network television in two ways. One is "upfront" and the other is "scatter."

Upfront is when you buy a 52-week deal with one or more of the networks, with certain cancellation options at each quarter. This gives the network an order for a 52-week period, and it gives the advertiser the guarantee, on a cost-per-thousand viewers, of a choice of inventory in the more desirable programs at the most desirable times.

That is the quid pro quo. It requires, of course, that the advertiser is committing a certain amount of money through the year, in order to get these benefits. He is guaranteed so many viewers at the given cost, and if the programs don't fulfill the guarantee, the network repays the advertiser in "make-goods" or free inventory.

Scatter is usually purchased on a quarter-to-quarter basis, and generally speaking, a scatter plan costs more. There's no guaranteed cost-per-thousand and the scatter advertiser has to be satisfied with what is left to be sold after the networks finish their upfront selling. The advantage is that scatter purchasing does not require any more financial commitment than on a quarterly basis.

What has changed most in recent years is the onset and growth of cable TV and syndication. Those and additional national networks. So advertisers have many more choices than what used to be only the three major networks.

Attractive as is the greater availability of buying options through the multiplying number of cable stations (and in some instances their ability to target specialized audiences), cable does not provide full exposure for national advertisers. There is not, at this writing, any one cable network that reaches more than 52 or 53 percent of the country's television homes. And, of course, cable stations reach fewer people than do the national network programs.

In each market, the national networks have "affiliate" stations. The syndication people do not have such predictable coverage:

They take their program and they try to place it in each market individually—whatever station will carry that program. Usually these programs are sold to national advertisers where they retain one or two units in the program to sell. The other commercial units in the program are used to make the deal with the stations. Those commercial availabilities can then be sold by the stations to local advertisers.

How the TV Buyer Uses Knowledge, Judgment, and Creativity

Everything in life involves some form of trade-off, where we make choices between the pros and cons. Where the expert TV buyer excels is in the fine art of negotiation. Frank explains:

The main negotiation from our side of the fence is to get the best possible programs for the lowest possible price, for the lowest cost-per-thousand guarantee. The network is just operating from the reverse—they want to sell you the least popular programs at the highest possible price and guarantee you the highest possible cost-per-thousand. So that's the area of negotiations. You've got to meet somewhere in the middle. Where you meet, to a large degree, depends on the marketplace conditions. If there is more money chasing the fixed inventory that the networks have, obviously it becomes a seller's market and the prices go up—just like any other commodity market. And the reverse is true. If there is less money than the inventory there is, then the networks need to sell that inventory at whatever price they can get.

So the negotiations are based primarily on that, and the other element of negotiations has to do with the ability of the buyers, namely us, to be able to read the marketplace, how it's going to be, *time* the marketplace, when the best and most opportune time to enter the marketplace will be, and that is something that is very difficult to predict.

The network program season starts in September, and there is a season for the cutoff of the upfront negotiations, usually in early spring, depending again on the health and nature of the marketplace—one could go all the way to the end of August, in some cases, but it usually starts right after the networks announce their prime-time schedule, usually around May. Soon after that, the upfront market begins to move.

In certain program categories, especially sports, there are large advertisers who buy sizable portions. They must buy a certain amount to be exclusive in their product categories, such as beers and cars. The majority of the advertisers buy what the stockbrokers call "dollar-cost averaging"—one buys some of the cheaper programming in order to be able to afford to buy some of the more expensive, higher-rated programming. It is the mix of those extremes, says Frank, that makes the negotiation successful or not.

"It's All in the Timing"

Unlike some commodities, the network TV media buyer is dealing with a fixed inventory. There are not any more commercial times available than what the networks can schedule. This fixed inventory is what all the advertisers and agencies are going after. In a "soft" marketplace, one can legislate terms, but in a "tight" marketplace the timing becomes even more important. It is not always advantageous to buy in early, certainly not in a soft marketplace, because the timing becomes very crucial. If the networks have inventory to sell, the closer it gets to premiere time in September, the more urgent it is for the seller to dispose of the inventory, and therefore the cheaper it will be. If it is a tight marketplace, with more money pursuing the same inventory, the buyer who commits early knows that he or she will get the inventory but therefore will have to pay a higher price. In that case, if the buyer waits too long, other people will have bought the best, and you have missed the opportunity for the time slots you would prefer. So it is a question of *timing* the marketplace as well as *knowing* the marketplace.

Smaller Advertisers and Network TV

At this time, it would be unlikely that a smaller advertiser could attempt to buy national network time on the "Bill Cosby" or "L.A. Law" shows. "However," says Frank,

there are areas in TV that can accommodate the low-budget advertiser. A product targeted to at-home housewives might buy into daytime network TV, which is considerably cheaper. There are different dayparts that cater to specific types of audiences, such as the evening news, which usually skews toward older consumers and more to men than to women. The early morning shows reach a good audience of both men and women—including working women, who may not be available during the daytime. And these shows are all cheaper on a cost-per-unit basis. . . . In any case, the whole business of TV buying is geared to price based on viewership—what kind and how many viewers watch the kind of television you are pricing.

How to Be a Creative TV Media Buyer

Throughout this book, we are discussing "the basics," plus something more. Frank Zingale expresses it as follows:

No matter what media you are buying, whether it's network television or a local radio spot, the basics are essentially the same . . . which are, first, you've got to know what it is you want and, second, you've got to know the language.

You don't have to be a mathematical wizard, but if you hate to work with numbers, you'd better do something else, because they are a large part of our language. You don't just negotiate with words, you negotiate with numbers, dollars, audience numbers, cost-per-thousand, GRPs [gross rating points].

However, just having a good knowledge of those things does not make you a very good buyer. You have to have an instinct of where the marketplace is, and the only way you do that is to find out, by every possible means. That kind of data is not published anywhere. You have to be totally up to date—not just what the situation was last week, but what it was an hour ago, before you determine whether it's the time to go in and make a buy.

You have to know, for example, how you're going to approach each of the networks if you believe, for example, that inventory is scarce. There are no rules in such a situation. It depends a great deal on the relationships you have been able to establish and maintain with the media salespeople. You learn information.

These things are going way beyond the "scientific" part of our business (what ratings you should be using, the background, the history of the particular time period you are looking at). You have to make judgments. If this particular program has been doing this kind of number in the past, will it *continue* to do that, or is there going to be some stiffer competition with the program opposite this year? Is there something you read or heard about the change in the cast? This is all part of a buyer's "creativity"—knowing and feeling what is *going* to happen. Our business is not based on what happened yesterday, it is *always* in *the future.* Yesterday's unsold commercial is useless to everybody, it's gone. A buyer must anticipate, estimate properly, accurately, what is *going* to happen. That is what makes a buyer terrific versus terrible—creative versus just a number-cruncher.

Above all, the enthusiastic media buyer is one who looks forward to each day's hurly-burly of *negotiation.* Frank explains how, when interviewing young applicants, he will ask them, not just about their background and experience, but how they have gone about dealing with people. "It's not enough for them to say, 'Oh, I like dealing with people,' but how well they can *persuade* people to their point of view." He might ask them some such question as: "Have you ever bargained to buy a used car? Never mind what kind of a deal you made, but did you *like* doing it, did you *enjoy* it?" If they didn't, they would never make good media buyers.

A Business of Trust

In a field which, to the general public, might seem on occasion to be a "cutthroat" business, it is a phenomenon how much negotiating is based on mutual trust:

The interesting thing about network television, and syndication, and cable, is that there is no such thing as a rate card. You go in and negotiate the best possible price. It's usually done on the 'phone, and our words are as good as our bonds.

With all the countless *billions* of dollars that have been spent in television, I can't remember a written *contract* that was executed by both parties at the point of making the deal. It's absolutely a gentleman's agreement—everything is done on the 'phone, the deal is made on the 'phone, seldom face-to-face, and you honor that word, because if you don't you don't last in this business.

Examples of Broadcast Media Creativity

Frank tells, with pride, of an example where his intuition *and* the result of having his ear to the ground resulted in a media buying coup for his client, the soft drink Dr Pepper. This product's advertising budget was small compared with those of its major competitors Pepsi and Coke, but they were all three interested in targeting a young audience, and he had heard through his grapevine of a brand-new program idea by George Schlatter called "The American Comedy Awards," which has become an annual event with a high rating among that target audience.

The program had not even been time-slotted when he called his contact at ABC and made a firm offer for the exclusive Dr Pepper sponsorship: "Believe it or not, only twenty minutes after my call, one of those major competitors' media buyers called with the same offer. But it was too late—the network had to honor our Dr Pepper first offer."

Creative media buying of that nature is, of course, only one of the ways that media people are innovative. For inspiration, here are some of the ways, including savvy buying, in which Y&R has innovated with broadcast media in the past:

☐ In 1928, the Radio Household Institute was organized to buy large blocks of radio time from NBC, which were then resold as individual time segments to clients and their advertisers.

☐ In 1951, for Jell-O Pudding & Pie Filling, Y&R produced and placed the first TV color commercial, with the soon-to-be obsolete CBS "field sequential" system.

☐ Y&R was the first to buy time on all three networks for the same special show (sponsored by General Foods).

☐ Tailoring network TV to a small client's needs, in the 1950s, Y&R secured regional sponsorship of one of the nation's top TV shows, "Sing Along with Mitch," in markets of prime importance to the J. H. Filbert Company, a regional marketer.

☐ When, in 1964, Y&R was limited to purchase only weather or news telecasts for Gulf Oil, Y&R Media bought into weather shows in 100 markets around the country. Where there were none, particularly on independent stations, the agency created 5-minute weather shows.

☐ In the early 1960s, Y&R created a unique broadcast franchise for its Gulf client, who wanted to create a public service image but to avoid identification with run-of-the-mill TV shows. In collaboration with NBC, Y&R developed a plan for sponsorship of special, unscheduled, headline news telecasts. A similar plan was subsequently negotiated with CBS for another client, an insurance company.

☐ In 1971, for Arrow Shirts, all network :60s available in the three leading late-night network programs, were purchased on the same evening—to maximize retailer impact and visibility of the fall fashion line. It was the first time that any advertiser managed to dominate all TV viewing by purchasing a full time period as a roadblock. (Retailers were requested to purchase local spots with co-op funds in the same program, and, in many markets, this client was the sole advertiser on the station for a full 90 minutes.)

☐ In 1972, a series of nationally televised "rock concert" specials was purchased for Dr Pepper. "Good Vibrations from London" was the first contemporary special to be simulcast on network TV and FM radio stereo stations in major markets. That same year Y&R developed the idea of the "New Year's Rockin' Eve" show for Dr Pepper to offset the lack of New Year's Eve programming for the young adult audience. Dick Clark, the young people's music guru, produced it, and the first show aired on NBC on December 31, 1971 to January 1, 1972, from 11:30 P.M. to 1:00 A.M. In 1984, the Independence Day holiday became the catalyst for a radio roadblock on youth-oriented networks, called "The 4th of July Blast." Product exclusivity was negotiated and local bottlers were able to tie in with point-of-purchase displays at the start of the peak period for the soft drink industry. Consistent ideas like these, together with the highly popular Dr Pepper commercial executions, have been largely responsible for the franchise that a hitherto small regional beverage has won—contending successfully with Pepsi and Coke for the youth market.

▫ In 1977, the first halftime show for college basketball games on TV was created for Met Life's exclusive sponsorship.

▫ In 1978–1979, Y&R secured the first commercial position for two clients in any overtime or extra-inning opportunities on AFC football and World Series games on NBC-TV, at a cost about half the rate card price.

▫ In 1981, for the U.S. Postal Service, Y&R conceived and created a series of drop-in vignettes called "The Spirit of Christmas." These ran prior to the Christmas season as part of the mail-early campaign. Each 90-second vignette featured a famous face. As part of the deal, USPS received replay rights and they ran again in 1982.

▫ In 1982, to maximize the impact of the introduction of the new Mercury Capri car, Y&R made the single largest-ever commitment in a miniseries sponsorship ("Masada") and used 100-second commercials in Screenvision in movie theaters. The introduction was the most successful in Ford history.

UNDERSTANDING MAGAZINES AND PLANNING FOR THEIR USE

Six subjects are covered in a seminar about the magazine medium:

I. Magazine trends

II. Reader dynamics

III. Magazine characteristics versus other media

IV. Magazine planning

    A. Basic guidelines

    B. Selective criteria

        1. Quantitative

        2. Qualitative

V. Creative considerations

VI. Magazine futures

Some of the information covered is the following:

Magazine trends

Circulation of consumer magazines grew 114 percent between 1950 and 1984, primarily due to a growth in new titles (statistics and categories of major growth).

Reader dynamics

The average reader tends to be younger, more upscale than TV viewer (data) . . . spends two to three reading days per issue (length of time to reach total audience for weeklies, biweeklies, and monthlies).

Magazine planning

Basic guidelines for evaluating magazines. Planning selection criteria (coverage, composition, cost per thousand, product usage, reach/frequency analysis).

Creative considerations

Positioning; unique/multiple units, special issues/advertorials, couponing, inserts, tie-ins, split runs, microfragrances.

Magazine futures

Continued proliferation of special interest publications; video magazines; videotex.

SUMMARY: **Magazines provide selectivity, extended reach, authority, permanence, involved readers, merchandising.**

This seminar presents a detailed case history of General Foods International Coffees, in which the plan involved 40 percent bulking books and 60 percent vertical. They present the magazine analysis, the evaluation/selection criteria—quantitative and qualitative—lists and complete data for the bulking, vertical, and military magazines, discussion of a set-aside budget for special interest publications, to be planned at a later date, and the flowchart in Figure 13–2.

How to Use Unusual Space Shapes in Print

Creativity in the use of media can go beyond the creative use of research and media selection. It's one thing to identify the right magazines, and to buy space there—it's quite another to stand out in that space, head and shoulders above your competitors. Often you can

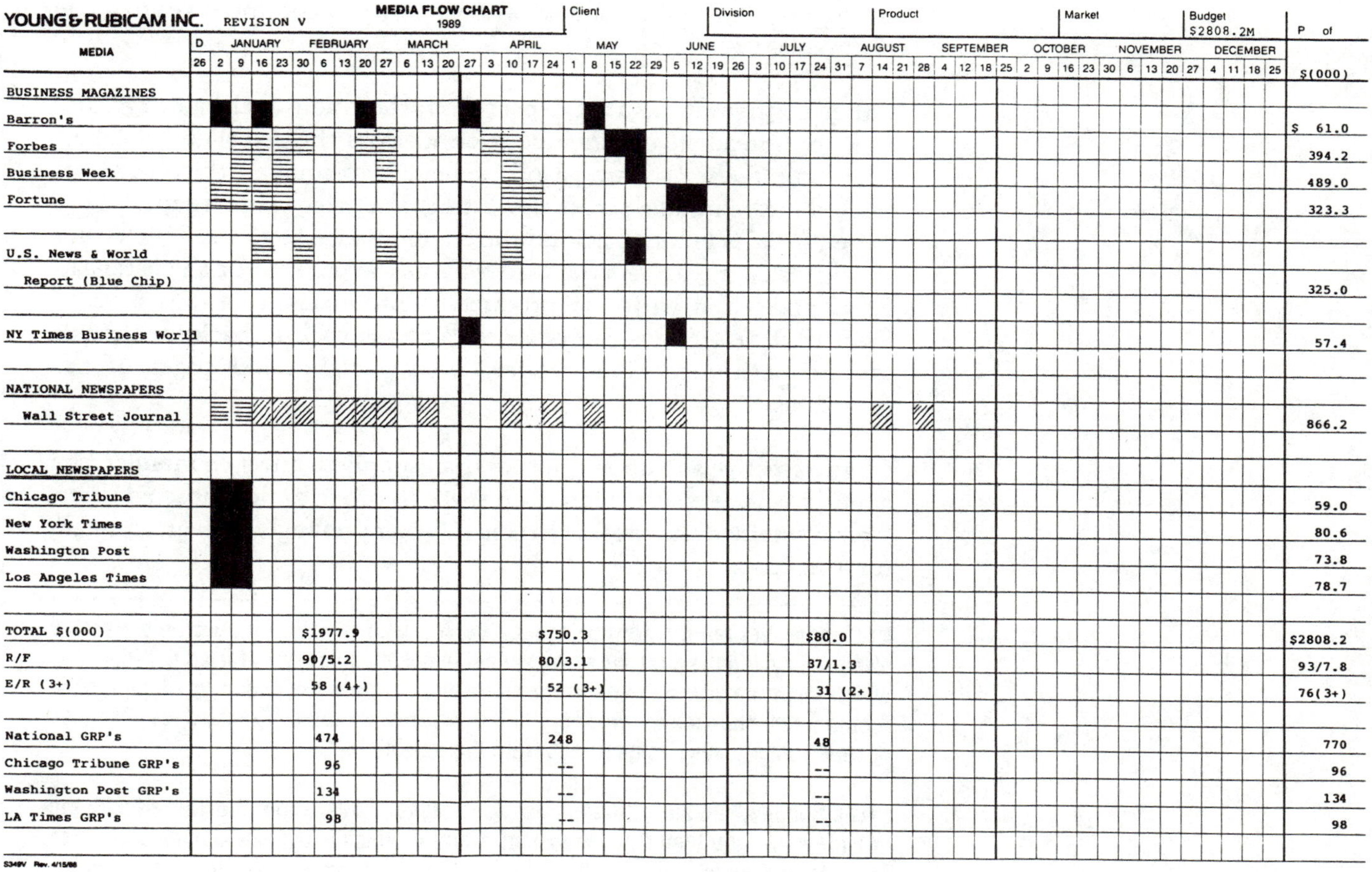
YOUNG & RUBICAM INC.
REVISION V
MEDIA FLOW CHART
1989
Client
Division
Product
Market
Budget
$2808.2M
P of
MEDIA
D JANUARY FEBRUARY MARCH APRIL MAY JUNE JULY AUGUST SEPTEMBER OCTOBER NOVEMBER DECEMBER
26 2 9 16 23 30 6 13 20 27 6 13 20 27 3 10 17 24 1 8 15 22 29 5 12 19 26 3 10 17 24 31 7 14 21 28 4 12 18 25 2 9 16 23 30 6 13 20 27 4 11 18 25
$(000)
BUSINESS MAGAZINES
Barron's $ 61.0
Forbes 394.2
Business Week 489.0
Fortune 323.3
U.S. News & World Report (Blue Chip) 325.0
NY Times Business World 57.4
NATIONAL NEWSPAPERS
Wall Street Journal 866.2
LOCAL NEWSPAPERS
Chicago Tribune 59.0
New York Times 80.6
Washington Post 73.8
Los Angeles Times 78.7
TOTAL $(000) $1977.9 $750.3 $80.0 $2808.2
R/F 90/5.2 80/3.1 37/1.3 93/7.8
E/R (3+) 58 (4+) 52 (3+) 31 (2+) 76(3+)
National GRP's 474 248 48 770
Chicago Tribune GRP's 96 -- -- 96
Washington Post GRP's 134 -- -- 134
LA Times GRP's 98 -- -- 98
S349V Rev. 4/15/88

FIGURE 13–2

do this through a unique use of the print, so that, in effect, the medium literally becomes the message, or at least the unique carrier for the unique message.

In June 1988, *The Wall Street Journal* ran a major feature, "ADVERTISERS SEE BIG GAINS IN ODD LAYOUTS—Page Position Can Make Ads More Prominent." Y&R has long been aware of this advantage and for years has conducted a special seminar about it. It's a show-and-tell session, for the Advertising Skills Workshop, about ways to use unconventional spaces in print to make a smaller budget look bigger and/or to dramatize copy points.

Magazines will make available space shaped like an L, a T, an upside-down T, or a U, or space split apart into whatever configuration suits your fancy.

If you take advantage of such shapes, the reader usually has a better chance of seeing your ad. If you use the U shape or the upside-down T, the readers read down into your ad four times. Or when you use the L shape, one can't miss your ad when he or she continues reading the editorial content.

Other configurations that depart from the traditional half page, full page, or spread shapes include such ideas as the so-called "checkerboard" unit; the "square island" spread (two squared third-page ads floated in the middle across the gutter); the "free form" shape, where the editorial is tailored around the ad; multipage sections, which offer strong visual impact. As the reader turns the page, he or she is repeatedly confronted with the product or products in various uses or formats. The sections can be a series of ads back to back, or the ads can be positioned consecutively on the right-hand pages of the magazines.

From a creative standpoint, rather than simply to effect economies, the concept is to use and manipulate space in order to dramatize ad units. At this seminar, the speaker makes this point tellingly with an architectural analogy:

I recently overheard a former agency person who is now a magazine's creative director say, "In the past, when we set out to design an ad, we started to draw lines which might vary in size and proportions, but they always ended up as square or rectangular, one reason probably being that *magazines* are rectangles. But also because we always designed ads from the outside in."

"Traditionally," he said, "that's how we designed houses too. We started with the outside walls and then fitted the room inside—which is why most homes are also squares and rectangles. But then," he continued, "some smart contemporary architects came along and said we ought to design from the inside out. We ought to plan each room separately. First, making each one the size and shape it *ought* to be, for its own purpose; then put them together, and let the form follow the function—let the shape come out however it does, to serve the purpose. In other words, the outside shape is whatever you *need* to make the inside work best—which is why we make these special units available."

Examples of Innovative Uses of Magazines and Newspapers

□ Y&R was the first to use editorial-style color comic strips for advertising, in 1931 for General Foods.

□ Y&R was also the first to use a phonograph record in a mass circulation weekly. This was a Christmas promotion for Remington shavers in *Look* magazine, 1959. Incidentally, to justify the high cost of this one-shot spectacular (which served the double purpose of high readership and trade merchandising to push distribution), the creative staff used imaginative approaches to persuade the best possible stars to perform, which resulted in the featuring of Bing Crosby, Rosemary Clooney, Louis Armstrong, and the Hi-Los on this one entertaining record. The caliber of these performers resulted in a high degree of participation as consumers tore out the record and played it—often many times over.

□ In 1961, Y&R was the first to use the cover photo of a magazine continued onto the back cover as an ad. At no extra cost we bought both the front and back cover of *Teen* magazine for Bondex, which started a teenage fad and caused a big sales boost for the product.

□ The first sample product affixed to a magazine page was a Y&R innovation: Johnson & Johnson's introduction of Band-Aid Brand Sheer-Strip Bandages in 1958, through a four-page spectacular with 1,200,000 actual samples of the product in the *Saturday Evening Post* newsstand circulation. In 1961, the first food product sample carried in magazines was a four-cup sampling of Sanka, in the newsstand distribution of *TV Guide* and *Family Circle* magazines. In 1961, the first sampling of a liquid—J & J's First Aid Cream—was placed in *TV Guide* by Y&R Media. Such samplings cost less than samples by direct mail or point of sale.

□ In the 1950s Y&R created the first four-page gatefold advertisement in magazine publishing history, with an insertion in *Better Homes & Gardens*. This stimulated a series of gatefold ideas. For example, a gatefold for a Remington shaver ad was used in the 1950s to dramatize the shaver's superior size and smooth shave. With the right-hand page gatefold closed, the man looked fully bearded. When the reader pulled open the gatefold, it revealed the man with a big clean-shaven swathe on his face. The gatefold turning created the sense of a "moving ad," since the man's hand went from one position on his cheek to a lower position.

□ In 1958, Y&R developed and pioneered preprinted full-color, magazine-quality inserts for newspapers. These inserts (which Y&R dubbed "Hi-Fi") featured a continuous design layout to accommodate a random cutoff at the newspaper. The idea required a new imaginative method for creating ads (wallpaperlike art and copy). At the same time, Y&R predicted the so-called "SpectaColor," to follow their invention, when special control equipment would be installed by newspapers, and this came about within four years. From the beginning of 25 million impressions in 1962, SpectaColor grew to over 900 million by 1969.

□ In 1968, the Print Production Department in Y&R's Chicago office developed a method of coating a newspaper page with Scotchgard to demonstrate how clean even a newspaper page could be kept. The headline: "Spill your coffee on this page and see how effective Scotchgard really is."

□ It was Y&R's media department which pioneered split-run advertising (in 1959 for Northern Tissue in *Life* magazine), to give its regional client the benefit of advertising in a major weekly magazine.

□ Believed to be the first four-page pop-up color insert ad in a magazine of large circulation was the Kaiser Aluminum & Chemical Corporation 1963 ad in *Machinery Magazine* and *Automatic Machining*.

□ In 1962, Y&R used the first Answercard in a supplement (*Parade*). It was a redemptive coupon for Minute-Rice, pasted on the center-spread, easily pulled off, and sturdy enough not to be easily lost or mutilated, as an ordinary coupon clipped from newspaper. Redemption return from the first one was 4.9 percent versus the norm of 2.5 percent.

□ Y&R pioneered the use of small ROP color ads in newspapers which previously permitted only 1,000-line units, so that clients with limited funds could have the benefit of ROP color.

□ And some twenty years later—a dramatic breakthrough for the advertising industry—Y&R Media negotiated and coordinated the first newspaper rate-cutting for national advertisers.

□ In 1982, Johnson & Johnson Baby Products Company was seeking an authoritative and selective environment for its advertising. Y&R, in conjunction with 13/30 Publishing Group, developed three corporate vehicles, *Pre-Parent Advisor*, *New Parent Advisor*, and *Parenting Advisor*.

□ General Foods Corporation wanted a way to reach the youth market. An annual promotion in *Seventeen* magazine, which was previously open to all advertisers, was negotiated on an exclusive basis for General Foods. The promotion is now called "Seventeen-General Foods Now You're Cooking National Competition" and comprises magazine space, collateral material, sampling, awareness research, and GF participation with high school home economics teachers.

□ In 1986, AT&T began to sponsor a full-page unit in *USA Today's* International edition during the heavy overseas travel period (May–September). The unit gives useful information regarding international telephoning, embassy addresses, coping with medical emergencies, and so on. This AT&T Traveler's Assistance Directory appears three times per week in *USA Today* and is also distributed on overseas flights and by hotels, travel agents, consulates, and visitor centers.

Other Media, Other Innovations

The following are a few examples of unique uses of other types of media:

□ Outdoor advertising in the Northern states suffers from a dearth of business during the winter months. In 1963, Y&R negotiated a two-week showing of every available panel in the New York market for a drink mix (Tang). Plant operators were persuaded to leave the copy up until the panels were resold. Many panels remained up and in good condition until April 1964—all for the price of a two-week showing. This idea was repeated for other clients at later dates.

□ In 1970, Y&R helped to develop a new concept in transit advertising—called Basic Bus. The idea: all interior space in the bus to be used *by a single advertiser*.

◻ In 1972 advertisements in paperback books were tested for Sanka. Ads ran in 500,000 copies monthly, mostly in adventure and travel dual-audience titles.

◻ In 1980, to advertise the Lincoln/Mercury Capri to its primary demographic audience of young adults, Y&R Detroit used Screenvision advertising in an estimated 2,000 theaters. The humorous commercial was 100 seconds long and was shown between features.

UNDERSTANDING THE NEW ELECTRONIC MEDIA AND PLANNING FOR THEIR USE

Seminars about these emerging media have covered the following five subjects:

"Enhanced" television: Cable TV; LPTV (local TV with a total broadcast signal range of 10 to 15 miles); DBS, MDS, and SMATV (satellite TV services); pay-per-view (through an addressable decoder which enables a viewer to unscramble the desired program)

Home video (videocassette recorders)

Home electronics (personal computers)

Computer-based on-line services (videotex)

Out-of-home electronic systems (interactive videodiscs)

Regarding the first, *cable*, the basic cable services are growing rapidly, projected to be in more than half the national homes by 1990. Pay cable, at a slower rate because of the competition of VCRs, will be in one-third of the homes.

Of all the new TV technologies, pay-per-view currently offers the most promise for the near future, and is now in 40 to 50 cable systems.

Videocassette recorders are already in half the homes, projected to 60 percent by 1990, 75 percent in key demographic groups. Most commonly, video is viewed as an extension of ongoing "service" communications. In addition, sponsoring feature-length "blockbuster" movies is becoming an option, and special promotion cassettes are also being used effectively.

Personal computers are now in some 20 percent of homes, projected to one-third by 1990. Of those, some have modems that allow information to be delivered over phone lines from one computer to another. The opportunities are at present only in videotex involvement. But advertisers may consider the potential for producing consumer computer software.

The current status of *videotex* as a consumer medium is directly linked to modem penetration, which has been slow, but should be some 50 percent by 1990. Consumer usage of videotex includes accessing information/data bases, sending electronic mail messages, playing games, and doing telebanking and teleshopping.

As a home video entertainment technology, the *videodisc player* has had limited growth, primarily because they are unable to record programming. Interactive out-of-home videodiscs, however, have transactional capabilities, as well as demonstration ease, and interactive videodisc kiosks are rapidly being placed in a variety of locations nationally. Consumers use them to access computer information that is depicted with photographic quality on a screen, providing product demonstrations, simulations, single product features, color selections, teleguide systems, and so on.

Getting a Legup on the New Media

If you have an innovative attitude, you can gain experience and a valuable franchise for those clients who are also far-seeing. Y&R got its feet wet in cable TV with such innovations as the following:

☐ The first venture by a major agency into cable TV programming occurred in 1970 and 1971. Y&R collaborated with Cox Cable in Warner Robins, Georgia, to develop 27 hours of original programming per week, construction of a rate card and time sales to local retailers.

☐ In 1976, 13 Y&R clients participated in the first live commercial cablecast distributed nationally by satellite, using the Madison Square Garden Sports Network. In 1977, 3 Y&R clients were the first advertisers to support that sports network. Part of the package buy was the Nielsen–Y&R audience research of the cable viewers of Madison Square Garden programming.

☐ In 1980, based on unique proprietary research about cable TV, Y&R negotiated an opportunity for our clients to gain franchise advertising promotions in Cable News Network. The short-term advantage over rate card exceeded 50 percent.

☐ In 1981, Y&R orchestrated a long-term purchase for General Foods on the new WTBS Super Station, including diminishing CPM guarantees. The contract was at a minimum of five years.

☐ In 1982, for General Foods, Y&R produced and copyrighted the weekly cable program "Woman's Day USA," written and produced in cooperation with the editors of *Woman's Day* magazine.

☐ In 1982, to gain greater insights into cable television, Y&R fielded a multiclient cable study which provided those clients with unique and proprietary information.

▫ MTV was a natural vehicle for Dr Pepper. However, it was important that a presence be developed to give the brand the competitive edge. In 1984, a program idea, taking advantage of the national interest in the game Trivia, was developed for Dr Pepper's sponsorship. As an ancillary benefit, it provided the Dr Pepper Company with names and addresses of those submitting questions, which could then be used for market research purposes.

▫ In 1984, a new idea in cable programming was developed for General Foods—90 seconds of "helpful hint" programming and a 30-second commercial, playing on five cable networks. The program, named "Shortcuts," was targeted at the young, employed adult who wants quality but doesn't have a lot of time.

▫ In 1985, to target the appropriate audience, a 5-minute program segment entitled "The Information Age" was developed for NYNEX to run on the *Financial News Network*. The segment ran ten times per week, with program emphasis on happenings in the areas of data communications and information transmission.

▫ In 1986, as a showcase for the new adidas line of clothing, named for the basketball star Patrick Ewing, a guest appearance was negotiated on MTV where Ewing appeared wearing the adidas product.

With these, and many more activities, Y&R has become by far the major agency in cable TV sponsorship. The medium has long ago passed the one-third coverage key factor, and the Y&R Media creativity that went into its inception is paying off handsomely for clients and agency.

Here are a few innovations in some of the other new electronic media covered in that seminar:

▫ In 1972, Y&R published and *sold* "VIDEO CASSETTES," the first comprehensive agency report on the new medium.

▫ In 1982, Y&R was involved in the CBS/AT&T videotex experiment in Ridgewood, N.J., that began on behalf of J & J and General Foods. This included activities ranging from advertising message development to program creation and merchandising.

▫ In 1982, a major brokerage (Merrill Lynch) and motor inn chain (Holiday Inns) received free commercials in "Tel-E-Pictures," an in-flight news program shown before the movie on Western Airlines. Y&R negotiated the arrangement, which used two of the three available commercial breaks.

▫ A confectionery company was one of the first advertisers featured in Videophile—a home video advertising vehicle located in video rental stores. Video rental outlets sell snacks, which provided point-of-purchase exposure. The use of Videophile also provided them with an excellent tie-in for their *Back to the Future* movie promotion, new on videocassettes.

A SEMINAR ON MEDIA MERCHANDISING

The overview for this seminar explains the subject as follows:

Merchandising is a tool to provide extra *awareness* to the trade, sales force, or consumers, of a product or service beyond the traditional scope of advertising.

Merchandising is the result of a joint effort on the part of the various media and the advertiser to promote both the media and the product or service being advertised in that media.

Pricing varies from medium to medium. Some vehicles have established percent allowances based on total expenditures. Others provide merchandising services at cost.

Following the overview, the subjects discussed are

☐ Types of merchandising

☐ Merchandising traits of various media

☐ Function of media planners in merchandising

☐ Examples

☐ Outlook

For the outlook, the seminar points out that media suppliers are shifting away from merchandising allowances, due to prohibitive costs and the media's tendency to discourage advertiser interest. Therefore, "Creative merchandising programs are the *responsibility* of the planning function" and "Be proactive—innovative merchandising opportunities can frequently be secured if they are solicited and can often contribute to increasing a product's sales."

A Seminar About "The Perfect Media Planner and Sales Representative Relationship"

Remember how media buyer Frank Zingale stressed the importance of TV media "rep" relationships. Acutely aware of such personal considerations, the Y&R media training program has conducted a seminar on the subject, stressing two dirty words: "supplier" and "buyer." The relationship should, instead, be a respectful collaboration. The following are some of the subjects covered:

☐ *What I want to learn from your visit.* Agency/sales relationship, the ideal salesperson, what I expect from you, what you should expect from me, how to answer my basic questions.

□ *The ideal agency media planner.* Advertising person, investor, approach to media.

□ *What I expect from you during the call.* Ask me what I do, find out what I need, give me information, give me good ideas.

□ *What I expect from you after the call.* Don't forget me, don't take the order and run—service the business, be responsive—follow up, don't be afraid to challenge me.

□ *What you should expect from me.* Accessibility, courtesy, an open mind; sharing information, explanation of why you are not or why you are getting the business.

□ *How to answer my basic questions.* How do I know I'm really getting what I'm paying for; who the readers are; explicitly, what visibility the ad will get (compatible editorial, franchise positions, opposite well-read feature/column, etc.).

A sympathetic postscript listed these things to keep in mind: "Not all agencies are alike. Assistant planners and media directors don't have the same needs. Agency people reincarnate many times (a sales call that doesn't produce an order today is not unproductive). Remember that we are all salespeople."

OTHER SEMINAR SUBJECTS

The Media Department's "traveling workshops" have included dozens of subjects, everything from A (Attentiveness and Arbitron Methodology) to Z (Zapping and Zipping). Among the most important new subjects, of course, are those seminars about evolving media, some of which could become dominant the way print, radio, and TV grew in their day. In addition to those described already are seminars about "Advertising in Catalogs" and "Teleshopping Overview." Other subjects of special contemporary importance are "Support Advertising" (i.e., the use of a secondary ad for the purpose of calling attention to a direct response advertisement) and "Commercial Avoidance" (i.e., both active and passive behavior of consumers which we must increasingly cope with through our creative ingenuity). Perhaps the most important workshop, as this chapter is being written, is the following 1988 addition:

───

"What Factors Have Caused Us to View the Media Planning Process Differently?—Now versus 1975"

───

The seminar covers the following seven subjects:

□ Higher media costs (CPM, out-of-pocket)

□ Network audience erosion

□ Increased media choices

□ Improved data retrieval and analysis

□ Different approaches to setting target audiences

□ Clients' increased need for accountable marketing efforts

□ Reduced product differentiation, coupled with reduced consumer brand loyalty

Each subject is accompanied by charts that illustrate the points made and details the causes and implications. The seminar then concludes with the following realistic summation:

It's a tougher world out there. The media dollar does not go as far, competitors are more formidable, Wall Street is more demanding, and consumers are more demanding. *But* there are *more opportunities*—more sophisticated ways to collect and analyze data about the audience and about consumers by groups and as individuals. And there are many more media to reach those consumers.

To realize those opportunities, we need to continue to push for innovations. And these can be achieved by more synergy in all marketing efforts, by partnerships between agencies and clients (and among agencies), by a greater willingness to take risks, and by recognition that the world will continue to change.

IN CONCLUSION

In April 1988, after a fierce competition among some of the leading advertising agencies, the Revlon Group assigned some $30-35 million in ad spending to Young & Rubicam. One of the main reasons for the choice was Y&R's media capabilities.

To determine the extent of Y&R's buying capabilities, Revlon gave the agency tests that paralleled buys other agencies had made and compared the results for effectiveness.

A report in *Advertising Age* cited the remarks of Arthur Cohen, Revlon executive vice president of advertising worldwide: "The upfront market doesn't move without Y&R. Their media buying is super, their strategic thinking is excellent, and the creative they put on the table is excellent."

And that conclusion brings this chapter full circle, back to where it began, with Alex Kroll's insistence that: *Media is a creative function.*

- -
CHAPTER CHECKLIST
- -

1. First requisite: understand your media.

2. Organize your internal and/or external media sources to provide the fullest and most current information for understanding.

3. Seven functions summarize the objectives of comprehensive media knowledge.

4. Media planning is based on four criteria of media research.

5. Consider the multiplying options in TV media buying and the best characteristics for a creative TV media buyer, including skillful timing and agility in negotiation.

6. For inspiration and guidance, review some examples of past innovation in broadcast media purchase and use.

7. Print media planning and buying (e.g., magazines) involves six areas of consideration. Unusual uses of space in magazines and newspapers is an example of creative use of print media.

8. Review examples of creative print media innovations.

9. Among important current and future media options are the multiplying forms of electronic media, including in-home and out-of-home forms of video and computers.

10. A vital consideration is the human relationship between media sellers and buyers.

11. Consider seven areas that are currently altering the ways of looking at media and providing new problems and opportunities.

12. Remember, whatever the medium, creativity is the key to successful media planning and buying.

- -

CHAPTER **14** The Whole Egg and the Whole Globe

THE WHOLE EGG

"We are betting the firm on this concept," said Peter Georgescu, president of Young & Rubicam Advertising, referring to integrated communications (IC), for which Y&R had used the metaphor "The Whole Egg."

Young & Rubicam had been founded to create compelling *advertising* that would help to sell clients' products. And because of familiar identification, I have often referred to Y&R as an "advertising agency."

It is no longer sufficient, however, to refer to Y&R as only an *advertising agency*. Certainly, the company still creates and places over $4 billion worth of advertisements. But a member of the Y&R family (public relations agency Burson-Marsteller) also helped to develop and operate the AT&T 1984 Olympic Torch Run. Another, Wunderman Worldwide, creates direct communications for the Columbia Record and Tape Club. One of the Y&R companies, Krown, Inc., even places clients' products in Hollywood movies.

In this diversity, Y&R has evolved from an advertising agency into a *communications agency*. Although Y&R was the first major agency to pursue the concept of a total communications agency, many of its competitors soon followed suit, with "Ogilvy Orchestration" as perhaps the best known example.

Defining the Goal

The concept of a total communications agency is a kind of "philosophers' stone" that has the power of transforming basic metals into gold. In this case, the "gold" would be the achievement of that same "Golden Ruler" I mentioned in Chapter Two, as Y&R defined it many years ago: "To reach the best possible prospect with the best possible message at the least possible cost." Or, as Y&R has refined it now, in the context of integrated communications,

To deliver to the right prospect

The most relevant message

At the appropriate time

Through the correct vehicle.

This simple statement captures the essence of modern communications—that advertising, public relations, direct response advertising and sales promotion must be driven by a thorough understanding of the customer, who he or she is, what message may be compelling, and when that message will be welcome or relevant.

People do need the kind of information marketing communications can provide. They want it, however, in a form and at a time that suits *their* needs.

Starting to Implement the Goal

Y&R formally announced the Whole Egg goal at a Board of Directors meeting in San Francisco, in October 1980. Although I was by that time a consultant, rather than a full-time employee, I was invited to attend the sessions and was gratified to find that they had drawn the inspiration for the phrase from a chapter in my book *The Compleat Copywriter*, published 14 years before. In the frontispiece of the soon-to-be-distributed "Whole Egg Catalogue," they quoted from my book as follows:

The presentation, made by this writer to the management of a major corporation, began with a bit of showmanship. Reaching into his suitcoat pocket, and holding the exhibit gingerly so that it would not break, he revealed the white, spherical form of an egg.

"If I were to ask you what this object is," he said, "what would you answer?"

"Would you say that it's albumen? Yoke? A paper-thin shell? Or would you say it is an *egg*?"

The point being made was that the advertising campaign about to be presented was supposed to be a unified, integrated whole. While it had many different aspects—just as the egg was composed of different elements, like albumen, yoke, and shell—the sum of the parts were supposed to add up to "the whole egg."

At that meeting, Art Klein, then the newly appointed marketing director, dramatically visualized the concept by putting together a giant jigsaw puzzle, in the shape of an egg, with the pieces representing the specialized members of the Y&R partnership.

The Ideal Components of a Whole Egg

The conception of what became The Whole Egg had begun almost a decade before that 1980 meeting. Ed Ney described this development:

In October of 1972, we had a very important meeting for this company. We decided at that time that we would go horizontally in the world of commercial communications, that we would get into public relations, design, sales promotion, medical advertising, business to business, corporate world, direct marketing, a whole range of activities.

There were, of course, sound business reasons for taking that historic step. Each of these communication specialties was in its infancy. This reason was important, but not sufficient.

For a company such as Y&R, dedicated to professional client service, growth for growth's sake is a poor foundation for a business strategy.

There had to be *added value* for the client to use the multiple communication disciplines Y&R had acquired. This added value for clients is found in the concept of integrated communications. As Ed Ney said, after the addition of the Burson-Marsteller network in 1979:

As we got all the companies together, it became obvious that we'd have to have integration. Intelligent integration of all these various services. . . . We've now got all the parts together to make it happen.

Jim Dowling, president and CEO of Burson-Marsteller, defined the new goal as follows:

True integration happens when we apply a bundle of disciplines to a common problem in such a way that to unbundle these disciplines would be to produce a lesser result than the totality of the bundled services. To use another metaphor, integrated communications should function like a symphony orchestra. When the different instruments are combined in a carefully orchestrated whole, the result is something greater than the sum of the parts.

It was inevitable (because IC was an idea whose time had come) that other major agencies would attempt the same concept. Each used a different term to describe it. As mentioned, Ogilvy & Mather adopted the analogy Jim Dowling had used, "orchestration." Omnicom called theirs the "networking concept." Saatchi & Saatchi, the British newcomer which, in a few short years, had become a "mega-agency" through acquisitions, dubbed their activity "a synergy of specialty services."

These versions of integrated communications, however, are not all the same. They are executed with greater or lesser enthusiasm, depending on the company's strategy and capabilities. In its simplest form, IC offers no more to a client than "one-stop shopping"—the convenience of using one agency to supply multiple services. A comprehensive article in *Marketing & Media Decisions* described this idea as "the umbrella principle"[1] and clearly indicated that this is as far as many agencies have taken the idea. Y&R and one or two of its competitors are developing a more complete vision of the value IC can bring to clients. First, I'll discuss this evolving theory of integrated communications; then, I'll move on to a look at the theory in practice.

The Pros and Cons of Integrated Communications— Theory and Benefits

Jim Dowling outlined six benefits of IC as captured by Y&R's Whole Egg strategy:

First, *it gives multiple perspective to the client's need*. The client gets the benefit of having his problems examined from many different views and each view is involved in the evaluation of the total problem.

---

[1] See Rebecca Fannin, "The Umbrella Principle," *Marketing & Media Decisions*. July 1988.

Two, *unified strategic thought.* The integrated solution should be better than a series of separate solutions which may in fact conflict with one another. Each individual element will be more sharply focused because it was conceived from the broad base of the total problem.

Three, *in an integrated program, it's possible to weigh each discipline's potential contribution against the whole.* We can direct client resources to the most productive combination of communication executions to achieve that total strategy.

Four, *interactive elements.* The total resolve of an integrated communications plan should be better because each part is designed to work with the other. Each part not only contributes individually but can bolster the effectiveness of all other parts.

The fifth benefit is *complete and effective management.* An integrated program is accountable not only for its separate parts but for its totality as well. So it should be more efficient for the client to manage, easier to measure, and more cost effective.

Lastly, *the client gets Y&R at its best.* We can offer the best integrated solution because individually, our separate specialties are the leading edge of the respective discipline, and when they're integrated in a single program, the client automatically becomes more important to all of Y&R.

If an integrated communications agency can deliver these benefits to a client, the agency will clearly prosper along with the client.

In 1985 Joe De Deo, president of Y&R Europe, summarized the opportunities for agencies at an international conference. He reviewed the benefits for clients and then listed the following eight reasons why agencies should want integrated capabilities:

□ Deeper understanding of client's business

□ Synergy: improved thinking from involvement in other disciplines

□ Expanded client relationship: more and higher points of contact

□ Stronger hold on the account

□ Involvement in faster-growth areas, more of client's marketing funds; networking

□ More stable account profitability

□ Expanded career opportunities for people

□ *Some* competitive advantage in new business

Risks

However, said Joe, there are definite risks to the client and the agency if the agency fails to deliver:

For clients

☐ Not getting the best in each discipline.

☐ Lack of disinterested counsel.

☐ Lack of competitive pricing.

☐ Wasted time and money due to infighting among "sister" agencies.

☐ Being sold unneeded services.

For agencies

☐ Distraction from primary client relationship (usually advertising or public relations).

☐ Costs of setting up, running a group of companies.

☐ Difficulty of getting, maintaining quality in all disciplines.

☐ Endangering the whole account with bad performance in any one area.

☐ Headaches of parochialness in individual companies: disputes about territory, income, pecking orders, crosscharges, client conflicts.

Finally, Joe listed what Y&R had learned:

☐ You can't fake it.

☐ Go out and buy the best practitioners you can find in each field and leave them alone.

☐ Up to a point.

And other obvious lessons:

☐ Not all clients need agencies to do it.

☐ Not all clients who need it can take it.

☐ Don't push it too hard—it will happen organically, naturally.

☐ Almost never put the advertising agency manager in charge of the other companies.

☐ Try not to worry about the mechanical techniques of communications and focus on the purposes.

Finally, looking to the future, he listed these conclusions:

□ Total communications is with us to stay—it's not going to go away.

□ Stand-alone advertising will continue to be the dominant way agencies develop their income for the rest of this decade.

□ However, the future belongs to those who can transcend the traditional "craft" barriers and deliver strategically integrated communications to their clients.

The Pros and Cons of Integrated Communications— in Practice

By 1988, Joe's predictions had proved to be accurate, and it was clear that integrated communications was a difficult row to hoe. *Marketing & Media Decisions* assessed the difficulty with brutal candor: "The mega-shops are opening up their ad businesses through acquisition and development to provide total marketing-service coverage. It's a nice theory, but so far it's proved full of holes."

Important point: **Those holes exist because many of the agencies are ill-prepared to integrate their services.**

For example, wrote *Marketing & Media Decisions*, "The new supermarkets are not really prepared to sell these services aggressively to current agency clients. The agencies rely on account executives to uncover opportunities for related marketing services. But very often the account executives aren't familiar with the range of services their agencies offer and/or may not be knowledgeable about the other fields. Moreover, many account executives have a built-in bias against recommending other marketing services. Every dollar that moves from advertising into sales promotion, for instance, dilutes the power of the account executive's own domain."

Another detriment to agency growth with integrated communications: reluctance on the part of many clients to use the same supplier for the many services. Some clients believe that the best work in such specialties can be done within their own organizations. Others desire independent counsel, particularly in such specialties as public relations. Finally, there is the problem of "overpromise" on the part of some agencies that has left clients wary of committing to integrated communications after a disappointing experience.

Important point: **However difficult a "Whole Egg" is to attain, it behooves client and agency to pursue the goal, because *all* the communications about the product or service you are dealing with should, ideally, be related.**

As I described the process in my book, "The whole egg is a tenuous thing:

> What people want dictates it; the kind of people they are dictates it; the nature and function of the product or service dictates it; the shape of the product, the color of the product, the name of the product, its packaging, distribution, and price dictate it; the words and pictures and what they are going to cost dictate it; and, of course, all the media through which the consumer gets the communication dictate it.

All those aspects are *communications,* and they should speak with one voice.

COMMITMENT TO THE WHOLE EGG

Achieving our philosophers' stone takes a lot of time, patience, and a gambler's iron gut. In the *Marketing & Media Decisions* article, Peter Georgescu went on record for Y&R as being irrevocably committed, when he said, "We are betting the firm on this concept. . . . Advertisers better embrace this idea. Otherwise, we have bet wrong."[2]

Little by little, Y&R clients *are* embracing the idea, and at this writing some 10 percent of them have used the principle effectively. These clients include some of the largest and most sophisticated of today's marketers: adidas, AT&T, Jacobs Suchard, Du Pont, Ford, General Foods, Goodyear, Kodak, and Unisys.

SEVEN TESTED METHODS FOR ACHIEVING INTEGRATED COMMUNICATIONS

An examination of Y&R's experience over the past decade reveals seven factors in achieving full IC success:

1. Assemble the Best Possible Specialists

In effect, the specialists working on an IC program are an extended product group. So even if you are a small organization, without benefit of such acquisitions as mega-agencies have made, you can at least set out to assemble a team of specialists in the various disciplines this book has described.

2. Cultivate a "One-for-All and All-for-One" Attitude

Here is how Art Klein, in a Young & Rubicam *World* article, expressed it:

> All of our work toward providing integrated communications will not be fruitful unless we acknowledge that it may be necessary for us to give up something in the short term in order to integrate successfully.

> "The Whole Egg" is not some cookie-cutter concept to be taken as a prefabricated solution from one client's problem to the next. On the contrary, the biggest advantage of a multidisciplinary approach is that it gives us flexibility to bring a number of disciplines to bear, flexibility to concentrate on just one, flexibility to bring one

[2]Ibid.

unit in where another unit is not working out. The strength of an integrated approach is that it gives us the capability to deliver to a client or prospect whatever is needed to solve a problem; and there are as many different solutions as there are problems.

3. Let Everybody Know What Facilities Are Available

Y&R published "The Whole Egg Catalog" in 1981. (See Figure 14–1.) It was divided into 27 sections. These sections listed and described the resources that everyone could draw upon and the people to contact in the affiliated companies and departments to access the information.

FIGURE 14–1

Note: Inside the catalog was an impressive foldout with a locator card reading "This card is designed to assist you in matching units and capabilities. Simply align the right edge of the card with the office column you wish to examine."

Since the catalog appeared, the agency has distributed other publications and directories from time to time, as well as videocassettes, informing the organization at large of their growing resources.

4. When Feasible, Bring the Disciplines Together into One Place

Bringing together the family of the agency and its specialized services in one location makes for closer collaboration and helps to solve the problem of slow "turnaround." Example: Y&R began this communal living with an appropriate gesture, by designing a common headquarters in San Francisco, where they had first announced the concept.

In New York, Y&R put this idea to work when it won the communications assignment for the U.S. Army in one of the hardest fought new business battles of the 1980s. The company's integrated capabilities were a key factor in the win. To bring the full power of the network to bear, Y&R set up a dedicated multidisciplinary account team in offices separated from the rest of the agency. Called the Y&R Army Group, this "agency within an agency" includes 180 specialists from Burson-Marsteller public relations, Wunderman direct marketing, Cato, Johnson promotions, and Y&R advertising.

In the past ten years, the company has effected similarly integrated offices in Copenhagen; Sydney; Frankfurt; Milan; and Sao Paulo, Brazil.

5. Train Your Team Members to Understand and Respect One Another's Expertise

In addition to the workshops of the Y&R Resource Center and those of its specialized companies, Y&R instituted a cross-ruffing custom, whereby up-and-comers in the various companies apprentice in specialties for which they don't already have expertise.

Example The Swapper Program started in 1984, and the following year a "swapper" from Burson-Marsteller reported in the *World* publication about a three-month program (six weeks at each sister company):

The latest swap . . . was expanded to include our Chicago, London, and Paris markets . . .

Following an initial briefing from Corporate's Nick Rudd in New York, the group returned to their markets and reported to their new units for the first six-week stint. In New York, for example, I started with WRK (now Wunderman Worldwide), while Rick Bodge joined B-M (Burson-Marsteller).

In the beginning, all of us felt somewhat out-of-sorts. Suddenly, we were in a new location, meeting with new people who had their own work style and jargon.

With a combination of individual and group briefings, general observation, actual work assignments, seminar participation, and simple osmosis, we gradually got to know our new colleagues and their specialties.

The next six weeks were even better for most of us. For example, my schedule at Y&R NY was jammed. I spent three weeks in Account Management, plus a week each in Research, Creative, and Media. I attended internal and client meetings, interagency briefings, creative and media presentations, and a commercial shoot and editing session, watching work evolve on a number of important brands . . .

Cultivating a "New Breed"   People are the most important factor in successful communications. In the chapter of my book that followed the Whole Egg chapter, I had envisioned future da Vincis who would not necessarily be account executives, but the focal point for the creative executions of the whole egg:

The reconstructive kind of person must be the hub of our wheel. How he will be adapted to the present structure of corporations and advertising agencies remains to be seen. Some advertising agencies have "creative directors" who are approaching the ideal. But, at this writing, most of them have only to do with national advertising media rather than with the whole egg. The ideal . . . will be a new breed who, by temperament and experience, by deliberate training and assignment to the tables of organization, will be qualified to coordinate *all* **communication—whether it be name, shape, color, design, or packaging of the product; television commercials; direct mail; publicity; dealer shows; or sky projection. After all, the consumer neither knows nor cares how the communication gets there. All he knows is what he sees and hears, and that can be anything and everything.**

There are many difficulties with having a "hub of the wheel" or czar who dictates a single direction for all the communications. I've already cited some of them, not the least of which are pride of authorship, affiliate autonomy, and morale. *Another very sticky problem:* Each specialized company is expected by top management to be a "profit center," and to be selfless and objective about how the client budgets are distributed can run contrary to the pursuit of a strong bottom line.

One way to cope with these contrary forces: Have the wheel hub assignment handled by the communications specialists who, by the nature of the account, should have the lion's share of the billing. A Y&R example: If, after analysis, direct response should be the major thrust of an account, Wunderman Worldwide people would be the hub; if the major need is public relations, Burson-Marsteller; and if advertising *per se* is still the major part of the whole egg, Y&R's people would dominate.

A common way to finesse the coordination problem: Simply have the strategy-makers start the ball rolling and follow the effort's progress. *Marketing & Media Decisions* described that method as highly successful with the Ogilvy & Mather Ryder company account:

> Larrick [Jon Larrick, Ryder's group director of marketing services] is also pleased with Ogilvy's ease in coordinating the campaign. He notes that a senior account executive spells out Ryder's strategy to staff members in related disciplines and then monitors the creation of all the work. In this overseeing role, the executive also makes sure that creative teams work together but tries not to dictate to specialists within each discipline. . . . Compared to the previous à la carte method, this approach is much more efficient. Larrick says: "The account people pre-plan the work and they set up the timetable for its completion."

There is one other method by which integrated communication may be coordinated, and it is totally organic. This is the dominating power of *a big idea*.

6. Cultivate Big Ideas That Transcend Pride of Place and Media Choice

You and I, and all of us who enjoy this profession, have experienced how a great idea doesn't care who has it. Most creative people are egotistical and like to think that their ideas are the best. But when a truly *big* idea arises, everyone—even someone who acknowledges it grudgingly—climbs on the bandwagon. The idea has a force and momentum all its own. In fact, as I pointed out in Chapter Three, if we are really creative, *we* don't get the ideas at all—we're simply the *media* through which the problem solves itself.

An example of such an organic happening was the basis of the presentation to Goodyear which inspired my "Whole Egg" concept. The "Go Go Goodyear" idea had already started to have a dynamic life of its own. At that presentation, I attributed its rightness to the spirit of "Goism":

> All we have is a TV campaign, with relatively little exposure and a lot of disassociated other campaigns and ideas. . . . But we have stumbled on to something which has staggering possibilities—completely right for the product, the mood of our times, and the progressive spirit of the company. This is a fast-moving world. The automobile is the American symbol of mobility. Tires move at great speed. Go Go Goodyear is a marvelously propitious theme to express the most progressive tire company in the world. In fact, through this lucky inspiration, we have come up with a complete philosophy—a copy policy, if you will—with which we can set standards for everything we do that contributes to the whole egg.
>
> This philosophy is "GOISM." The campaign, in *all* its facets, should have the look, the sound, the feel of movement, of turning wheels, of vitality, of forward thrust.

From then on, the presentation outlined how the theme and the philosophy of "goism" should pervade all Goodyear's communications—its logo, the way its tires would be shown and filmed, its store signage, its exchanges on the telephone with customers, its sales promotion, direct mail, public relations, and advertising.

At the end of the presentation, the chairman of the board, then Ed Thomas, wagged an admonitory finger under the presenter's nose:

> "I understand what you're driving at. But it can't stop here. You've got to get everybody into the act."

The first person to understand the idea of an integrated campaign [continued the report in my book] was the chairman of the board, because it was he who saw his vast corporation every day from the top and it was he who was constantly questioning, "What are we? What do we add up to? How do we communicate it to our many publics?"

The proof of that pudding, of the organic power of an idea to transcend all difficulties, was this: At that time, 25 years ago, neither Goodyear nor its advertising agencies had any system or agreement for integrated communications. On the contrary, Goodyear had large internal departments in numerous divisions, devoted to different forms of communication, a number of advertising agencies, and many stand-alone communication suppliers. It did take a while before the Go Go Goodyear campaign eventuated, in almost all the facets of the company's communications. To show the persistent power of an idea, here is just one classic example: Eventually, every one of the hundreds of Goodyear retail outlets, with their stationary Goodyear diamond logo lighted signs, began to move. The words "Go Go Goodyear" were flashing everywhere in the evening sky.

That Go Go Goodyear integrated effort came about, and lasted for many years, despite the fact that there was no prior agreement and organization for the whole egg. One of the first examples of IC after Y&R had announced their whole egg mission was the effort for the brokerage house of Merrill Lynch. Eventually, Merrill Lynch used most of the Y&R specialties, but the efforts began piecemeal.

The first was for the merchandising and internal implementation of the "Breed Apart" theme line and logo. One asset of the theme was that it not only worked effectively against the target audience but also could set a standard for Merrill Lynch's own performance to live up to. Y&R pointed this out to the client and asked questions like these: Are the brokers and operational people delivering the caliber of service and product that meets the high performance level established by the theme line? Does the Merrill Lynch training program adequately prepare the broker to perform on that level? Is the visual image projected by the office design and interior decor consistent with the theme line?

After raising those questions, Y&R recommended to Merrill Lynch that we form a task force of Y&R, Burson-Marsteller, and other members of the Y&R family of companies. Burson was already working with Merrill Lynch; so this gave Burson-Marsteller another assignment.

The task force visited a range of offices, reviewed the training programs, interviewed management, and came up with a complete recommendation that included new office designs, company signage, and education programs for the client's account executives.

A second opportunity for integration presented itself when the investment banking arm of Merrill Lynch was about to establish regional directors to increase penetration in various parts of the country. They needed a selling presentation of their investment banking capabilities. For this assignment, Y&R, Burson-Marsteller and Cato Johnson worked together. Finally, after Y&R purchased Chapman, Lester Wunderman got them involved as well.

7. Collect Case Histories as a Guide for All

I have attempted, with all the precepts and guidelines discussed in this book, to provide as many explicit case examples as space and availability allow. This is because Y&R has always attempted to teach by inspiration and example rather than by formulas. Unlike some other large agencies like Ogilvy and Doyle, Dane, Bernbach in the old days, there has never been a "Y&R Look."

Important point: Every client's problem is considered unique, and the solutions are, therefore, different from one another.

The value of case histories, like the cases in a law book, is that they show and tell a wide variety of solutions to problems. We emphasize that no one is *the* way and encourage our teams to blaze new, original trails rather than simply to emulate a case history. However, the best case histories reveal how each, in *its* way, did its own trail-blazing. They inspire, encourage, help to give confidence to the would-be originator, and provide triggers for brainstorming in many directions.

I have already cited some case histories for our Whole Egg. Here are two more . . .

A European Case History[3]

Y&R in Belgium introduced Hegor shampoos back in 1974. At that time there were two basic products formulated to deal with dandruff and greasy hair produced by Richardson-Vicks and sold through pharmacies.

Recently, line extensions like special shampoos for blonde or red hair or fine hair added some cosmetic overtones and diffused the therapeutic image. In the interim, the main competitor, Klorane, had been taking share from Hegor with a similar therapeutic positioning, but it was reinforced by a special cleansing ingredient story, and this was hammered home very effectively in the advertising.

To counterattack, Richardson-Vicks decided to leave the old line unsupported and introduce, through Y&R Belgium, a new Hegor Mediker line of three shampoos, Hegor 1, 2, 3. Given the brand's heritage, we and the client decided to build Hegor's therapeutic image and to broaden it by positioning the new Hegor shampoos as the definitive line of products designed to help hair and scalp problems that are not currently addressed by normal shampoos.

Specifically, a new formula for greasy hair, one for dandruff, and a completely new product to get rid of hair lice were introduced. So Y&R worked out a carefully coordinated array of communications techniques, package design, consumer print advertising, point-of-sale brochures, and, of course, direct mail to pharmacists, pediatricians, and schoolmasters.

[3]As presented by Norman Kappler, then vice president and director of marketing, Y&R International.

In conjunction with Y&R Belgium, Cato, Johnson Brussels developed new packaging with a highly ethical and contemporary design. This reinforces the line's therapeutic benefits and supports both the product's efficacy and its newness. Y&R Belgium, using the normal disciplines of the SSO, the Creative Work Plan, and the brand personality, developed a print campaign to launch Hegor shampoo for the greasy hair and dandruff products. The advertising used double-page spreads which looked like pages from a laboratory research technician's handbook, with the copy and the sketches and the notes written on it. To further communicate the clinical heritage, the laboratory in which the products were developed was prominently featured.

Client and agency both believed that the antilice shampoo was better handled through point-of-sale material and direct response. So, utilizing the flexibility of the Whole Egg, Y&R Belgium arranged for Wunderman International to develop mailings to pediatricians and schoolmasters which included leaflets for the children. The mailings presented the 100 percent efficacy of Hegor's antilice product. To presell the line of products, Wunderman also created mailings to pharmacists to explain the full range of Hegor Mediker's benefits. Included in that mailing was a point-of-sale brochure developed by the agency, based on the print advertising.

The program was highly successful. The downward trend in sales was reversed, share increased, distribution expanded, and the sales of the antilice shampoo were significantly above the target.

A Successful New Business Presentation[4]

When CIT first approached Y&R and other agencies, their goal was to consider using consumer advertising, for the first time in their 71 years, as a means of establishing an awareness and an image which could build business. Our initial attack followed the routine of the past. We attended a client briefing on their perception of the problem. We conducted extensive research focus groups of borrowers and nonborrowers, then telephone interviews to quantify what we had learned. We tapped the Stanford Research Institute and its VALS material to gain further perspective on the life-styles and the values of people who borrow.

We accumulated information from the National Consumer Finance Association and from the National Association of Realtors. We contacted security analysts, and last, we made extensive visits to CIT offices in five cities to get a feel of their retail presence and the degree and caliber of their coverage.

From these pieces we gained insight into their business and their prospects. We established a series of hypotheses that were later used to set the stage for our alternate recommended strategy. It was then realized that communication disciplines other than advertising were going to be needed. For example, how was the often postponed and frequently threatening act of borrowing to be motivated? Our answer—through direct response and the talents of Lester Wunderman and his crew. Or how was CIT going to deliver an upscale second mortgage product to a homeowner audience when its storefront operations were handled by people accustomed to dealing with a more desperate kind of finance company customer? The answer here was Burson-Marsteller with its extensive training capability, a training capability that could be reinforced over time by their employee communications expertise.

[4]For CIT Financial Services, a subsidiary of RCA which specializes in loans, mortgages, and other types of financing. As presented by John H. Hatheway, then senior vice president and group director, Y&R New York.

Both Wunderman and Burson-Marsteller were made integral parts of our product group and of the solicitation process, a process which involved the presentation of integrated communications strategies, even an integrated direct response television commercial.

This integrated approach very clearly differentiated us from our worthy competitors and Y&R was awarded the business. Since we've had this assignment, we've defined still further opportunities for the communications expertise of our specialty companies. From what started out to be just an advertising solicitation, we have broadened the definition of the problem, and ultimately our own involvement, not only through advertising and direct response, but also in Yellow Pages advertising, in training, in storefront design, in publicity, even an exploration of new distribution systems.

The presentation of this case history concluded with these words:

The Whole Egg concept works. Never underestimate the value of an integrated communications attack in creating a differentiation for Young & Rubicam and in helping Y&R win business. And once that's accomplished, in involving it in the totality of that business.

THE WHOLE GLOBE

A second kind of integrated communications is that which has been promoted by some advisors for corporations that market their goods or services worldwide.

With the opening of Russia to more liberalized worldwide connections, the economic aspirations of Third World countries, and the 1992 goal of removing trade barriers among the 12 nations of the European Community, global marketing has become of accelerating concern.

At Y&R, training for international advertising began as long ago as the 1930s, when Y&R established its first overseas offices. It continued when, during the 1970s and 1980s, the agency's worldwide offices expanded from hardly more than a dozen to more than 200, including the first joint ventures with the Chinese and Russians.

The controversy of a single global communications effort versus strictly local advertising grew most heated in the 1980s, when Professor Theodore Levitt, of the Harvard Business School, became the global marketing guru, preaching universally common campaigns.

Global Marketing: Myth or Reality?

This 1986 Y&R seminar, by Niels Menko, an international management supervisor, gave an overview of the situation with an agenda that covered four major points: (1) pressure toward "global marketing" is growing, but (2) there is no agreement on what it is; (3) its executions in the real world vary widely; as do (4) real examples at Y&R. The following are his explanations of each point:

A. Pressure toward "global marketing" is growing due to

  1. *Consumers*

    a. Cheaper travel, increased exposure

    b. Global communications

      (1) Satellite TV

      (2) Print

      (3) Entertainment programs

    c. Immigration

    d. Education

    e. Choice of local and foreign goods in metropolitan cities

    f. Increasing knowledge, sophistication in purchase habits

  2. *Marketers*

    a. Instant communications worldwide

    b. Short-lived product advantages owing to

      (1) Know-how

      (2) Technology

      (3) Financial support

        (all globally available)

      (4) Less protective patents

    c. Immediate and global competition

    d. Requirements for greater "global" control and economies of scale

  3. *Clients*

    a. As marketers start to look at the world as "one," managing it efficiently becomes a concern

    b. Agency consolidations are one result

      (1) Better control

        (a) One central contact

        (b) Another worldwide communication chain

      (2) Marketing

        (a) Improved global planning

        (b) Transfer of experience/knowledge/ideas

        (c) Efficiencies

          (i) Clustering of markets

          (ii) Production efficiencies

The presentation then cited recent examples of centralized global campaigns for specific clients by Y&R and such agencies as McCann, Ogilvy & Mather, and Bates, including the example of world marketer Philips consolidating from 137 to 5 agencies worldwide.

The overview continued:

B. *But what is "global marketing"?*

   1. Ted Levitt is the best known proponent.

      a. But he overlooks differences in cultures, stage of category development, consumer segmentation.

      b. And Philip Kotler, Kenichi Ohmae, Jerry Wind, and others disagree with him.

   2. Client philosophies vary widely—from centrally imposed strategies and executions to local management control.

   3. Stage of development of any industry may vary widely from country to country.

   4. To Y&R

      a. "Global marketing" is not to be confused with one advertising campaign worldwide.

      b. "Global marketing" is

         (1) An awareness of the world as a single marketplace.

         (2) Centralized organization and planning.

         (3) The standardization of products, whenever possible, to achieve economies of scale.

         (4) Marketing a similar product, with a similar strategy, appealing to consumer segments with similar attitudes and values in multiple markets (possibly with similar communications).

We call it "cross-cultural marketing."

**Y&R
Seamless Network**

This presentation outlines how Y&R organizes to assist clients with a "cross-cultural" marketing effort, rather than simply hit-or-miss global campaigns. For the internal organization,

   1. Advertising executive committee meets four times a year.

   2. There are regular worldwide/area managers meetings.

   3. Majority equity is fully 100 percent.

   4. A client handling matrix system pervades all Y&R Inc.'s companies.

The seminar then outlines the training and tools which help to create a "seamless" organization—the Advertising Skills Workshop, Strategy Skills Workshop, Effective Management Workshop, Unit Manager Workshop, and Creative Management Program to improve product—all of which give a homogeneity to Y&R people at thousands of miles separation from one another.

Finally, the seminar described the organization and teamwork which combined to offer clients the kind of integrated communications described in the preceding pages.

The presentation also outlined how global marketing can have four degrees of "directed" accounts/clients:

1. "Loose" coordination, with exchange of information and local management decision making

2. "Formal" direction, with exchange of information, pressure from headquarters for a similar strategy/positioning, a so-called matrix decision making between local and HQ management, and often similar strategies with local executions

3. "Strict" direction, with exchange of information, HQ direction, leading, and decision making, the same strategy unless exceptions are approved, and often the same creative concept with similar executions and local production possible

4. "Worldwide" advertising—HQ imposed, same executions, "central" production, and only rare exceptions

Mary Alice Kennedy, a stalwart in the New York International headquarters, compiled a reel of commercials that illustrates the whole spectrum of advertising ranging from "decentralized coordination" (for Kodak) to "centralized coordination" (for Coca-Cola).

Building Businesses Across Cultures

In September 1988, Y&R distributed an explanation of its global methods and philosophy, in its newsletter entitled "Dispatch," to a specially selected list of clients and prospective clients. Written by John P. McGarry, Jr., chairman of Client Services Worldwide, the bulletin explained why globalization should not be used as shorthand for "Why can't we run the same ads everywhere?" that Y&R has found that there are few instances where a single global execution is either efficient or wise:

Marketers who underestimate cultural and market differences run the strong risk of breaking their connection with consumers. The simple truth is, nothing is really global. There may be regions, areas, clusters of markets where some common factors apply. In our view, what is possible—and where real opportunities exist—is cross-cultural marketing.

Many companies—from Japanese cars to French cosmetics to American fast food—have proven that a well-thought-out and consistently executed concept can build sales and share of market on a worldwide basis.

Viewing the world as one potential marketplace is an attitude, a state of mind, if you will. And for companies whose home bases are saturated markets, it is a necessary perspective.

In managing a business globally, one side of the equation will always be the efficiencies that can be created from consolidating an area or a group of markets—efficiencies in purchasing, manufacturing, packing, distribution.

But if we approach globalization from a marketing standpoint, we must face it from the starting point of the consumer—adding value by creating a meaningful consumer connection.

How to Understand Your Consumer and Your Markets

By now, most companies have learned that a common language or geographic proximity does not necessarily imply a common market. Chileans are not Mexicans or Spaniards, Germans are not Swiss. To form a single appropriate target group there must be a more tangible common connection than language.

A cross-cultural marketing approach must take into account people's basic motivations, values, and life-styles, as well as demographics.

This means psychographics are as important as demographics. And you must have a common "yardstick" to measure the relevant consumer attitudes and values in different countries.

Y&R has made a multimillion-dollar investment in generating solid consumer-oriented research in half-a-dozen markets around the world. Our proprietary cross-cultural consumer tools have yielded quantitative data on consumer demographics and psychographics, which have paved the road to intelligent decision making about handling global accounts. Identifying common segments, fundamental commonalties about the human psyche, that cross cultures and countries, is the best way to start developing a multinational marketing strategy.

Critical to the development of such a strategy is the consideration of different market and competitive conditions. A common strategy will not work across a mixture of monopoly and highly competitive markets; across high-tech markets at the same time as Third World markets, or across unknown category markets and saturation markets. A global marketing strategy must identify markets with similar stages of category and brand development.

The cross-cultural marketing approach can lead you to many different solutions— a global strategy, or the development of two or three clusters of markets, each with its own strategy.

How to Add Value Through Communication

Peter Georgescu, president of Y&R Advertising, in a 1987 speech in Cairo, Egypt, explained that the value of products must be communicated in different ways to countries in different stages of development—that is, using a structure of attributes, benefits, and personalized values:[5]

This way of looking at consumer relationships to products is commonly used in our marketing analyses . . . and, in fact, has the name "laddering." . . . The historical state of an economy, in terms of its consumerization, more or less has dictated the basic content of advertising approaches: in *under*developed, or just emerging markets *information* about products, that is, their attributes. In developing markets, *education* about their benefits, for the purpose of consumer choices. And in mature, fully developed consumer marketplaces, the appeal of individuals' values through *personalizing* can be added to the equation.

Peter explained how, even in those countries where the *information* stage is advisable, a marketer can start building a franchise, so that as it does develop, he can move toward cementing his relationship, successively through *product benefit* and *personalized value* communication. Peter cited how a recent study of consumer brands in the United States revealed that in more than 20 categories, the brand that was number one in *1923* is still number one today (such brands as Ivory, Johnson & Johnson, Hershey, Kellogg, etc.). This is because those brands consistently added to their productivity by making these successive consumer connections. His tip to marketers who, perhaps like yourself, are just getting their feet wet in global marketing:

The most important implication for a developing marketplace is the advantage of knowing *ahead of time* what we had to learn *over time* . . . the tremendous assets of productivity and equity that can be yours when you plan and program marketing efforts toward building "consumer meaning" into everything you do.

"Being There"—How to prepare for the "Consumer Flashpoint"
Taking a long-range view, Alex Kroll, in a 1987 speech entitled "The New World," likened the global marketer's horizon to the atmosphere of the 1600s, when European merchants looked westward, hearing reports by Cartier, Cortez, and Cabot of a rich new world for the picking:

That is where we stand today. We merchants and salespeople stand at the banks of a great sea, facing the possibilities and perplexities of a "New World," the last new world we shall ever know.

It is a world as big as the one we have now. As populous as the one we have now. Where our sales may multiply ten or a hundredfold over the next decade.

But there are no good maps. No reliable reports. Should we go? Where? When? And how?

The only difference between us and the wool merchant (of the 1600s) is that our New World is not west, but east, and it is populated by 2 billion people who— sometimes clumsily, sometimes swiftly—are being ejected from the prison of the "command" economies into the freedoms and perplexities of "demand" economy.

[5]Peter Georgescu, president of Y&R Advertising, in a 1987 speech in Cairo, Egypt.

As the "command" economic experiments of the 20th century end, millions of Indians, Mainland Chinese, Russians, East Germans and other Eastern Bloc-ers stand somewhat bewildered but ravenous after a long drought and famine, for material goods and services.

Kroll cited a recent survey which revealed that Chinese youth want "eight big things": color TV, refrigerator, stereo, camera, motorcycle, modern furniture suite, washing machine, and an electric fan.

Kroll cited a whole series of evidences in China and Russia of the whetting of consumer appetite, largely due to the enormous power of television. And he emphasized that the time is *now*, with increasing urgency, to start answering these appetites:

While conventional wisdom says the New World is a long way from being profitable or even interesting to Western consumer companies, *I offer the opposite vision.*

There is considerable evidence that the New World will rush at the Old World's goods and services. It's later than you think.

I believe we will see, soon, probably within five years, a *consumer flash point* in each of these nations. A consumer flash point when a significant number of people become "consumer ready," interested in choosing specific brands, not just generic products. Meaning they will select goods and services not just for functional needs, but for symbolic, personal or emblematic needs. . . . Not what the cigarettes or slacks or sodas do for me, but what they say about me. That's value-added marketing, where we merchants make the money.

These people—call them the leading edge, or the early adopters—are not a lonely crowd. Perhaps 70 million in India, 60 million in the Soviet Union, 100 million in China. They will have the means, and they will either *have* or increasingly *demand* access to consumer goods.

The warning Kroll was giving to his audience was that "when the flash point occurs, the battle for brand position could be largely over." The reason, he emphasized again, is that ever-expanding eye on the world, TV:

The Chinese have opened the door and slammed the door to the West, rhythmically, in the 20th century. But the door is not the means of passage any longer. The signal comes through the roof.

It is the roof where the signal comes in, and now that hundreds of millions of Chinese view at least two hours of TV per day, the door to the mind is opened for good. For both the Chinese and the Soviets have given in—reluctantly—and allowed the installation of . . . modern communications systems.

It is a fact that information breeds the need for more information. It is irreversible. The appetite grows. The results are unpredictable. The system outside the system grows . . .

The government is pouring on the coal itself—the Soviets have made a major commitment to "information technology"—microelectronics, computerization, in order to keep their weaponry competitive and improve their industrial output and "quality of life."

But . . . once you make that commitment to disseminate computers, word processors, copiers, etc., and place the means of "information technology" in people's hands, you shake hands with the devil. The means of state control of information passes from your hands.

He then outlined the encroachment of satellite TV systems into the New World—three new satellite systems that in the next five years, would reach into Eastern Europe, and how, beyond the need to install a dish to receive those stations, "an electronic doo-dad, a miniature tube that makes the antenna viable" was being readied by Western scientists and would be available within a couple of years:

Ultimately, the effect of media is to create consumers. These symbols which pass through the air carry a compulsion to be acquired. Be it a fashion, or a feeling of being in the world—of being modern.

In this free-flow, free-for-all of information and media, brand building, and brand share building is going on with a vengeance . . . right now in the New World.

We are seeing the extraordinary event of brands gaining a *dominant position in minds of a market before they can be bought by the majority. Before the flash. Which suggests the biggest change of all. You've got to sell them, before they are able to buy you.*

Kroll cited examples of marketers who had already realized, and profited by, this phenomenon—how in India Colgate had achieved a lock on the toothpaste market, Lux on soap, and Gillette on the battle of the beards—how Pepsi is already preferred in the USSR—and how the Japanese have "all but conquered China in electronics and autos: Toyota is preferred to a Rolls, regardless of price." Finally, he emphasized that there are other media besides the electronic: "There is the human media. The tourist. The ubiquitous walking, talking, eating demonstrators of 'modern' ways."

Kroll gave us this warning "way back in 1987." As I write this chapter, it already seems dated and a truism given the events of this past year, with the further opening up of that New World. There has been a setback in China, to be sure, but even the current repressive government would prefer to continue its economic reforms. The marketing prospects, with 350 million consumers enjoying the free trade and common currency of the new European community, are illimitable. We have seen the rising expectations of Poland and Hungary and of other previously "Iron Curtain" countries. The magnetic attraction of the free enterprise system is gaining power in many more countries all over the world.

I think it is fair to predict that by the time this book is printed and in your hands, that *flash point* Kroll referred to will have continued to ignite and spread . . . like *wildfire*.

. . . .
CHAPTER CHECKLIST
. . . .

THE WHOLE EGG

1. Integrated communications (IC, or "The Whole Egg") is more than just advertising, but the entire scope of many forms of commercial communication—each used and coordinated according to each client's needs.

2. Its purpose—to communicate to the right prospect with the right message at the right time through the right medium.

3. Ideally, all forms of communication about a product or service should support, complement, and supplement one another, to create a unified whole.

4. The advantages of IC to marketers include unified strategy, for all forms of communication, better management of the total communications program, and the fact that the total effect of IC is greater than the sum of its parts.

5. The advantages to agencies include greater understanding of a client's business, broader communications experience, expanded career opportunities for employees, and, potentially, greater profitability.

6. There are seven tested methods for achieving true IC:

   a. Assemble the best possible specialists in each form of communication.

   b. Cultivate the ultimate in teamwork.

   c. Keep all the specialists fully informed of the capabilities and activities of one another.

   d. Bring all the specialists into the closest possible proximity with one another.

   e. Familiarize the specialists with one another's methods and practices, if possible providing direct experience for all in one another's craft.

   f. Cultivate basic ideas which can be central to all communications, regardless of which specialties are brought to bear.

   g. For inspiration and guidance, collect and disseminate to all specialists, case histories of successful integrated communications.

THE WHOLE GLOBE

1. Global marketing is of increasing concern because of the expansion of the free economic systems and of consumer needs and wants all over the world.

2. Global marketing means different things to different people—varying from the desire to provide the same message, using the same techniques, in all countries, to the goal of providing the right message, with the right technique, for each individual country.

3. Y&R's approach, called "cross-cultural" marketing, varies, according to product, service, and need, from totally *decentralized* coordination, allowing each unit complete autonomy, to totally *centralized* coordination, with one headquarters in charge.

4. Y&R believes that no communication can be totally global, but that it is sometimes possible for any and all to have a common strategy and the same basic idea shared by all.

5. Depending on the state of each given economy and consumer life-styles and attitudes, there are three stages of communication that might predominate:

   a. To provide *information* about your product or service.

   b. To provide *education* as to its benefits.

   c. To *personalize* your approach, appealing to individuals' values and desires.

6. There may well be, in the near future, a "flashpoint" at which developing economies become mature.

7. To profit at such a time, marketers should pave the way, to establish their equities, through creative communications in advance.

Index

A

B